Yale French Studies

NUMBER 66

The Anxiety of Anticipation

Yale French Studies

Sima Godfrey, *Special editor for this issue*

Liliane Greene, *Managing editor*

Editorial board: Charles Porter (Chairman), Peter
Brooks, Paul de Man, Karen Erickson,
Shoshana Felman, Karen McPherson, Richard
Goodkin, Fredric Jameson, Roddey Reid

Staff: Karen Erickson, Elise Hsieh

Editorial office: 315 William L. Harkness Hall.

Mailing address: 2504A Yale Station,
New Haven, Connecticut 06520.

Sales and subscription offices: Yale University
Press, 92A Yale Station, New Haven,
Connecticut 06520 *or* Yale University Press,
Ltd., 13 Bedford Square, London, WC1B 3 JF,
England.

Published twice annually by Yale University Press.

Designed by James J. Johnson and set in Trump
Medieval Roman by The Composing Room of
Michigan, Inc.

Printed in the United States of America by The
Vail-Ballou Press, Binghamton, N.Y.

ISSN 0044-0078

ISBN for this issue 0–300–03180–7

The Anxiety of Anticipation

This issue on "The Anxiety of Anticipation" addresses the energy peculiar to the vectors of French literary history. As the title suggests, it takes as its point of departure the persuasive theory of English literary history that Harold Bloom has advanced over the past ten years in his extended elaboration of "The Anxiety of Influence."[1] However convincing Bloom's theory has been for mapping out the continuous dynamic of English and American poetry, it has proved curiously inadequate for charting the productive tensions that are built into the writing and reading of French literature. This for reasons that are implicit in the avowedly American bias of Harold Bloom and his similarly avowed disinterest in the specificity of French culture and intellectual history.

The creative conflict that Bloom has identified at the psychic core of English poetry is born out of the sublimation of an evasive dialogue between individual authors that informs the ongoing process of Anglo-American writing. "Gnostic and elitist, a strong reading, like Emerson's, champions the isolate individual, the solitary construer, a Dickinson, a Thoreau, a Whitman."[2] The dialectical energy that underwrites the production of French literature, on the other hand, is organized less around a dialogue between individual authorial voices than about a more generalized debate with an inherited tradition of *authority* itself. The French artist seeks not so much to domesticate a precursor's influence through a transumptive act of poetry as to anticipate substituting his own proleptic programme for

1. Harold Bloom, *The Anxiety of Influence* (New York: Oxford University Press, 1973).
2. Harold Bloom, *Agon: Towards a Theory of Revision* (New York: Oxford University Press, 1982), p. 21.

a closed system of poetic convention. In so doing, he strives to become the new authority who may open the critical trajectory for future poetic moves. Simply put, if according to Bloom's ratios the English poet is always looking anxiously backwards at his precursors, within the strong tradition of French poetry, the French poet looks anxiously forward(s) to his successors. Whereas in our reading of English poetry we have been trained to listen for echoes of the past (the voice of Milton in Wordsworth, or the voice of Keats in Tennyson), the reading of French poetry is governed by a prospective strategy that alerts us to echoes of the future (the poetics of Verlaine in Baudelaire, Valéry in Mallarmé, etc.)

Within Bloom's revisionary map, the question that preoccupies English and American poets is: "How can I become (overcome) Milton or Wordsworth, Whitman or Dickinson?" The strong voices of French art ask another question that Bloom himself sees as central to the enterprise of literature: "What is a classic?"[3] A question that is rephrased through personal anxiety to read: "(How) shall I become a classic?" Inside a tradition that is historically conditioned by the centrality of a powerful neoclassical ideology, the question of becoming *a classic* necessarily presupposes a confrontation with the magisterial authority that is predicated upon the status of *the classic*. And this is as true of French writers as it is of French painters, for whom we have isolated Boileau and Poussin respectively as distinctive (though impersonal) "sources" of modern preoccupation.

Even today, we continue to read the urgency of French disputation with totalizing systems of monolithic authority and logocentric closure in the powerful deconstructive enterprises that have given continued momentum to the practice of writing in France. Indeed, it is only in light of this debate on the primal scene of French instruction that we can understand, for example, the varied yet constant career of one of France's most recent poets of belatedness, Roland Barthes. Harold Bloom, emerging from struggles with his own pragmatic and individualistic sources, has been quick to note that the deconstructive enthusiasms of present-day Continental poetics are in their own "Franco-Heideggerian" way themselves monolithic,[4] despite all protests to the contrary. We cannot, however, dismiss

3. Harold Bloom, *A Map of Misreading* (New York: Oxford University Press, 1975), p. 34.
4. Bloom, *Agon,* p. 19.

such strategies, as Bloom casually does, as "only another residuum of the now wearisome perpetual crusade of intellectual France against its own upper middle class,"[5] for they represent a profound native struggle with (academic) authority that goes back to the intellectual anxieties of French culture, anxieties that may be located in the heuristic principles of the seventeenth century. And it is from this perspective, in particular, that Barthes' early book *On Racine* becomes a strong statement of critical polemic. By emphasizing his personal Gnostic interpretations of English literature, Bloom has deliberately evaded the trajectory more familiar to French literature that engages consciously in an agonistic struggle with the priority of the Classics. It is this struggle that dramatized the poetic debates of the seventeenth century (giving rise to the paradigmatic Quarrel of the Ancients and Moderns), and by extention, still characterizes (less consciously, perhaps) the ideological debates of modern French poetics.

This is not to suggest that Bloom's pragmatic model for antithetical reading must fail in its assessment of French poetry; on the contrary, the structure that it advances of negation, evasion and extravagance remains a forceful one for reading the inherent anxieties of a tradition so unlike his own. The dissimilarities lie rather in the identification of the public nature of the power, authority and tradition that are transferred in every strong act of misreading; a conflicted nature which directs the reader of French literature to strong critical precedents that attempt, belatedly, to theorize and legislate their way out of the historic closure of academic orthodoxy and onto the open field of the timeless *classic*.

At a more private level, the strong poems of French literature remain all, like the strong poems of Bloom's own tradition, "lies against time," and as such they anticipate anxiously the final authority that all poets as human beings must face—the authority of death. For this, Harold Bloom refers to his own critical predecessor, Vico: "Vico, who identified the origins of poetry with the impulse towards divination (to foretell, but also to become a god by foretelling) implicitly understood . . . that a poem is written to escape dying. Literally, poems are refusals of mortality."[6] "Combining Vico and Freud

5. Ibid.
6. Bloom, *Map*, p. 19.

teaches us that the origin of defense is its stance towards death, just as the origin of any trope is its stance towards proper meaning . . . death is the most proper of literal meanings and literal meaning partakes of death."[7] Maurice Blanchot, another decidedly strong French poet of our day, puts it this way in *l'Espace littéraire:* "the writer is the man . . . who derives his power from an anticipated relation with death."[8] The revisionary model of writing thus inscribes the uncertainty of a performative act of poetic *will* in the double desire for some sort of mastery (*volonté* and *maîtrise*) and the legacy of a testament for posterity. The modern French poet, in sublimating his own critical ancestry, aspires to a position of future authority through an indistinguishable act of critical legislation and poetic legacy: to write the *preface* of the future.

For the French author, the patriarchal line of strength opens backwards to include not only Montaigne, Pascal, Hugo, Baudelaire, Mallarmé, Valéry, Gide and Breton, but also—as for Bloom—the mythological paternity of Nietzsche and Kierkegaard, who have become in our own belated time "inescapable points of origin." Bloom defers to Oscar Wilde for his insight that "criticism is the only civilized form of autobiography."[9] In reconstituting the temporal imperatives of all autobiographical writing, both Nietzsche and Kierkegaard have reoriented our Post-Modern reading of poetic anxiety by translating a general apprehension in the face of the inevitable manhandlings of our critical and poetic thoughts that are themselves born of the repetition of prior misreadings.

This is the same anxiety that Maurice Blanchot, anticipating the "always future reader," locates in the shifty territory of a "literary space" that surrounds the artist on all sides—"the violent emptiness where everything repeats itself eternally."[10] A space haunted by the blurred echoes of the "wandering word": "It [*la parole errante*] resembles an echo, when the echo repeats aloud not only that which was first murmured, but becomes confused with the whispers of immensity [*l'immensité chuchotante*]; it is the silence become reverberating space . . ."[11] Blanchot anxiously fills that risky space, how-

---

7. Harold Bloom, *Poetry and Repression* (New Haven: Yale University Press, 1976), p. 10.
   8. Maurice Blanchot, *L'Espace littéraire* (Paris: Gallimard, 1955), p. 92.
   9. Bloom, *Agon,* p. 48.
   10. Blanchot, *L'Espace littéraire,* p. 213.
   11. Ibid., p. 46.

ever, with the implicit value judgments of a culture that predetermines the assignment of works of art to categories of conventionalized taste: "It [the work of art] is judged a success or failure in view of the rules, precarious as they are today, that may constitute instances of an aesthetic. . . . It is said to be rich or poor in view of a culture that compares it to other works . . . that adds it to the national, human treasury or sees in it only the pretext for discussion and teaching."[12] The qualification of the work of art as the pre-text of the future fills the violent emptiness of literary space with poetic potential and defies the moment of death by giving birth to the unstable hazards of new communication: "The distance that places the work outside our grasp and outside the reach of time . . . exposes it also to all the adventures of time, showing it to be ceaselessly in quest of new form, a new conclusion, complacent to all the metamorphoses which, by attaching it to history, seem to make of its own distancing the promise of a limitless future."[13] That limitless future Blanchot finds in Mallarmé's project of "le livre à venir." The book of the future—the ultimate work of poetic negation—would be organized through a premeditated, perfectly defined and hierarchized architecture that leaves nothing to chance (1885, 1868); it would eliminate past and future and the personality of the poet all together to discover the eternal present that is the timeless space of the nameless classic, a space that escapes the fatal closures of time and interpretation in the dissemination of plural effects.

It is the dream of achieving a universal (as opposed to personal) work of timelessness in literary space that we may characterize as the anxiety of anticipation. Blanchot affirms that the "essence of literature is precisely to elude all essential determinations, all stabilizing, even actualizing assertions; it is never there, it must forever be rediscovered or reinvented."[14] His post-Romantic articulation of the ambitions of the strong poet thus assumes a swerve not away from the fact of any specific authorial presence, but from the totalizing systems of authority itself that might reduce literature to a positive set of proven axioms. At the same time he insists upon his "oft-repeated . . . suggestion . . . that literature asserts the improbability of any reduction to a unifying principle . . . which is why we can

12. Ibid., p. 211.
13. Ibid., p. 214.
14. Maurice Blanchot, *Le Livre à venir* (Paris: Gallimard, 1959), p. 244.

approach it only indirectly through a series of negations."[15] The anxiety of modern French poetry ultimately resides in the unsettling contradictions of a historicized desire to negate and transcend history: not to be a Classic, to be a classic.

One last remark on Bloom's evasive disregard for the radical difference of other cultures. In *The Map of Misreading*, Bloom has stated that "American poets are the most consciously belated in the history of Western poetry."[16] Like most cultural generalizations this one is highly suspect; for in his grand sweep, Bloom has manifestly excluded the many colonized voices that have for at least the past thirty years sought to articulate their own belated place in a patriarchal history that both is and isn't their own. I could take as a final illustration an example from women's writing, but that case has already been persuasively argued by many feminist critics. Instead, I turn to an example by a Québécois author, Hubert Aquin. His first novel, *Prochain épisode*,[17] was published in 1965, at a critical moment when *séparatiste* movements were unquietly mapping out the "Quiet Revolution." Aquin's persona in the book is a young novelist who has been arrested by the police for his terrorist activities in Montréal. To distract himself during his period of incarceration, he sets about to write an adventure novel that he locates in the neutral Francophone setting of the Swiss Alps—a landscape that is "neutral" politically but overdetermined for him literarily by the memories of Benjamin Constant, Rousseau, Musset and Byron that invest it; forebears who are not really his own, yet exert over him an inescapable influence. Just as he has been paralyzed by impersonal, collective political authorities in his attempt to write the "prochain épisode" of his country's future, he is equally paralyzed, as a belated, disinherited author, in his attempts to write the "prochain épisode" of his own novel, and of literature in general. The two anxieties merge in a hallucinatory passage at the center of the book.

> Nothing here is free, nothing. . . . I sense that my improvisation is plunging into an atavistic mould, and that my river of spontaneity is banked with ancient alluvium. I am not writing, I am written. The

15. Maurice Blanchot, *L'Entretien infini* (Paris: Gallimard, 1969), pp. 594–95.

16. Bloom, *Map*, p. 53.

17. Hubert Aquin, *Prochain épisode* (Montréal: Cercle du Livre de France, 1965). English translation, Penny Williams (Toronto: McClelland and Stewart, 1967).

gesture I have yet to make has been waiting for me for a long time. . . . I create only what has preceded me and make the footprints I have yet to trace. . . . I run in vain; my past has traced my future path and offered the words I thought I had invented.

I have long dreamed of creating my own movement and my own rhythm; of discovering a road for others to follow. All these years, I have dreamed of the triumphant outburst I would produce. . . . But I have only managed to trace words already shaped. . . . Caught in a bed of clay, I follow the path. . . . This disorderly book and I, we are the same. This mass of pages are the product of history, an unfinished part of myself and consequently a flawed witness to the hesitant revolution which I continue to proclaim in the way open to me—institutional delirium. . . . Suddenly I dream of my disordered epic becoming part of the national calendar of a people without history! . . . The inevitable disorder is already capturing me and moulding my spirit. . . . The great earthquake is beginning, in us and through us . . . [Pp. 67–71]

Aquin's belated persona expresses the anxiety of a writer and political "agent" consciously trapped in his own rereadings of a past history that anticipates his every move. He dreams of a "totalitarian art, in constant genesis," of forging a radically new path, but this too is a hallucination predicted by the Romantic past that catches him in a bed of clay. The metaphor he appropriates for his own break out of history (for a people without history) is "institutional delirium" and this is the metaphor that I would finally like to propose for the anxiety of anticipation, in all its French (and Francophone) reverberations: "Cet amas de feuilles est un produit de l'histoire, fragment inachevé de ce que je suis moi-même et témoignage impur, par conséquent, de la révolution chancelante que je continue d'exprimer, à ma façon, par mon *dé-lire institutionnel*"[18] (my emphasis). The unruly misreading of institutional authority recalls a similar poetic appeal a century earlier for the "de-regulation" of all meanings and it provides the strong poet with a tentative place in the hesitant revolution that anticipates the open path for art and constant genesis. "But I am certain of the future. Already I feel the irresistable pressure of the next episode . . . everything will resolve itself in beauty."[19]

SIMA GODFREY

18. Aquin, p. 124.
19. Ibid.

To Become a Classic

SIMA GODFREY

The Anxiety of Anticipation:
Ulterior Motives in French Poetry

> Nos disciples et nos successeurs nous en apprendraient mille fois
> plus que nos maîtres, si la durée de la vie nous laissait voir leurs
> travaux.
>
> —Paul Valéry

Harold Bloom has in recent years organized the development of English Romantic poetry around a dynamic of anxiety which he calls the "Anxiety of Influence." His model for reading the English poets in the wake of their predecessors may be a convincing one for some literatures, but oddly, not for French. Whereas other literatures had "strong" poets early in their history to direct and frustrate future generations in an Oedipal way—this for instance is the role that Bloom assigns to Milton for the English Romantics—the French, despite persistent efforts to do so, never managed to produce a major epic poet of equivalent force or stature.[1] In the formative centuries of modern French literature, the period extending roughly from Ronsard to Chénier, the epic poem maintained a *theoretical* supremacy in the canonized hierarchy of genres,[2] and French literary observers continually sought out a national contender for epic stardom. But the genre never succeeded in dominating aesthetically the literary production of that age—nor of the subsequent one—yielding precedence to tragedy, the lyric and the novel.[3]

1. I am deliberately referring here to the modern era, dating roughly from the 16th century. The medieval tradition, while rich in epic poems is not so (for reasons that are obvious) in "strong" individual poets whose personal apotheosis would guarantee privilege in the patriarchal history of poetic lineage.

2. Many references could be cited here. The following quotation from Fontenelle's "Description de l'empire de la poésie," 1678 (*Oeuvres*, Paris: Brunet, 1761), v. ix, p. 404 is not atypical: "Cette grande ville que la carte vous représente au-delà des hautes montagnes que vous voyez, est la capitale de cette Province, et s'appelle le Poème épique."

["The great city that is indicated on the map just beyond the high mountains that you see is the capital of this Province and is called Epic Poetry."]

3. Cf. William Calin, *A Muse for Heroes: Nine Centuries of the Epic in France* (Toronto: University of Toronto Press, 1983).

From the midsixteenth century through the eighteenth century, an era marked by the proliferation of literary theories that concentrated on the rediscovery and rereading of the classical theorists in general, and of Horace (the *Ars Poetica*) and Aristotle (the *Poetics*) in particular, the epic poem was widely considered to be the noblest of literary genres, and the only one capable of conferring utter glory upon a nation, a language or a writer. Nevertheless, even in the seventeenth century, at a time of the most intense theorizing on the superior merits of the epic, none of the neoclassical epic poets could produce a work on a par, for instance, with the dramatic works of Corneille, Molière or Racine.[4] In the eyes of posterity, it would seem equally fair to judge the sixteenth- and eighteenth-century epic poems of Ronsard (the *Franciade*) and Voltaire (the *Henriade*)—literary figures who otherwise dominate their age—as relatively mediocre by comparison to the *Aeneid* which they sought to emulate.

So implicit was the preoccupation with creating a French epic and the anxiety over a possibly inherent inadequacy to do so, that in the most famous prescriptive doctrine of literature, the *Art Poétique* of 1674, Boileau subtly altered the hierarchical order of genres in the third canto to place tragedy, a classical genre in which the French had excelled, ahead of the epic.[5] In so doing, Boileau was not demoting

4. The mid-seventeenth century saw the publication of a singular abundance of epic poems by authors who aspired to no less than giving France the Homer or Virgil she had been waiting for. Even a partial list is impressive:

Le Père le Moyne, *Saint Louis*, 1653 (7 cantos), 1658 (18 cantos)
Saint-Amant, *Moyse Sauvé*, 1653
Scudéry, *Alaric*, 1654
Chapelain, *La Pucelle*, 1656 (first 12 cantos), 1682 (last 12 cantos)
Desmarets, *Clovis*, 1657 (24 cantos)
Louis le Laboureur, *Charlemagne*, 1664
Coras, *Josué, Samson, David, Jonas*, 1665
Charles Perrault, *Saint Paulin*, 1675.

Cf. Marcel Hervier, *L'Art Poétique de Boileau* (Paris: Mellottée, 1949).

5. The "adjustment" did not go entirely unnoticed. Pierre Claude François Daunou, Boileau's most active defender in the early nineteenth century, passes over the structural inversion of genres hastily in a telling deflection: "il nous peint au troisième chant la tragédie, l'épopée, la comédie. Cet ordre n'est peut-être pas le plus naturel; mais rien jamais dans un poème didactique et sur de tels sujets, n'a égalé la magnificence de ces trois tableaux." ["in the third canto he describes for us tragedy, the epic and comedy. This order is perhaps not the most natural; however, nothing in a didactic poem on such subjects has ever equaled the magnificence of these three tableaux."] "Discours préliminaire," in *Oeuvres de Boileau Despréaux* (Paris: Dupont, 1825), p. xxv. (Unless otherwise indicated, all translations are my own.)

the epic to second rank; on the contrary, he still maintained its pre-eminence above all literary genres. However, in the face of the evidently inferior epics that were being produced at that very time (Chapelain's lengthy *La Pucelle* is the repeated subject of mockery within the *Art poétique*), it seemed tactically prudent to begin the literary exposition of neoclassical forms by emphasizing the genre of the *tragic*, in which the gap between classical tradition and contemporary taste had been more successfully bridged.

Similarly, in the French version of his "Essai sur la poésie épique" (1733), Voltaire notes in France the surfeit of critical discourse surrounding the epic that overshadows and underscores the decidedly unsatisfactory *literary* performance by the French within that genre. Asserting the predominence of theater as the form best suited to the French imagination, he does not even assume the position of his own *Henriade* in the canon of posterity.

> Nous n'avons point de poème épique en France, je ne sais même si nous en avons aujourd'hui. . . . Il est honteux pour nous . . . qui avons réussi en tant de genres [d'être] forcés d'avouer, sur ce point, notre stérilité et notre faiblesse. . . . Il faut avouer qu'il est plus difficile à un Français qu'à un autre de faire un poème épique. . . . Oserai-je le dire? C'est que de toutes les nations polies, la nôtre est la moins poétique.[6]

6. "We have no epic poem in France and I am not even sure that we have any today. . . . It is a shame that we . . . who have succeeded in so many genres are obliged to admit on this point our sterility and our weakness. . . . One must admit that it is more difficult for a Frenchman than for anyone else to create an epic poem. Dare I say it? Of all the refined nations, ours is the least poetic." "Essai sur la poésie épique," in *Oeuvres complètes* (Paris: Garnier, 1877), vol. 8, p. 360. Two pages later Voltaire adds: "The geometric spirit that has taken hold of literature in our day has created yet another obstacle for poetry. . . . *Method* is the quality of our writers . . . The general taste that they have . . . formed quite clearly excludes the epic imagination."

Two centuries later, Paul Claudel in "Réflexions et propositions sur le vers français," (*Oeuvres en prose*, [Paris: Gallimard, 1965], p. 43) makes a similar observation on the absence of epic poetry in France.

> Un long poème est tout autre chose qu'une collection de poèmes courts. . . . Tout ce qu'il y a en français d'invention, de force, de passion, d'éloquence, de rêve, de verve, de couleur, de musique spontanée, de sentiments de grands ensembles, tout ce qui répond le mieux en un mot à l'idée que depuis Homère on se fait généralement de la poésie, chez nous ne se trouve pas dans la poésie mais dans la prose . . .

> A long poem is something quite different from a collection of short poems. . . . In French, everything that shows invention, strength, passion, eloquence, dreams,

Voltaire clearly identifies *poetic* talent with epic poetry, and in admitting a potential national weakness, he alludes indirectly to the success of the English, and more notably Milton, a success he had emphasized in the earlier English draft of this essay (1727). But in the following passage from the French text, he makes his most emphatic statement regarding the epic in France: "Vous entreprenez un ouvrage qui n'est pas fait pour notre nation; les Français n'ont pas la tête épique."[7]

Indeed, even during the height of French Romanticism, when authors were straining most consciously to overthrow the generic precepts and value judgments of the neoclassical tradition, the preoccupation with epic poetry looms large. To be sure, the range of epic poetry was radically transformed, from the heroic expression of a national heritage to the vehicle for alternately intimate or humanitarian sentiments; nevertheless, the period extending from 1800 to 1860 represents quantitatively the summum of epic production in France, eclipsing by far the Middle Ages and the Baroque.[8] Within the poetic output of the nineteenth century one needs to be reminded periodically of Lamartine's lyrical epics, *Jocelyn* and *La Chute d'un ange*, Vigny's *Eloa*, *Le Déluge*, *La Colère de Samson*, and Hugo's *Légende des Siècles*, *La Fin de Satan* and *Dieu*, to name but a few of the most familiar epic poems of that period. And yet, despite this outburst of epic energy, written at a time of great poetic successes, one is inclined to agree with Voltaire that this is not where poetic strength lay. None of these poems, both by virtue of certain structural and rhetorical weaknesses and by their belated arrival in the canon, can be said to occupy the magisterial place assumed by Milton's *Paradise Lost* in the English tradition.

Bloom himself has recognized this disparity between the French and English poetic traditions: "French poetry lacks not only early

---

vitality, color, spontaneous music, the feeling for larger schemes, everything, in short, that best corresponds to the idea of poetry as generally conceived of since Homer, belongs in our case not to the realm of poetry, but prose . . .

7. "You are undertaking a work that is not made for our nation; the French do not have an epic spirit." Comment made to M. de Malezieux, whom he had consulted about his own *Henriade*, in Voltaire, op. cit., p. 363. In a slightly different line of argument, Baudelaire paraphrases Poe's "Poetic Principle": "Voilà évidemment le poème épique condamné," *Oeuvres Complètes* (Paris: Gallimard, 1975), v. 2, p. 332.

8. Cf. Calin, op. cit., chapter 13.

giants of the dimension of Chaucer, Spenser and Shakespeare, but it is also devoid of any later figures whose strength could approximate Milton, Wordsworth, Whitman and Dickinson";[9] but his conclusion, that the French tradition is *weak,* may be too hasty. The absence of a poetic "giant" does not entail the absence of a paternal authority, with which Bloom would have all strong poets grapple in the achievement of their own distinctive voice. There does exist indeed a powerful father figure of modern French poetry, but his strength is derived not so much from his role as a poet, which he was, as from his role as a *critic.* I refer to the same dogmatic author of the *Art poétique,* Boileau, whose influence was in fact so great that it was not until 1894, after generations of attack on the sacrosanct alexandrine, that Mallarmé could stand up and announce: "J'apporte en effet des nouvelles. Les plus surprenantes. Même cas ne se vit encore. On a touché au vers."[10]

Modern French poetry may thus be said to emerge not so much from the struggle with individual poetic precursors as from a struggle with poetic theory as codified and embodied in the neoclassical precepts of the *Art poétique.* Boileau's poem stands in the history of French poetry less as an example of patriarchal authority in verse than as a model of patriarchal authority *on* verse: it is the inscription of doctrine in poetry that initiates a tradition of critical discourse that would accompany all subsequent poetic production in France. While Boileau the poet may drop out of the master schema of French literary history early in the eighteenth century, the "effet Boileau" (what Bernard Beugnot has called "le monument Boileau"),[11] based on the immutable "gloire scolaire" of the *Art poétique,* is one with which

---

9. "The Breaking of Forms" in *Deconstruction and Criticism* (New York: Seabury, 1979), p. 13.

10. "To be sure, I come with news. Of the most surprising kind. Nothing of the sort has ever been seen. The line of verse has been shaken." "De la Musique et des lettres" (*Oeuvres complètes,* Paris: Gallimard, 1945), p. 643. By emphasizing Boileau's critical as opposed to poetic legacy, we return to Voltaire's implied opposition between "method" and "poetry." (See footnote 6, above.) Indeed, Boileau's *Art poétique* can be read as a "discours de la méthode poétique," exemplifying the "geometrical spirit" that for Voltaire characterizes the French mind. Harold Bloom has suggested, rightly I think, that Boileau may be troping on Descartes. Nevertheless, for the purpose of this discussion of poetry, it is clearly *Boileau's* name that "figures in large on the standard," to paraphrase John Keats ("Sleep and Poetry," 11. 203–06).

11. Bernard Beugnot and Roger Zuber, *Boileau; visages anciens, visages nouveaux* (Montréal: Presses de l'Université de Montréal, 1973).

each generation of poets would have to come to terms in the definition of its own literary heritage and destiny. Boileau's *Art poétique*, a poem which every strong poet-critic (and not just Gautier or Verlaine) would rewrite as the programme for the future of poetry, thus initiates a tradition of "art critique" in France, a tradition that reorients the production and reception of French verse down to our own day.[12]

To the extent that it is the valorization of a critical perspective that governs the writing and reading of French poetry, the anxiety that is produced is both similar and inverse to that suffered by Harold Bloom's poets—an anxiety of *anticipation*. Just as each French poet must set out to rewrite the critical "preface" for modern verse, we the readers of French poetry are trained to identify in the writing of its "strong" authors the articulation of a critical "prise de conscience" that seeks (risks) to define and chart the poetic path for literary developments to come, in defiant repetition of Boileau.

To go a step farther, if the energy peculiar to French poetry does not originate in the strategic relations engendered by a belated encounter with epic poets, it can be said to derive from the inscription of poetry in a tradition that has been—at least since the seventeenth century—marked by the monumental presence of *epic critics*, of whom Boileau serves as the paradigmatic example. By the same

---

12. In singling out Boileau's "Art poétique" as a "source" of modern poetic anxiety (and by modern, I refer primarily to the Romantic and post-Romantic traditions), I do not mean to ignore Boileau's many predecessors nor his own "sources." Like his contemporaries and immediate predecessors, Boileau's productive preoccupations are focused on a general attempt to come to terms with the "master works" of classical antiquity and in particular the documents of classical theory. From the sixteenth century on, numerous versions of the "Art poétique" were produced in response to the rediscovery of Horace, including translations, commentaries and variations (Vida, 1527; Jacques Peletier du Mans, 1544; Sebilet, 1548). Du Bellay's *Défense et illustration de la langue française* of 1549 urged young poets to look to the ancients for poetic models and he particularly emphasized "le long poème," to which he devoted a separate chapter. "Choisis-moi quelqu'un de ces beaux vieux romans français comme un Lancelot, un Tristan ou autres; et en fais renaistre au monde une admirable Iliade et laborieuse Enéide." (Pt. 2, ch. 5.) There were many other such Renaissance versions of the "Art Poétique" including Ronsard's *Abrégé de l'Art poétique* of 1571, but perhaps the most important precursor for Boileau was Vauquelin de la Fresnaye, whose *Art poétique* appeared in 1605. One might add to these various treatises on poetics the many prefaces to epic poems, in which authors offered the promise of matching the ancients in the noblest of genres. If we insist upon Boileau's *Art poétique* above all, it is not by virtue of its singularity or originality, but specifically because of the lasting historic influence it produced on literary debate and production throughout the eighteenth, nineteenth and ultimately twentieth centuries.

token, the strong voices of modern French poetry, which are also the strong voices of modern French poetics—and we may turn back from Boileau to Ronsard, Du Bellay and the Pléiade as well as look forward to Baudelaire, Mallarmé, Valéry and so on—do not so much struggle to find their place among the poetic "giants" of a forbidding past that is anxiously closed, as to secure a tentative place in a critical tradition that is anxiously open; open to the uncertain validation that can only come from the testimony of the future. "La valeur des oeuvres de l'homme ne réside point dans elles-mêmes, mais dans les développements qu'elles reçoivent des autres et des circonstances ultérieures. . . . Nos disciples et nos successeurs nous en apprendraient mille fois plus que nos maîtres, si la durée de la vie nous laissait voir leurs travaux." The strong poets of the French tradition must also be strong critics to pre-face the eventual poetry of the future. For this reason it becomes an axiom of French poetry that: "Tout véritable poète est nécessairement un critique de premier ordre."[13] The critical gesture that is built into the constant revision of the "art poétique" thus repeats a literary wager with posterity that is fraught with anxiety and risk.[14]

13. "The value of the works of man does not reside within them, but in the developments they are subjected to by other, ulterior circumstances. . . . Our disciples and our followers could teach us a thousand times more than our masters if the span of a lifetime allowed us to see their works." "Every true poet is necessarily a critic of the first rank." Paul Valéry, "Choses tues" in Oeuvres (Paris: Gallimard, 1957), v. 2, pp. 477, 479; Variété 5 (Paris: NRF 1944), p. 157. Cf. Baudelaire: "tous les grands poètes deviennent naturellement, fatalement critiques. . . . il est impossible qu'un poète ne contienne pas un critique." "Richard Wagner," Oeuvres complètes (Paris: Gallimard, 1975), v. 2, p. 793.

14. Cf. Bloom: "Every poet begins (however 'unconsciously') by rebelling more strongly against the consciousness of death's necessity than all other men or women do. . . . Poetic anxiety implores the Muse for aid in divination, which means to foretell and put off as long as possible the poet's own death." (The Anxiety of Influence, New York: Oxford University Press, 1979, pp. 10, 61.) In assuming the voice of critical authority, the poet runs the risk of being proved insufficient and of being relegated to the deathly ranks of the "not-quite." This, for instance, is the case of Théophile Gautier, whose willful, imperative poetics ("L'Art") are surpassed and subsumed by the poetry of his own disciple, Baudelaire, who illustrates both how strong and how weak his mentor can be. In a gesture typical of the anticipatory anxiety that invests critical readings of French poetry, Claudine Gothot-Mersch, one of Gautier's most recent and sympathetic editors Emaux et Camées (Paris: Gallimard, 1981) also inscribes Gautier's reputation in the list of poetic "almosts." She ends her prefatory appreciation of Gautier as follows: "ce recueil dont on goûte . . . l'art mineur mais parfait, mérite bien aussi d'être considéré pour ce pas qui s'y fait vers quelque chose de neuf."

An insistence upon the "Art poétique"—a poetic genre explicitly infused with a critical purpose—as the master poem underlying modern French poetry thus implies a critical preoccupation with poetics that would precede the more strictly literary preoccupation with poems. At the same time, however, it also evinces a response to collective and institutional convention—such as that established by the most French of institutions, the Académie Française.[15] Likewise, the periodic revolts against institutionalized authority have also tended in France to be organized under the collective banner of self-conscious movements or "schools" (from the "Cénacle" to "Tel Quel," to note but two modern instances) which articulate theoretical platforms and proclaim their own status as alternate institutions of literature. In this the pattern differs significantly from the individual dialogue with a forebear that is Bloom's model for English verse.

This difference has not gone unnoticed. Such an otherwise unimaginative critic as Brunetière in his essay "Sur le caractère essentiel de la littérature française" (1892), contrasts the essential "sociability" of French literature with the individualism of the English: "Par rapport à la littérature française, définie et caractérisée par son esprit de sociabilité, la littérature anglaise est une *littérature individualiste.*"[16] With a finer poetic instinct, Paul Claudel articulates

15. The reference to institutional convention alludes directly to the ideological and aesthetic substructures of seventeenth-century French neoclassicism that determine the distinctive "personality" of a much larger tradition. It should be recalled that the Académie Française, founded in 1634 by Richelieu with the royal patronage of Louis XIII, was officially charged "de travailler premièrement à un Dictionnaire de la langue françoise, et ensuite à une Grammaire, à une Rhétorique et à une Poétique." (Preface to the first edition of the *Dictionnaire de l'Académie française,* 1694.) The preface to the seventh edition of the dictionary (1877) resumes the history of publication and emphasizes the recognized permanence of its merits that were not challenged by the French Revolution itself despite the temporary suspension of the Academy. "Quelque libre, grâce au ciel, que soit aujourd'hui la concurrence en cette matière, le dictionnaire de l'Académie a toujours eu, néanmoins, et aura toujours une sorte de caractère officiel." The official lexical encoding of the "mother tongue" (that was to be followed by an official grammar, rhetoric and poetics) was thus transmitted through two centuries as the normative product of a paternal tradition emanating from a cardinal and his king and presided over by an official institution chartered by them.

16. "By comparison with French literature, which is defined and characterized by the spirit of sociability, English literature is an individualistic literature." *Etudes critiques sur l'histoire de la littérature française V* (Paris: Hachette, 1907), p. 273. Brunetière does make notable exception in England for the generations of Congreve, Wycherley, Addison and Pope.

the French commitment to convention [17]in the "Réflexions et propositions sur le vers français": "Les mêmes principes qui déterminent la vie du Français l'ont guidé quand il s'est agi de donner à ses idées une forme officielle et une expression définitive. La poésie classique française a ses canons . . . et la musc de Boileau Despréaux sort tout entière comme un fleuve rafraîchissant du Jardin des Racines Grecques." "J'honore dans Boileau . . . un de nos écrivains *canoniques*, je veux dire un de ceux qui ont redigé et mis en lumière les lois et les formes essentielles de notre expression."[18]

Just as seventeenth-century neoclassical doctrine reoriented an earlier Renaissance revision of the Ancients to focus on the order of classical *theory*, its own status derives from its position as the critical model for future revisionist structures in French literature. Accordingly, it is not so much the individual poems of Boileau that later generations rewrite, but the academic theory and canonical glory that he is seen to embody as "Législateur du Parnasse."

While none of these conclusions are particularly surprising to readers even moderately familiar with French literary history, they bear repeating at a time when the specificity of literary history is being actively questioned along with all forms of history writing and their attendant fictions. To the degree that history itself has been reassessed in terms of inherent textual strategies, it is important to acknowledge the nature of the textual dynamic and critical anxiety that underpin the structures peculiar to the history of French poetry. André Gide, one of the twentieth century's most self-conscious proponents of "art critique" resumes the historical energy indigenous to French literature in his response to an "enquête" published in the *Figaro* in 1940. The *Figaro* presented him with five questions pertaining directly to the nature and future of French literature, of which

17. The commitment to convention is equally evident in the persistent militance against specific doctrines that are denied only to be replaced by new doctrine. Cf. The initial article by Alexandre Guiraud in the Romantic journal, *La Muse Française*, "Nos Doctrines" (1824). This statement of the theoretical convictions of French Romanticism begins, significantly, with a quotation from Boileau.

18. "The same principles that determine the life of a Frenchman have also guided him in giving an official form and definitive expression to his ideas. Classical French poetry has its canons . . . and the muse of Boileau Despréaux emerges in full from the refreshing river of the Garden of Greek Roots (Racines)." "In Boileau I revere . . . one of our *canonical* writers, that is, one of those who organized and brought to light the essential laws and forms of our expression." Claudel, *Oeuvres en prose* (Paris: Gallimard, 1965), p. 9; second quotation from "Boileau" (1911), op. cit., p. 437.

this was the fifth: "Dans quel ordre d'importance actuelle classez-vous les divers genres: roman, essai, critique, poésie? Vers lequel vous semblent devoir aller les préférences du public?"

This was his answer:

> Dans cette palingénésie et nouvelle enfance de la culture, la poésie sera son expression la plus naturelle. Les autres "genres" que vous citez ressortissent peut-être davantage au passé. Souhaitons pourtant que la France meurtrie ne se désaisisse jamais de sa qualité maîtresse: la critique. Je parle de la critique non point comme d'un "genre," mais comme une qualité . . . où la France se montre incomparable et qui se révèlait naguère aussi bien dans les tragédies de Racine ou les poèmes de Baudelaire. . . . Une vertu qui n'empêche pas la poésie, mais lentement l'amène à l'art . . ."[19]

In support of his argument for the critical strength of French literature, Gide isolates examples from the seventeenth and the nineteenth centuries. In charting the anxiety of anticipation that is inherent in a literary tradition emerging from the energy of critical debate, I propose to do the same. A brief overview of the reception of Boileau's *Art poétique* in the nineteenth century may illustrate this point.

"L'EFFET BOILEAU"

In his book *L'Art poétique de Boileau,* Marcel Hervier summarizes the dynamic response to Boileau as follows: "Quoique Boileau n'eût rien inventé, c'est sous son nom que la postérité met les règles classiques . . . c'est son autorité que l'on combat."[20] He points to the per-

19. "In what order of present-day importance would you class the following genres: novel, essay, criticism, poetry? In your opinion, towards which of these genres should the preferences of the public lean?"—"In this moment of rebirth and rejuvenation for our culture, poetry should be its most natural expression. The other 'genres' that you cite were perhaps more prominent in the past. Let us nonetheless hope that despite the bruises she has suffered, France never lets go of her master quality: criticism. I refer to criticism not as a 'genre' but as a quality in which France has proved herself to be incomparable. In the past this quality revealed itself in the tragedies of Racine as well as in the poems of Baudelaire. . . . A virtue that does not stand in the way of poetry, but slowly leads it to art . . ." "Réponse à une enquête," in *Attendu que . . .* (Paris: Charlot, 1943), pp. 25–27

20. "Although Boileau invented nothing new, it is under his name that posterity placed the rules of classicism . . . it is his authority that is attacked." *L'Art Poétique de Boileau* (Paris: Mellottée, 1949), p. 228.

sistence of Boileau's authority in the enduring controversies of the eighteenth and early nineteenth centuries that are epitomized by the 'Concours de l'Académie de Nîmes'' whose prize was awarded to Pierre Claude François Daunou in 1787 for his response to the question: "Quelle a été l'influence de Boileau sur la littérature française?" Daunou, who was a staunch advocate of the neoclassical precedents established by Boileau, prefaced his 1825 edition of that author's works with the following *avertissement:*

> Nous nous estimerions heureux si nous pouvions contribuer à per- pétuer l'influence de ses leçons et de ses exemples; c'est un soin qui n'est malheureusement pas superflu, en un temps où le dessein semble pris de substituer, on ne sait quelles théories étrangères, à celles qui ont fait briller d'un si pur et si vif éclat notre littérature nationale.[21]

The defense of Boileau in the early nineteenth century is articulated in terms of an argument for genealogical purity that directs readers back to a national (and natural) father whose role, in the nineteenth century, was being usurped by foreign pretenders. Sainte-Beuve, a poet and the critical godfather of French Romanticism, attacked the premises of Daunou's conservative stand in his essay on Boileau (1829): "le concert de si dignes efforts n'a pas suffisamment protégé Boileau contre ces idées nouvelles, d'abord obscures et dé- criées, mais croissant et grandissant sous les clameurs. . . . Il est bon, à chaque époque littéraire nouvelle, de repasser en son esprit et de revivifier les idées qui sont représentées par certains noms devenus sacramentels, dût-on n'y rien changer, à peu près comme à chaque nouveau règne on refrappe monnaie et on rajeunit l'effigie sans al- térer le poids."[22] Sainte-Beuve does not structure his account of the

21. "We would consider ourselves pleased if we might help perpetuate the influ- ence of his lessons and his examples; such a service is unfortunately not superfluous at a time when there seems to be a design afoot to substitute all sorts of foreign theories for those theories that made our national literature shine with such pure and vital brillance." Daunou, *Oeuvres complètes de Boileau Despréaux* (Paris: Dupont, 1825), p. vii.

22. "Noble concerted efforts have not sufficiently protected Boileau against these new ideas, first obscure and discredited, but now growing and expanding with every hue and cry. . . . In each new period of literature, it is good to review in one's mind and to reanimate those ideas that are represented by certain names that have become sacred,—even if in the end nothing need be changed. Just as with every new regime, new coins are struck; the effigy on the coin is refreshed while the weight remains unaltered." "Portraits littéraires," in *Oeuvres* (Paris: Gallimard, 1956), p. 657.

Romantic "revolution" in terms of a violent liberation of letters from the repressive hold of authoritarian rule (this is the metaphor that Hugo would later exploit); he does so rather in terms that imply a polemic reformulation of the Quarrel of the Ancients and the Moderns. In his call for the introduction of a new symbolic currency into the economy of literature, he stresses a system that will be based, once again, on *new* rather than *no* constraints.

First, however, the tarnished image on the coin had to be effaced. Mme de Staël had already begun the work for him by actively attacking the image of the inhospitable father in *De l'Allemagne*, suggesting that the dissemination of Boileau's word had caused the miscarriage of poetry in France. "Boileau, tout en perfectionnant le goût de la langue, a donné à l'esprit français, l'on ne saurait le nier, une disposition très-défavorable à la poésie."[23] Gérard de Nerval, in 1830, was already promoting a new model in his rediscovery of Ronsard, the forgotten father of French poetry (and poetics),[24] and he was busy launching his own attack on Boileau for having choked the natural voice of French verse. Sainte-Beuve would participate in the erection of this new effigy in his famous sonnet to Ronsard:

> A toi Ronsard, à toi, qu'un sort injurieux
> Depuis deux siècles livre aux mépris de l'histoire,
> J'élève de mes mains l'autel expiatoire
> Qui te purifiera d'un arrêt odieux . . .[25]

Boileau's paternal authority had to be discredited absolutely and Sainte-Beuve undertook this task in no uncertain terms. At the beginning of his 1829 essay on Boileau, Sainte-Beuve alludes to the suspicious anecdotes that had been circulating, regarding the poet's "insensitivity"; and he mentions in particular a remark by Helvétius,

23. "Even as he perfected the taste for language, Boileau bequeathed the French spirit—it cannot be denied—with a very unfavorable disposition towards poetry." In *Oeuvres complètes* (Paris: Treuttel and Würtz, 1820), v. 10, p. 267.

24. In 1830 Nerval published an anthology of Pléiade poems and in 1831 the essay "De l'Ecole de Ronsard au 16ᵉ siècle" (in the *Mercure de France*). Ronsard had been largely repressed from the French tradition as a result of Boileau's hostile attack in the *Art Poétique*.

25. "For you, Ronsard, for you, whom an unjust fate / For two centuries has relegated to the scorn of history, / I erect with my hands an altar of expiation / That will purify you of this hateful sentence."

which he does not expand. Informed readers of 1829 would have been familiar with Helvétius' note:

> On lit dans *l'Année littéraire* que Boileau, encore enfant, jouant dans une cour, tomba. Dans sa chute, sa jaquette se retroussa; un dindon lui donna plusieurs coups de bec sur une partie très délicate. Boileau en fut toute sa vie incommodé; et de là peut-être, cette sévérité de moeurs, cette disette de sentiments qu'on remarque dans tous ses ouvrages; de là sa satire contre les femmes . . .[26]

Sainte-Beuve, in invoking the anecdote of Boileau's impotence, cuts off the source "d'un si pur et si vif éclat" at its point of origin. The myth of Boileau's physical impotence becomes the myth of his poetic impotence—the impossibility of generating a pure line of sons and poets. Sainte-Beuve then proceeds to a critical assessment of Boileau: "Ce n'est pas du tout un poète, si l'on réserve ce titre aux êtres fortement doués d'imagination et d'âme. . . . Boileau, selon nous, est un esprit sensé et fin, poli et mordant, *peu fécond.*"[27] (my emphasis) The genealogical line was now open to reinterpretation and the election of a new father, and while it would appear that that place was reserved for Ronsard, it is equally clear that Sainte-Beuve, the aspiring Romantic poet and critic, was himself preening for the new role as "Législateur du Parnasse."

It would seem therefore that at the height of French Romanticism, in the mid-1830s, Boileau might long since have abdicated his rule. In the "Preface to Cromwell" (1827) Victor Hugo too had ranked him among the adversaries of the new art and called for his deposition. Throughout the generation of the forties and fifties, the brotherband of late Romantic poets continued nonetheless to wrestle with the father, whose "art poétique" remained a standard both to be waved and overthrown. Indeed it seems that his high profile was sustained to provide the visible target for attack by a discourse that was self-consciously critical in the face and image of its antagonist.

26. "We read in *l'Année littéraire* that while still a child, Boileau was playing in the yard and fell. When he fell down his frock rolled up: a turkey pecked him several times on a very delicate part of his body. Boileau suffered from this indisposition all his life. Hence, perhaps, his severity of manner and the want of sentiment that one notes in all his works; hence his satire against women . . ." *De l'Esprit*, 3, 1, note 1.

27. "He is not a poet at all, if we maintain that title for those people who are forcefully endowed with imagination and soul. . . . It is my opinion that Boileau has a fine and sensible mind, caustic and polished but not very fertile."

"L'EFFET HUGO(HÉLAS!)"

Flaubert in 1843 called Boileau a pedantic "pisse-froid" who had eclipsed Ronsard and seduced the French with his critical opinions.[28] In 1852, he writes to Louise Colet, here with tempered admiration for Boileau, "ce vieux crouton de Boileau vivra autant que qui que ce soit, parce qu'il a su faire ce qu'il a fait."[29] Nevertheless, two months later he is indignant that Boileau's reputation should have surpassed that of Perrault, and that France's purest poet, Ronsard, should still remain unknown. Even Théophile Gautier, whose Parnassian taste for formal perfection should have made him sympathetic to the aesthetic ideology of Boileau, joined in the general Romantic swerve from the neoclassical "father." Brunetière himself expresses surprise at this reaction: "Et je m'étonne sans doute que Gautier . . . n'ait point vu qu'en donnant des leçons de son art, il en revenait tout bonnement à ce Boileau qu'en toute autre occasion il maltraitait si fort."[30] What surprises Brunetière, who remains despite his historical prestige a naive reader of French literature, is that Gautier should reject the formal precepts of Boileau to propose formal precepts of his own. Indeed, the status of the *Art poétique* as the master poem that all belated poets misread and rewrite called for a necessary "mistreatment" by Gautier in his years of poetic apprenticeship.

Similarly, in his mythical autobiography, *Les Contemplations,* Victor Hugo specifically inscribes his own violent struggle with Boileau in two poems, "Réponse à un acte d'accusation," (Livre I, 7) and "Quelques mots à un autre" (Livre I, 26). The poems were written in 1854 and 1855 respectively, but Hugo deliberately assigns them the fictive date of 1834, so that he may choreograph his own heroism into the meaningful years of the "Romantic Revolution." In the "Réponse . . ." he celebrates his single-handed victory over academic principles in bombastic verse that evokes the huge sweep of the French Revolution.

28. Letter to Ernest Chevalier, Sept. 2, 1843, *Correspondance,* 1, (Paris: Conard, 1926), p. 145.

29. "That old stick-in-the-mud Boileau will live as long as anybody, because he knew how to do what he did." Sept. 13, 1852, *Correspondance,* 3 (Paris: Conard, 1927), p. 21.

30. "And I wonder indeed that Gautier . . . did not see that in preaching the lessons of his art, he was simple returning to Boileau, whom on another occasion he mistreated so badly." "Théophile Gautier," in *Questions de Critique* (Paris: Calmann-Lévy, 1888), p. 200.

Et sur l'Académie, aïeule et douairière,
Cachant sous ses jupons les tropes effarés,
Et sur les bataillons d'alexandrins carrés,
Je fis souffler un vent révolutionnaire.
Je mis un bonnet rouge au vieux dictionnaire . . .
Boileau grinça des dents; je lui dis: ci-devant,
Silence! et je criai dans la foudre et le vent:
Guerre à la rhétorique et paix à la syntaxe! . . .
Et j'ai battu des mains, buveur du sang des phrases,
Quand j'ai vu, par la strophe écumante et disant
Les choses dans un style énorme et rugissant,
L'Art Poétique pris au collet dans la rue . . .

Without addressing the falsification of dates, we can see that the poem is troubled by its own internal duplicities. The metrics of the poem may occasionally illustrate some of Hugo's experiments in versification; for the most part, however, the poem is written in "alexandrins carrés," with good, solid caesuras at their core. And for a poem that wages war on Rhetoric, it is quite overwhelmed by its own rhetorical inflation. In "Quelques mots . . ." Hugo posits an interlocutor who fervently defends Boileau against the young Romantic upstart and to whom he responds as follows:

Vous déclarez Boileau perruque indéfrisable;
Et, coiffé de lauriers, d'un coup d'oeil de travers
Vous indiquez le tas d'ordures de nos vers . . .[31]

31. "Reply to an Act of Impeachment," in Victor Hugo, *Poems* (Boston: Estes and Lauriat, 189-), v. 2.

Then on th'Academy—staid dowager,
Hiding "tropes" 'neath her petticoats away,—
And on the Alexandrine's close array
I turned the revolutionary wind,
The "Red Cap" on th'old dictionary bind . . .

Then Boileau ground his teeth. "Be still," said I,
"You're out of date!" Then through the storm I cry,
"To rhetoric, war! To syntax peace assured." . . .

Drunk with the blood of phrases, I applaud,—
Seeing the strophe foaming, raging proud
Speaking its thoughts in thundering voice and loud,
Seize roughly on th'old rules of poetry. [*l'Art Poétique*]

From "Several words to Another": "You declare Boileau an unshakeable bigwig;/And, wreathed in laurels, looking askance,/You point to the rubbish heap of our verse . . ."

Hugo encodes the myth of his own poetic genius in verses that do not simply do away with poetic doctrine, but redefine a doctrine and a rhetoric that are both specific and dogmatic. That he should still be haunted by Boileau in the fifties (he had been writing poetry, successfully, since 1824) is telling. If Sainte-Beuve set about to castrate the father, Hugo would attempt to behead him, thereby cutting himself off (along with the rest of the nineteenth century whose spokesman he chose to be) from the spirit of French classicism that he could not escape. "Le dix-neuvième siècle ne relève que de lui-même; il ne reçoit l'impulsion d'aucun aïeul; il est fils d'une idée . . . mais le dix-neuvième siècle a une mère auguste, la Révolution française."[32] Having presumably done away with the father (but has he? Both poems are overdetermined by a dialogic structure that conjures up a necessary paternal antagonist), ten years later Hugo indulges in the supreme Romantic myth of the poet: the myth of self-creation. "A strong poet . . . must divine or invent himself, and so attempt the impossibility of *originating himself.*"[33] The poet imagines himself and his century born not out of a continuous paternal lineage, but from the discontinuous Romantic chaos of a mother who is revolution. And he will reclaim the language of that mother—*la langue maternelle*—by attacking first, the dictionary, symbol of the normative order imposed by the French Academy[34] and the *Art poétique:* "Tous les mots n'avaient pas droit à la langue. Le dictionnaire accordait ou n'accordait pas l'enregistrement. Le dictionnaire avait sa volonté à lui. . . . Les perruques-soleil faisant loi en poésie, les *Arts poétiques* qui oublient La Fontaine, . . . Boileau et La Harpe; tout cela est du passé."[35]

---

32. "The nineteenth century springs from itself only; it does not receive its impulse from any ancestor: it is the offspring of an idea . . . but the nineteenth century has an august mother, the French Revolution." "Le 19e siècle," in *William Shakespeare,* (1864), (Paris: Flammarion, 1973) p. 301; trans. A. Baillot (London: Hurst and Blackett, 1864), p. 325.

33. Harold Bloom, *Poetry and Repression* (New Haven: Yale University Press, 1976), p. 7.

34. Cf. footnote 15.

35. "Words did not all belong by right to the language. The dictionary granted or did not grant the registration. The dictionary had a will of its own . . . the brilliant nonentities fixing laws on poetry, the *Arts poétiques* which forget Lafontaine . . . Boileau and La Harpe; all that, although official and public teaching is filled and saturated with it, all that belongs to the past." *William Shakespeare,* op. cit., pp. 248–49; trans. pp. 264–65.

It is significant that Hugo projects his wishful dream of a Romantic present, liberated from the weight of the past, in an essay on
William Shakespeare, who throughout the decades of French Romanticism, stands as the model for the "individual genius" that the
French poet would (but cannot) be; the genius who, as Bloom puts it,
"belongs to the giant age before the flood,"[36] an age historically
contemporary to, though radically separate from, the classical age of
French literature that the nineteenth-century Romantic tries to flee.
But his flight is fatally circular; everywhere along his path he runs
into the inevitable shadow of Boileau.

By 1852, Sainte-Beuve, still aspiring to the position of strength that
would implicitly link him to the figure of the seventeenth-century poet-
critic, was revising his earlier judgment of Boileau. "Depuis vingt-cinq
ans, le point de vue en ce qui regarde Boileau a fort changé. . . . Aujourd'hui . . . nous revenons à lui avec plaisir. . . . Boileau est un des
hommes qui m'ont le plus occupé depuis que je fais de la critique, et avec
qui j'ai le plus vécu en idée."[37] He adds that what the Romantic poets
lacked in their initial period of promise was "un Boileau," implying
perhaps his own failure to fill that magisterial role. Similarly, in
1852–53, Flaubert was becoming more and more preoccupied with the
wisdom and success of Boileau, whose attention to style and devotion to
formal perfection served to inspire his own aesthetic convictions. His
letters to Louise Colet during these years are full of references to an
obsessive rereading of "ce vieux père."[38] On September 7, 1853, he
writes:

36. *The Anxiety of Influence,* p. 11.
37. "For the past twenty-five years, the point of view with regards to Boileau has
changed a great deal. . . . Today . . . we return to him with pleasure. . . . Boileau is one
of the men who has most preoccupied me since I began writing criticism, and one with
whom I have lived most closely in spirit." *Causeries du lundi* (Paris: Garnier, n.d.), v. 6,
p. 494.
Sainte-Beuve's criticism of Boileau in the later essay is marked by a measure of
humility that is absent from the youthful charge of 1829—the reflection, perhaps, of a
more mature self-image that has in some way failed to match up to the stature of his
predecessor. As in the case of his early attack against Boileau, however, some fifty years
later Sainte-Beuve the critic would be similarly erected to antithetical status by Marcel
Proust in his writings *Contre Sainte-Beuve.* It is both ironic and—within the scheme
here proposed—not entirely surprising that the polemic with Proust rather than
Boileau should have justified the critical authority of Sainte-Beuve in the nineteenth
century.
38. Letter of Sept. 30, 1853, *Correspondance,* 3, p. 360.

Je relis maintenant du Boileau, on plutôt tout Boileau, et avec moult coups de crayon aux marges. Cela me semble vraiment *fort*. On ne se lasse point de ce qui est bien écrit. Le style c'est la vie! C'est le sang même de la pensée! . . . que d'Art il a fallu pour faire cela et avec si peu! Je m'en vais ainsi, d'ici deux ou trois ans, relire attentivement tous les classiques français et les annoter, travail qui me servira pour mes *Préfaces* (mon ouvrage de critique littéraire, tu sais).[39]

Here Flaubert articulates the dilemma of all potentially strong poets in France, who are continually caught (consciously or unconsciously) in the obligation of rereading Boileau; for indeed Boileau cannot be read, he can only be reread in a perpetual dynamic of misprision and revision. In explicitly aspiring to the strength of his precursor ("Cela me semble vraiment fort.") he announces his own project of "art-critique," a collection of *Préfaces* to French literature that will be the culmination of his career,[40] a series of critical projections that inscribe him in the proleptic tradition of the *Art poétique*.

If Hugo then still insists upon his radical swerve away from the father in 1854 and again in 1864, it suggests a certain immaturity in the definition of his own poetic growth; it is as if his poetic development were arrested at an initial revisionary stage that is evoked in his nostalgic return to the youthful "triumphs" of 1834. And it is for this reason that Bloom is wrong in suggesting that he is the strong poet of the French tradition. "French poetry lacks not only early giants of the dimension of Chaucer, Spencer and Shakespeare, but it is also devoid of any later figures of strength who could approximate Milton and Wordsworth, Whitman and Dickinson. There is also the oddity that the nearest French equivalent, Victor Hugo, remains absurdly unfashionable and neglected by his nation's most advanced critics."[41]

---

39. "I am presently rereading Boileau, or rather, all of Boileau, and with many pencil notes in the margin. It seems really strong to me. One never tires of what is well written. Style is life! It is the very blood of thought! . . . So much Art was necessary to produce this and with so little! In the next two or three years I thus plan on rereading all of the French classics and annotating them, an endeavor that will serve me for my *Prefaces* (my work of literary criticism, you know)." *Correspondance*, 3, p. 336.

40. Cf. Letter to George Sand, July 5, 1868 (*Correspondance*, 3, p. 386): "Quand je serai vieux je ferai de la critique. . . . Personne mieux que moi, ne comprend les indignations de Boileau contre le mauvais goût." ["When I am old, I shall turn to criticism. . . . No one better than I . . . understands Boileau's indignations at bad taste."]

41. "The Breaking of Forms," op. cit., p. 13.

While it is true that Victor Hugo is by virtue of his enormous corpus[42] and popularity with the general reader a poetic giant, and true also that he is in a curious way equivalent to the English poets Bloom cites, Hugo ("hélas!") lacks the critical insight to be *the* strong poet for French poets. In his refusal to come to terms with Boileau, to allow the "dead" (in whose death he is proudly complicit) to return, he never achieves the legislative status of the poet-critic. He continues to write the epilogue for Romantic poetry and in so doing never succeeds in producing the Preface that will ensure his lasting strength.

In the energetic words of the young Rimbaud (a stronger poet in many ways than Hugo, but one whose career was cut short before the poetic cycle was complete) the poet must be "absolument moderne." Hugo, by clinging to the faded fiction of a Romantic rupture, never advanced fully to the dialectical integration of classical (critical) consciousness and Romantic (poetic) inspiration that would guarantee him his lasting gianthood.

To be a strong poet in the continuous tradition of French literature, is to commit oneself, anxiously, to a discontinuous vision of the future; to draw on a critical tradition of the past in order to legislate the order of the new and the modern. It is to inscribe oneself not simply in a virile line of poetic tradition but more precisely in the shifting *zig-zag* of critical authority. Roland Barthes, a modern "poet-critic" whose strength derives paradoxically from the early confrontation with neoclassical doctrine that impelled him to look forward, has characterized the "disruptive" dynamic of French literature as follows: "Reactive formations: a doxa . . . is . . . posited; I find it unbearable; in order to escape it, I postulate a paradox; the latter thickens, becomes itself a new concretion, a new doxa, and I must proceed further toward a new paradox."[43] The energy that generates the strength of French poetry emerges from the paradoxical need to be *absolutely modern* in a tradition where the conditions of modernity are commanded (anticipated) by the past.

The same Rimbaud who dismissed Hugo as "trop cabochard,"

---

42. A corpus whose greatest influence, nevertheless, is limited to specific moments in the critical development of French literature, most notably, the 1830s, the "heroic" age that Hugo persistently returns to.

43. "Doxa/Paradoxa," in *Roland Barthes* (Paris: Seuil, 1975), p. 75.

nevertheless recognized in his late verse a vision that opens onto new poetic possibilities.[44] Significantly, late in his career, there are hints of Hugo's return to the dogmatic Boileau he had been wrestling with for forty years. Flaubert writes in a letter of 1874: "Il n'y a guère qu'avec Victor Hugo que je peux causer de ce qui m'intéresse. Avant hier il m'a cité par coeur du Boileau. . . . Cela m'a fait l'effet d'un cadeau, tant la chose est rare."[45] The Romantic Hugo whose poetic memory is haunted by the voice of Boileau offers in this "rare" moment the image of the poetic ideal that Flaubert defines elsewhere as follows: "Il faut montrer aux classiques qu'on est plus classique qu'eux et faire pâlir les romantiques en dépassant leurs intentions. Je crois la chose faisable, car c'est tout un."[46]

The strong poet must aim beyond the polemic distinctions of Classical will and Romantic whim to neutralize the burden of ulteriority—the anxious opposition of past and future—in the transcendant achievement of present voice. Ultimately, this poetic achievement cannot be located in the gigantic body of Hugo; it does define, however, the reputation of the nineteenth-century's most powerful poet, and the poet whose "effect" has become synonymous with modernity: Charles Baudelaire.

"L'EFFET BAUDELAIRE"

In April 1864, Alcide Dusolier, a minor critic writing in *Le Nain jaune*, summarized the poetic character of Baudelaire in the title of an article that has become famous for its antithetical stance: "Charles Baudelaire ou Boileau hystérique." Though the epithet was clearly intended to ridicule the poet, there is a certain aptness in the juxtaposition of contraries that suggests the coupling of a Classical critic and Romantic poet to produce the strong artist that Flaubert envisioned. Boileau, the virile figure of paternal authority and self-control, guarantor of a continuous

---

44. Letter to Paul Demeny, May 15, 1871, in *Poésies* (Paris: Gallimard, 1973), p. 204.

45. "Except for Victor Hugo, there is hardly anyone else with whom I can discuss what interests me. The day before yesterday he quoted some Boileau for me by heart. . . . I felt as if I had just received a gift, so precious was that moment." Letter to George Sand, Dec. 2, 1874, *Correspondance*, 7, p. 224.

46. "We must show the classics that we are more classic than they, and outshine the Romantics by surpassing their intentions. I believe this can be done, for it is all the same." Letter to Louise Colet, June 26, 1853, *Correspondance*, 3, p. 249.

tradition, is modified by *hysteria*, the utterly feminine image of chaos and disruption that was so often used to discount the passionate energy of the Romantic imagination. While Boileau stands as the Classical father of French poetry, "hysteria" characterizes the Romantic mother that Hugo honors in his essay of the same year.

The marriage of "l'esprit critique" and "l'imagination poétique" that characterizes all of Baudelaire's writings determines more precisely his most daring literary experiment, the "Petits poèmes en prose." Poem 32, "Le Thyrse," is dedicated to the genius of Franz Liszt. Its language combines the rigorous theoretical idiom Baudelaire had developed in his critical essays with the sensuous imagery of the *Fleurs du Mal*. The central image of that poem, the Thyrsus, exemplifies in its own internal tensions the force of Baudelaire's poetry and the genius of Liszt, the strong artist who is destined for immortality: "philosophe, poète et artiste." The integration of philosophy and poetry (to produce the artist) is translated in a union of masculine and feminine opposites; will and fantasy, mastery and passion, straight line and zig-zag—Classic and Romantic.

> Le bâton c'est votre volonté, droite, ferme et inébranlable; les fleurs c'est la promenade de votre fantaisie autour de votre volonté; c'est l'élément féminin exécutant autour du mâle ses prestigieuses pirouettes. Ligne droite et ligne arabesque, intention et expression, roideur de la volonté, sinuosité du verbe, unité du but, variété des moyens, amalgame tout-puissant et indivisible du génie, quel analyste aura le détestable courage de vous diviser et de vous séparer?[47]

Baudelaire's essays on modern art stress in an analogous way the simultaneous engagement of the artist with the paternal authority of the past (le "verbe magistral"[48]) and the adventures of a maternal imagination ("reine des facultés"). And in his double commitment to Classical restraint and Romantic expansion, Baudelaire synthesizes the academic doctrines of Boileau and the individualistic (anti) doc-

---

47. "The rod is your will, steady, straight, and firm, and the flowers, the wandering of your fancy around your will, the feminine element executing its bewitching pirouettes around the male. Straight line and arabesque, intention and expression, inflexibility of the will, sinuosity of the word, unity of the goal, variety of the means, all-powerful and indivisible amalgam of genius, what analyst would have the detestable courage to divide and separate you?" "The Thyrsus" in *Paris Spleen* (1869), trans. Louise Varese, (New York: New Directions, 1970), pp. 72–73.

48. "Salon de 1846," *Oeuvres complètes* (Paris: Gallimard, 1975), v. 2, p. 491.

trines of Hugo to produce the most powerful "art poétique" since the seventeenth century.

André Gide qualifies the strength of Baudelaire's "art poétique" in terms of the critical spirit that invests the master code of all French literature. "Car il n'est rien chez Baudelaire, qui ne réponde à quelque interrogation de son esprit critique, à sa constante investigation, et c'est bien par cette conscience de lui-même et de son art qu'il s'élève au-dessus des vagues et faciles transports de ses plus éminents contemporains. . . . C'était une révolution . . . que d'inviter *l'art* à maîtriser la poésie. . . . Je suis de ceux qui se plaisent, ou s'amusent, à voir entre Baudelaire et lui [Boileau], non certes une parenté de génie, mais des analogies de métier flagrantes."[49]

Paul Valéry, scion of the same line of poetic generation, also interprets the inescapable force of Baudelaire by enlisting him in a literary tradition that is determined by the critical order of the seventeenth century. "A quoi tient cette importance singulière? . . . c'est une circonstance exceptionnelle qu'une intelligence critique associée à la vertu de la poésie."[50] His appreciation of Baudelaire is marked by the anxiety of its own inherent contradictions: the historic force of French poetry derives from the association of critical intel-

49. "For there is nothing in Baudelaire that does not respond to some interrogation of his critical mind, to his constant investigation; indeed, it is by virtue of this consciousness of himself and his art that he rises above the vague and facile transports of his most eminent contemporaries. . . . His was a revolution . . . that invited *art* to master poetry. . . . I am among those who fancy seeing a link between Baudelaire and [Boileau], certainly not a relationship of genius, but startling analogies of craft." Preface to *Anthologie de la poésie française* (Paris: Gallimard, 1949), pp. ix–x, xxvii. Cf. also "Baudelaire et M. Faguet," in *Nouveaux prétextes*. The titles of Gide's two collections of criticism, *Prétextes* and *Nouveaux prétextes*, recall Flaubert's own critical project, *Préfaces*. The critical preface has a long and rich history in French literature that can only be hinted at here. Many critical prefaces gained early independent status as proleptic manifestoes for various literary movements. One could refer to Du Bellay's second preface to *L'Olive*, Racine's prefaces to his tragedies, etc. In the nineteenth century, some prefaces acquired a celebrity that actually outstripped the works they were meant to introduce, thereby rendering those works oddly superfluous to the general history of French literature. Among the more prominent examples, the prefaces to *Cromwell* (Hugo), *Mlle de Maupin* (Gautier) and *Pierre et Jean* (Maupassant). Here the critical gesture managed not only to "precede" the literary act, but to supersede it. On the precarious supplementarity of the preface, see Jacques Derrida, *La Dissémination* (Paris: Seuil, 1972).

50. "To what may we attribute this singular importance? . . . it is the exceptional circumstance of a critical intelligence associated with the virtue of poetry." "Situation de Baudelaire," in *Variété 2* (Paris: NRF, 1930), p. 143.

ligence and the virtue of poetry but that association, Valéry adds, remains the exception, an exception to whose rule he himself aspires. Baudelaire rises out of the tradition of "l'art poétique" to become "l'inventeur des combinaisons les plus neuves et les plus séduisantes de la logique avec l'imagination, de la mysticité avec le calcul, le psychologue de l'exception."[51] By locating himself in the differential space between the systems of an immediate Romantic context (Hugo) and the historically mediated context of French Classicism (Boileau), the poet succeeds in creating, in the words of Hugo, a "frisson nouveau," a vibration whose force would break the ground of French literature in the radical way Hugo himself had failed to do. "Il suffit de considérer les mouvements et les oeuvres qui se sont produits après lui [Baudelaire], contre lui, et qui furent automatiquement, des *réponses exactes* à ce qu'il était."[52] Baudelaire, like Boileau, effects through his disruption the generation of movement(s) that ensures the vital continuity of French poetry. In his apotheosis as the new figure of authority to whom all sons respond, he becomes a "classic." "Classique est l'écrivain qui porte un critique en soi-même."[53] Valéry's definition of the classic summarizes the essential nature of the strong poet in French literature. And while he points specifically to Racine who carried Boileau (or the image of Boileau) within him, the genealogy of French literature supports the more general claim that all strong poets harbor the image of that same father.

"Le propre de ce qui est vraiment général c'est d'être fécond . . . la véritable fécondité d'un poète ne consiste pas dans le nombre de ses vers, mais bien plutôt dans l'étendue de leurs *effets*."[54] It was the

51. "The inventor of the newest and most seductive combinations of logic and imagination, of mysticity and calculation, the psychologist of exceptions." Valéry, op. cit., p. 144.

52. "One need only consider the movements and the works that were produced after him [Baudelaire], against him, and which were, automatically, *exact responses* to what he was." Valéry, op. cit., p. 147.

53. "A classic is a writer who carries a critic inside him." Valéry, op. cit., p. 155.

54. "The property of what is truly general is that it be fecund . . . the true fecundity of a poet does not consist in the number of his verses, but rather, in the extent of their *effects*." Valéry, op. cit., pp. 160, 168. Cf. "La plus grande gloire de Baudelaire . . . est sans doute d'avoir engendré quelques très grands poètes" (p. 173). ["Baudelaire's greatest glory . . . comes no doubt from having engendered several very great poets."] Valéry, in defining the genealogical line of Verlaine, Mallarmé and Rimbaud, anticipates—anxiously—his own place in the future.

literary fate of two centuries of French poets to struggle with the authority of the "effet Boileau." In a repetition of that productive tension, all poetry since the midnineteenth century has had to struggle belatedly with the "effet Baudelaire." When he "broke the ground" of literary history in 1857, the poet of the *Fleurs du Mal* also redefined the poetic landscape[55] of the map for (mis)reading the ulterior motives of all strong French poetry: "Là, tout n'est qu'ordre et beauté." In the critical space between order and beauty lie epic strength and the anticipation of art.

"L'EFFET BLOOM"

The critical imperative of the French tradition translates into an open invitation that appeals to the reader (and potential writer) to participate in the dialectical process of a critical poetics where order may precede beauty. As such, it does not presuppose the Romantic nostalgias of individual triumphs or successful landings, but supposes only the ceaseless voyage out of an authoritative past into the hazardous future to which Baudelaire's speculative poems invite us. The poem "L'Invitation au voyage" dramatizes the characteristically Baudelairian invitation of a masculine intelligence to a feminine imagination to join with him on a voyage of poetry that celebrates their union. And the two versions of the poem (verse poem 1855, prose poem 1857) articulate in their very repetition the critical displacement of poetic discourse onto an expansive, uncertain space that is potentially idealized in a paradise where "le luxe a plaisir à se mirer dans l'ordre." In that exotic landscape the poetic anima rediscovers her own image in a textual tradition that is cultivated in the midst of botanical splendor:

> Fleur incomparable, tulipe retrouvée, allégorique dahlia, c'est là, n'est-ce pas, dans ce beau pays si calme et si rêveur, qu'il faudrait aller vivre et fleurir? Ne serais-tu pas encadrée dans ton analogie, et

55. Cf. Fontenelle's hierarchical map of poetry in footnote 2, above. While Fontenelle's map is organized around the strictly defined order of genres, Baudelaire designs his "map" (a *paysage intérieur*, as in the pocm(s) "L'Invitation au voyage") around the two aesthetic principles of *order* and *beauty* which articulate the axis of critical and poetic tension to the exclusion of generic restrictions. In the two versions of this poetic landscape, Baudelaire plays off the dualities characteristic of his general artistic system: the eternal and the ephemeral, calculation and spontaneity, etc.

pour me servir du langage de ces livres qui traînent toujours sur ma
table et qui te font ouvrir de si grands yeux, n'aurais-tu pas pour
miroir ta propre *correspondance?*[56]

The prose poem of 1857 situates the hypothetical garden of poetic
Eden in a world where Nature is edited by Art and incomparable
flowers (not yet fallen into Evil) find nevertheless their happy analogy
in the language of "ces livres qui traînent toujours sur ma table":
evidence of the cumulative past that plants the seeds for the *art
poétique* that will disseminate out of Baudelaire's own "Corre-
spondances."

French poetry with its implicit critical discourse that responds to
the tradition of the *Art Poétique,* concentrates on the processes of
poetic expression and production that remain endlessly open to plural and contradictory possibilities. The interrogative potentiality of
this poetry disorients the reader through strategies of indirection that
make the poetic voyage one that can promise only a movement—
with no fixed destination—"bien loin d'ici."

> Mais les vrais voyageurs sont ceux-là qui partent
> Pour partir; coeurs légers, semblables aux ballons,
> De leur fatalité jamais ils ne s'écartent,
> Et, sans savoir pourquoi, disent toujours: Allons![57]

In the final poem of *Les Fleurs du Mal,* "Le Voyage," Baudelaire poses
the dilemma of the modern poet who is caught at once in the fatality
of a finite past that cannot be escaped and committed to forging the
paths of an infinite and discontinuous future. He spins about—
"Nous imitons, horreur! la toupie et la boule"—striving for the momentum that will launch him outside the closures of time and space:

---

56. "Incomparable flower, rediscovered tulip, allegorical dahlia, it is there, is it
not, in that beautiful country, so calm, so full of dreams, that you must live, that you
must bloom? Would you not be framed there within your own analogy, and—to borrow
the language of the books that always lie scattered on my table and make you open your
eyes so wide—would you not see yourself reflected in your own *correspondence?"*
Baudelaire, *Oeuvres complètes,* 1, p. 1324.

57.   But only those who leave for leaving's sake
             are *travelers;* hearts tugging like balloons,
             they never balk at what they call their fate
             and, not knowing why, keep muttering, "Away!"

"The Travelers," trans. Richard Howard, *Les Fleurs du Mal* (Boston: Godine, 1982).

"singulière fortune où le but se déplace,/ Et n'étant nulle part, peut
être n'importe où!" The literary destiny of the strong poet is thus
projected "anywhere out of this world," into an idealized "espace
littéraire," unmarked by the contingencies of time and personal
struggle; a space where the work of the poet may eventually become
the classical body of depersonalized *effect*.[58]

Harold Bloom, in charting the design for English literary history,
enlists a reading of Romantic and post-Romantic poetry that adheres
to a myth of personal growth, culminating in the resolution of an
Oedipal crisis. His theory of influence and revision, based as it is on
the presupposed integrity of self and *oeuvre*, thus assumes the
closure of a totalized product that can be encoded in a *map*—complete with directions for reading the route to poetic self-reliance, self-
fulfillment and (individual) voice. Within the dynamic continuum of
French poetic history, however, the retrospective model of the map is
ultimately subordinated to metaphors of the indefinite but historically determined voyage on which a differently oriented tradition
plots its own advance. The collective anxiety that qualifies the paradoxical quest of the French poet subsumes the individual anxiety of
influence into anticipations of the new: translating the desire for the
unfamiliar in the familiar terms of a critical tradition that aspires to
sound the space beyond the map for the cultivation of future poetry.
In a corner of that hypothetical space, "Bien loin d'ici," Baudelaire's
flowers will continue to blossom, long after they have lost their
bloom.

58. Cf. Maurice Blanchot, *Le Livre à venir* (Paris: Gallimard, 1959).

RICHARD SHIFF

The Original, the Imitation, the Copy, and the Spontaneous Classic: Theory and Painting in Nineteenth-Century France

As the title suggests, this essay has four major divisions. Their order follows an obvious logic that is linear and yet circular: each of the four routes of investigation leads to the others, and any one of them could initiate a forward course; nevertheless, all seem bent on returning to a source. The concept of the "original," as the clearest reference to source or origin, becomes the most natural point from which to begin the intellectual journey. But here the highway already seems to degenerate into by-paths. The first section of the essay has priority, just as any origin, and cannot benefit from antecedents; it can only encircle its subject, remains fragmentary, and fails to reach any decisive conclusion. This admission comes not as an apology in advance of an incomplete argument, but rather as a polemical introduction.[1]

A deviated approach to (and from) the original may be the only appropriate one. Nineteenth-century artists often speak of their own originality uneasily, are uncertain over the essential nature of originality, and cannot hold that subject captive within a final definition. In general, nineteenth-century discourse recognizes the wildness of the original; and in the wavering motion of its consequent insecurity, it anticipates and evades the incisions with which critics today would undercut any rigid or seamless history of origins. To emphasize the point: nineteenth-century theorists will often survive attempts to dismiss their discourse as a *self-assured* metaphysics of

---

1. Elsewhere I have discussed originality more extensively; see my essays "Miscreation" (*Studies in Visual Communication* 7 [Spring 1981]: 57–71) and "Making a Find: An Argument for Creativity, not Originality" (forthcoming in *Structuralist Review*). In general, I associate the *modern* concept of originality with "finding," or the making of something (*seemingly*) out of nothing.

presence, as a resolute accounting of absolute and unique origins. In fact, many of them appear to have regarded originality just as problematically as critics do now; and it would therefore be judicious to note that the discourse of early modernism characteristically attains no further level of confidence than to be *self-assuring.* In other words, this discourse never becomes fully convinced of the position it espouses; it cannot manifest a self-assured closure; it only gestures toward it. Clearly it sought the original—but could it ever be certain of having found it? A (relatively sympathetic) reading suffices to reveal this anxiety over origins and authoritative authorship; indeed, the problematic of originality lies exposed, not only in the discourse, but on the very surface of nineteenth-century art.

As the theory and practice of early modernism is reviewed to determine the interrelationship of the concepts of "original," "imitation," "copy," and "spontaneous classic," the central but unsettling obsession with origins, sources, and the influence of tradition becomes ever more apparent. Eventually, I focus on the question of the *"anxiety of anticipation"* as I conclude that artists and critics of the nineteenth century sought to create or define a style which might insure from the start that any imitation or interpretation by another would be inadequate or simply impossible. These artists and critics sought a style outside history, one that would endure in its *original* state, long after the lifetime of its creator. Additionally, in the course of my argument, I make the following observations with regard to the theory and practice of painting in nineteenth-century France: (1) the meaning of "imitation" was shifted (sometimes rather abruptly) from a relationship of synonymity with "invention" to a relationship of synonymity with "copy"; (2) universality, as the essence of a desired artistic "ideal," was often replaced by individuality; (3) critics and theorists came to attend less to the representation of "ideas" (signifieds) and more to the means of representation (signifiers); (4) the exemplary modern artist (the "spontaneous classic") came to be seen as one who is inimitable.

Initially, three statements may serve to indicate the complex interaction of some of the senses of "original," "imitation," and "copy" to be encountered in nineteenth-century texts. The reader may find it difficult to pass from one of these three statements to either of the others without questioning one or both; it is apparent that the various concepts of "original," "imitation," and "copy" conflict. The fourth statement given below represents the anxiety of Paul Gauguin, toward whom the other sources cited in this essay move, as if having anticipated him. Gauguin marks our beginning and our end.

(I) We do *not* identify as imitation . . . the process by which two chairs, for example, are fabricated and rendered so like one another, that our eye cannot distinguish which was the model from which is the copy of it. [Quatremère de Quincy, 1837][2]

(II) The last word in imitation is to produce a copy that one could take for the original. [Charles Blanc, 1867][3]

(III) Two versions of one of the more troubling definitions of the noun *copy:* (a) the original writing, work of art, etc., from which a copy is made (Oxford English Dictionary); (b) in printing, the [original] manuscript text on which compositors work (Littré, 1863).[4] (In other words, the "copy" is the one and only "original" and is that which is to be copied.)

(IV) Well, despite the fact that nobody wants my work because it is different from that of others (strange, illogical public which demands the greatest possible originality from a painter and yet will not accept him unless he resembles all the others—and parenthetically, *I do resemble those who resemble me* [je ressemble à ceux qui me ressemblent], that is *those who imitate me*, yet you want to do business with me. . . . [Paul Gauguin, 1900][5]

I. THE ORIGINAL

When Gauguin wrote from Tahiti (his primordial "Eden") to the Parisian dealer Vollard, he expressed the irony of his situation: his

2. Antoine Chrysostome Quatremère de Quincy, *Essai sur l'idéal dans ses applications pratiques aux oeuvres de l'imitation propre des arts du dessin* (Paris: Le Clère, 1837), p. 309 (emphasis added). This book (hereafter cited as *Idéal*) is a compilation of articles previously published, for the most part, in 1805. Here, and elsewhere, unless otherwise noted, my translation.

3. Charles Blanc, *Grammaire des arts du dessin* (Paris: H. Laurens, 1880; orig. ed., 1867), p. 18.

4. Entry for "copy," *Oxford English Dictionary* (Oxford: Oxford Univ. Press, 1971); entry for "copie," Émile Littré, *Dictionnaire de la langue française* (Paris: Hachette, 1863–66).

5. Letter to Vollard, Jan. 1900, reprinted in John Rewald, ed., *Paul Gauguin, Letters to Ambroise Vollard and André Fontainas* (San Francisco: The Grabhorn Press, 1943), p. 33 (Rewald's trans.; my emphasis). Prof. Rewald kindly supplied me with the unpublished French version of the letter.

potential for commercial success seemed to depend on both his difference from others and his likeness to them. The fact that others imitated him would make his own work, otherwise so original as to be unassimilable, meaningful and acceptable to the public. Yet if he were copied, if he served as the original "copy" *for* others, he might lose his originality—both his singularity and his priority—and appear to be the copy *of* others. As if caught between distorting mirrors, the painter lost his position at the center, experienced a "mise en abîme," and saw that he resembled those who resembled him. Would his Parisian public be able to find the origin (the "reality") among the innumerable images?

In one respect Gauguin surely was not original: many of his predecessors had already recognized the implications of the problematic of originality. French artists, critics, and historians active during the nineteenth century—both those repeatedly revived in direct quotation or imitative pastiche (such as Gauguin) and also those quickly forgotten—often faced the disturbing realization that the original and the imitation could exist only symbiotically. Among those who pondered the problem, the theologian and history professor Hervé Bouchitté did not fare so well as Gauguin before the public; he may be counted as one of the large number of cultural agents who experience suspended animation—no one bothered to (mis)interpret or imitate him; he was ignored, his works withered. Bouchitté's contribution to the history of art was a comprehensive study of Poussin; it is mentioned but once in the present standard monograph on this artist, and there cited only in a footnote and unnecessarily.[6] Indeed, upon publication in 1858 Bouchitté's book received the kind of review intended to send it to an early, if not immediate death. Paul Mantz, writing for *L'Artiste*, complained that Bouchitté offered nothing new (i.e., was not original), omitted much available information (did not use the proper sources), and had studied inadequate reproductions instead of the original paintings.[7] But in defense of Bouchitté's effort, one might speculate that this author had simply *not been seeking to innovate;* for in passing he made this

6. H. Bouchitté, *Le Poussin, sa vie et son oeuvre* (Paris: Didier, 1858). The inappropriate citation is in Anthony Blunt, *Nicolas Poussin,* 2 vols. (New York: Bollingen Foundation, 1967), 1, 160.

7. Paul Mantz, "Un Nouveau Livre sur le Poussin," *L'Artiste,* n.s., 4 (23 and 30 May 1858): 39–40, 55.

rather conservative, yet provocative pronouncement: "Painting which would offer the viewer absolutely unknown ideas or completely unexperienced feelings (*des affections tout à fait inéprouvées*) could not be understood" (p. 331). Bouchitté seems to imply that the radically original should be avoided for the sake of communicating with a public.

Here Bouchitté was not anticipating the cause of Gauguin's commercial difficulties and his bitter wrangling with Vollard; his concern was not with the originality of a stylistic manner. The radical innovation he had in mind involved instead the experience of "ideas" and "feelings"; it would not be detected by comparing one work of art to another, but by relating art to one's knowledge of nature. In other words, the difference that troubled Bouchitté was in signifieds, representations of reality; in contrast, for Gauguin, who worried over maintaining personal stylistic identity, the problematic difference (and similarity) was in signifiers, indices pointing back to the artist as much as to a world he depicted. Gauguin held that artistic style—artistic language—determined all. As both modern primitive and modern classic, he attempted to render his images in a primordial style conceived as analogous to a universal mother tongue, one that maintained a clear sense of its roots or origins in human experience.[8] In his concern for discovering an appropriate means of expression and his intimation that his language would either limit or expand his knowledge of the world, Gauguin seems familiarly modern (but not "postmodern"). Bouchitté, however, chose to focus on the originality of "content" rather than of style; he assumed that "ideas" were more of an issue than the means by which they were known. Just as many other theorists of his time, he held the comforting belief that images might exist in the mind independently of the means to render them. Perhaps for this reason, his own text on Poussin seemed both unoriginal and unintelligent to Mantz, generated little long-term interest, and remains obscure (if not unknown) today. Possibly, in resisting or even challenging originality, Bouchitté became so idiosyncratically contrary that no one who engaged in a pursuit of the original could bear the paradox of acknowledging him.

8. See Gauguin's letter to August Strindberg, 5 Feb. 1895, reprinted in Maurice Malingue, ed., *Lettres de Gauguin à sa femme et à ses amis* (Paris: Grasset, 1946), pp. 262–64.

II. THE IMITATION

Bouchitté's remark on the incommunicability of the absolutely original follows upon his quoting the definition of "invention" offered by Antoine Quatremère de Quincy, a figure considerably less neglected than Bouchitté himself. Quatremère was an admirer of Winckelmann, a friend of David, and later of Ingres; he enjoyed a long and prolific career as an Academic theorist. As Academician (he served as Secrétaire perpétuel of the Académie des Beaux-Arts from 1816 to 1839), Quatremère dedicated himself to the teaching of art in terms of normative principles. Yet, ironically, these principles involved concepts, such as "invention", that were by no means discussed with universal agreement. In 1824 Quatremère had written that pictorial invention would "give birth to unknown ideas in the mind of the viewer, to unexperienced feelings in his soul, and present to his eyes images or combinations that nature never would have offered."[9] It would seem from this definition that artistic invention is revelatory—but of what? Not of a romantic self nor of the particularities of nature associated with the experiences and observations of the idiosyncratic romantic artist, for Quatremère opposed romanticism.[10] Instead, whether through new ideas, feelings, or visual images, artistic invention would reveal general aspects of nature—of "Creation"—not otherwise known. But how, then, could an invention be understood? Must it have some connection with familiar ideas and experiences? Bouchitté, on his part, seemed to think so; hence he argued that Quatremère had exaggerated the degree to which invention could be absolutely new.

9. Bouchitté (p. 331) quotes this passage from Quatremère de Quincy's *Histoire de la vie et des ouvrages de Raphaël* (Paris: Gosselin, 1824), p. 412. Quatremère revised the wording of his statement for a subsequent edition ([Paris: Firmin-Didot, 1835], p. 391). For Quatremère artistic invention retained an element of inscrutability associated with genius; see his *Essai sur la nature, le but et les moyens de l'imitation dans les beaux-arts* (Paris: Treuttel et Würtz, 1823), p. 181. (Hereafter cited as *Imitation.*)

10. On romanticism, cf. *Imitation*, pp. 79–81. Quatremère felt that the romantic artists (such as Delacroix) had confused mere innovation with genuine originality; see R. Schneider, *Quatremère de Quincy et son intervention dans les arts (1788–1830)* (Paris: Hachette, 1910), p. 256. Ironically, Delacroix often discussed artistic imitation by making exactly the same distinction that Quatremère would; he argued, for example, that Poussin did not imitate the material details of his source, but captured its "genius." See Eugène Delacroix, "Le Poussin" (1853), *Oeuvres littéraires*, ed. Elie Faure, 2 vols. (Paris: Crès, 1923), 2, 95.

Traditionally, inventions were regarded as *composites*, new artistic compositions of old and familiar elements; Quatremère's definition itself indicated this in its reference to "images or combinations."[11] Nevertheless, Bouchitté could not follow Quatremère's claim for the efficacy of artistic invention without hesitating, for he recognized that the *elements* of the new work (as opposed to its totality) would have to be known in advance to the viewer as well as to the artist. It is as if the viewer must be able to re-create the work out of its component parts in order to understand it. Such re-creation would be imitation.[12] Inventive *compositions* could be comprehended to the point of their being subject to imitation only when others recognized the elements and understood the principle of organization—a composition, according to Bouchitté, is a harmonious ensemble, determined by "the connection and subordination of groups, the correspondence of expressions, the just weighting of parts, the felicitous combination of lines" (p. 333). When one does not have knowledge of the parts and their interrelationships—that is, when the composite images are "absolutely unknown," unfamiliar in any view and impervious to any analysis—indeed one cannot understand the work of art *as an invention or composition*. Nor can one understand it *as an imitation*, for one does not know where or how to find its original. What is being imitated? Not even one source, among the several *combined* sources, seems available. Such is the nature of the "absolutely unknown": it has no recognizable parts.

Quatremère de Quincy had a manner of defining imitation so that this line of argument would be obviated; indeed he was much more concerned with the notion of imitation than with the (for him) secondary notion of invention. In his *Essai sur la nature, le but et les moyens de l'imitation dans les beaux-arts* (1823), he developed a definition of imitation that recalled the Aristotelian one: imitation was not a mere copy, but a made (or poetic) thing, an inventive creation or fiction. Quatremère wrote that "to imitate in the fine arts, is to produce the resemblance of a thing, but in some other thing which

11. Cf. Condillac's definition of invention (quoted in Kineret S. Jaffe, "The Concept of Genius in Eighteenth-Century French Aesthetics," *Journal of the History of Ideas* 41 [1980]:587): "In fact we do not create ideas; we can only combine, by composition and decomposition, those that we receive by the senses. Invention consists in being able to make new combinations" (my translation).

12. This is stated by Quatremère himself: *Imitation*, p. 122.

becomes the image of it."[13] This "image," associated with imaginative invention, could be understood in terms of identity and difference; the academic theorist argued:

> As regards imitation, I call all those objects identical, which do not present themselves to us as different; it being understood that it is not here meant to take the words *identity (identité)* and *difference (diversité)* in their absolute and mathematical acceptation: I will just remark here, that according to the rigid sense of the word, there is but one sole identity in nature [i.e., God]. . . . Those objects then are called identical, which simply appear to be so, as are all the works produced by mechanical operations [i.e., reproduction]. This kind of apparent identity, which is the cause of confusion between similar objects, is precisely that at which the imitation of the fine arts ought not to aim. Such resemblance ought not to be its end. Repetition by means of an image [i.e., representation] being the exact opposite of that by means of identity [reproduction], all imitation which has the latter in view tends only to destroy itself, since in so doing it no longer aims at appearing imitation. [Pp. 7–8; Kent trans., pp. 15–16]

Simply put, imitations should aim at being different from, not identical to, their original and each other.

If, as Quatremère implies, "similarity by identity [*similitude par identité*]" is readily attainable by means of the mechanical crafts, what accounts for artistic resemblance by difference or "by image [*par image*]"? According to Quatremère, the image is but an appearance of reality, never reality itself; and, more than that, it is an unequivocal appearance—it never deceives; it is no illusion or double. One sees the image for what it is, a work of art, a representation constructed in a particular medium according to appropriate conventions. In the case of a painting, one is aware of the *fiction* of the image's two-dimensional representation of a three-dimensional world. Artistic technique (convention) becomes the "difference" or differentiating medium that accounts for the "ideal" quality of an image, the product of intellectual composition. It would be wrong

---

13. *Imitation*, p. 3. The translation is from Quatremère de Quincy, *An Essay on the Nature, the End, and the Means of Imitation in the Fine Arts*, trans. J. C. Kent (London: Smith, Elder, 1837), p. 11 (italics eliminated). Hereafter, extended quotations from *Imitation* will be given as in the Kent translation, with references to both the French and English texts.

"to deprive every art, as much as possible, of that part of its fictitious and conventional nature [*sa nature fictive et conventionnelle*] which makes it appear art, by substituting, through a spurious fidelity, the character of reality for that of appearance, and similarity by means of identity for resemblance by means of an image" (pp. 13–14; Kent trans., p. 22).[14]

In sum, although the "image" is new, it is linked to the reality from which it differs by way of its conventionalized form. The conventions of art effect a transformation from the (known) "real" to the (unknown) "ideal" by means of metaphor—by means of the "transferring" which Quatremère notes is the etymological sense of the figure of metaphor. Quatremère calls metaphor a "means of recomposition"; and "as man is incapable of creating otherwise than by effecting new combinations, one cannot under any form of composition whatever, bring two things together which were not previously so, without transferring the one or the other and sometimes both" (p. 325; Kent trans., pp. 359–60). The manner of representation, that is, the artist's technical procedure, brings about the metaphoric transference, this creative representation in the form of an image. The "difference" so essential to Quatremère's sense of imitation thus reduces to what may otherwise be referred to as the artist's "style." And so it becomes apparent that if one shifts the focus from signified to signifier (as the Romantics did), it is the artist who makes the difference.

When Bouchitté criticized Quatremère, he did not suggest that one might explain the element of novelty in terms of the individual style of the author of a work. Quatremère himself would not want to make much of an issue of individuality because he was arguing for an art of generalized idealization (*Idéal*, pp. 42–43, 57). Yet he could not entirely avoid the subject:

> Take, for instance, in the imitation of the human body, any [individual] model you please. Have the most exact copy (*copie*) taken of it by all the designers in the world. Lo! you will find as many different copies as there are copyists. A certain proof that besides the local and individual model contemplated by all alike, each one has within

14. Cf. also pp. 267–68. Quatremère was aware of the etymological link between "imitation" and "image"; cf. entry for "imāgō," A. Ernout and A. Meillet, *Dictionnaire étymologique de la langue latine* (Paris: Klincksieck, 1939).

himself another, which he consults and imitates. [*Imitation*, p. 182;
Kent trans., p. 206]

Quatremère's argument here is commonplace, yet problematic. It is
not at all clear from his writings when one should judge the individuality of a copy as a sign of idealized imitation, and when it should
instead be regarded as evidence of mechanical incompetence in re-
production. Moreover, there is a third possibility that such individuality in copying may simply result from self-indulgence, a failure
to control one's own peculiarities of imagination—such a failing, of
course, was said to characterize romanticism. Quatremère suggests a
way of dealing with the problem when he writes that the classic
Greeks, who were masterful imitators, worked systematically and
with fixed principles (*Idéal*, pp. 42–43). Following Quatremère's observation on the Greeks, one might conclude that whenever regularity can be discerned in the technique of an artist, the "difference"
in his work is largely the result of generalized imitative idealization
rather than some unreflective assertion of the self.

Although Quatremère, colleague of Ingres, belonged to the
"Classical" camp, it is important to note that he and his Romantic
antagonist Delacroix, perhaps unknowingly, reached some agreement in relating regularity to classic style. Delacroix, on his part,
defined the works of the classic artist as those which "seem destined
to serve as models, as the rule in all their parts. . . . Shakespeare, by
this account, will not be classic, that is to say, suited to being imitated in his techniques, in his system"; Shakespeare is too individualistic and irregular to be imitated by others.[15] It seems, then,
that one characteristic of the classic artist is that he serves as the
model, both the original and the "copy" for others, and that others
imitate not his individuality, but his technical system. Delacroix
implies that a classic, who is without predecessor, initiates a sequence of (necessarily inferior) imitations; he establishes a canon and
a doctrine. A nonclassic artist keeps his originality to himself. Shakespeare, who exhibits nothing but idiosyncrasy, remains inimitable.
Now Quatremère, on his part, argues similarly (but with some difference); he notes that an imitation *without rule or system* will result
from an artist who relies only upon himself and is "as if without

15. Entry for 13 Jan. 1857, Eugène Delacroix, *Journal*, ed. André Joubin, 3 vols.
(Paris: Plon, 1950), 3, 22–23.

predecessor." Such an artist corresponds to Quatremère's notion of the modern realist or romantic who either becomes a mere "copyist" or "opens up the paths of his art solely to himself." In contrast, the classic (Greek) artist provides the traces of a system others can follow as a means to *ideal* imitation (*Idéal*, pp. 42–44, 89 ff.).

Quatremère speaks of the idiosyncratic artist as a kind of realist obsessed with trivial detail and the accidents of nature, or alternatively, as a fantasizer, dependent on the unpredictable surges of his inspiration. Clearly, such an artist is "without predecessor." But in another context, Quatremère finds also that the classic Greeks had "no predecessors" (*Idéal*, pp. 44, 103). They *initiated* a tradition characterized by system and principle and served as an *absolute* origin, not a mere member, like any other member, of a sequence of copies. For Romantic critics, the notion of an absolute stylistic origin was at least as important as it was for Quatremère, if not more so. For the Romantics, however, the originality of the idiosyncratic or unsystematic artist was of greater interest than that of the law-giving classic. Hence, Théophile Thoré wrote that original artists were "the sons of no one, but they all have the same origin, that is to say that they proceed from their own innateness [*innéité*]."[16] How does the working of this inborn quality differ from the process of intellectual idealization (resulting in the "image") to which Quatremère would refer? On the one hand, it is more clearly identified with the self, or the individual "temperament" of which, with a progressively greater sense of particularity, Romantics and naturalists such as Stendhal, Baudelaire, and Zola would speak.[17] On the other hand, this innateness or instinctiveness generates a more direct "copy" than does Quatremère's process of "imitation."

Thoré's Salon reviews reveal this shift in the relation of the work of art to imitation and to copying. Although Thoré sometimes speaks of a poetic transformation in a work of art just as Quatremère does, he makes two assertions that the academic theorist could never affirm

16. Théophile Thoré (Thoré-Bürger), "Salon de 1846," *Les Salons*, 3 vols. (Brussels: Lamertin, 1893), 1, 289–90.

17. See, e.g., Charles Baudelaire, "De l'Idéal et du modèle," in "Salon de 1846," *Oeuvres complètes*, ed. Claude Pichois, 2 vols. (Paris: Gallimard, 1976), 2, 454–58; and my discussion of "tempérament" and "idéal" in "The End of Impressionism: A Study in Theories of Artistic Expression," *Art Quarterly*, n.s., 1 (Autumn 1978): 338–78, esp. 357–59, 365–66.

without fundamentally reassessing his notion of imitation. First, he directly contrasts "imitation" to poetic invention: "Poetry . . . is exactly the opposite of imitation" ("Salon de 1844," I, 20). Here Thoré may simply be demolishing the arguments of Quatremère and others at a single stroke by denying the specialized meaning they had given to the classical term. Second, and more significantly, in a discussion of Clésinger's sculpture, Thoré argues that nature is often

> in charge of *composing* images, fully ready to be reproduced in a form of art. A landscapist stops at the corner of a forest path and finds there a complete picture, with a central effect and well-organized lines. He has but to paint the landscape directly made by nature. Never would the academicians have invented this variety and this harmony. A sculptor has his model take a pose, and all at once a shape appears to him which exalts and impassions him. The sculpture is made. It remains only to draw this figure out from a block of marble. ["Salon de 1847," 1, 538–39]

Here, it seems that the *process* of artistic imitation involves no invention, no composition. The complete image is immediately conceived as a whole—or rather not "conceived," but simply "seen." The landscapist or sculptor merely renders *in a technical or even mechanical fashion* something seen to exist in nature. Needless to say, stylistic predecessors are not required when the presence of the natural model is so strong. Although different artists will be struck by different natural images, each one in making his representation performs what Quatremère would have to call a "copying"—not a copying of another's art, but of nature itself.

III. THE COPY

Within the meanderings of Romantic criticism Quatremère's distinction between "imitation" and "copy" got lost. Nor was it later to be found within Academic theory itself, at least not in the form Quatremère had considered traditional and had sought to sustain. Charles Blanc, whose *Grammaire des arts du dessin* (1867) was the most comprehensive statement of the theory and practice of the visual arts within its period, cited Quatremère's works and held many of his views, but did not employ his language. For Blanc, imitation was tantamount to copying: "What is imitation? It is a faithful copy, and nothing more. . . . The last word in imitation is to produce

a copy that one could take for the original" (*Grammaire*, pp. 17–18).
Blanc argued that the Aristotelian doctrine of imitation should be
replaced by what he regarded as a more intellectualized (Neo)Plato-
nism. He suggested that both Classical and Romantic theorists, despite other differences, had indeed accepted "the Platonic formula
[that] art is the interpretation of nature," and not its "copy" or (what
is, for Blanc, the same) its "imitation."[18] Implicitly, he demanded a
reconsideration of Quatremère's terminology. He placed his own emphasis on the quality of "style," associating it with artistic invention
and opposing it to imitation. The artist, according to Blanc, should
aim for stylization of the generalized sort, the quality of idealization
to be found in classic art. Although Blanc's "style" is analogous to
Quatremère's "ideal" that results from imitation, this concept of
style is clearly associated with the appearance, or form, of the work
(as signifier) rather than with the image that appears in the work (as
signified). Quatremère had preferred to speak in terms of the image or
idea itself. For Quatremère, imitation represents the appearance of
something in a form different from its reality; the viewer might ignore the technical conventions or formal manner responsible for this
difference so long as the difference *of the image itself* were evident.
Quatremère argues that the act of *comparing* the ideal image to the
real affords intellectual pleasure, and such pleasure constitutes the
"aim" of imitation (*Imitation*, p. 5). For Blanc, however, the particularity of a style seems more directly identified with the content of a
work; it is the "imprint of human thought on nature" (*Grammaire*, p.
20). One must attend then to the manner of imaging, or the style of
representation.

Both Blanc and Quatremère identified art with idealization; nevertheless, they would dispute the central issue that a theory of art
must investigate—for Quatremère, it is imitation; for Blanc, style.
Yet, on the question of the classic, the two Academic theorists would
have no difference; for in this case, style becomes invisible (or, in
Winckelmann's metaphor, "tasteless"):

> The Greeks [attained] absolute style, that *impersonal* and sublime
> art [concerning which] Winckelmann uttered these profound words:
> "Perfect beauty is like pure water, which has no particular taste."
> [*Grammaire*, p. 21; emphasis added.]

18. Charles Blanc, Introduction to *Histoire des peintres de toutes les écoles: École
française*, 3 vols. (Paris: Renouard, 1865), 1, 45–46.

In the case of the art of the classic Greeks, the question of stylistic identification or differentiation will not arise so long as the represented image reveals its universal quality. This art is "impersonal"; its originality is not that of a single author, but belongs to all who "imitate" (Quatremère's term) or to all who "design" (Blanc's term). Blanc opposes design to imitation and equates imitation with copying, but refers nevertheless to an ideal much like Quatremère's:

> Design [*dessin*] is not a simple imitation, a copy mathematically conforming to the original, an inert reproduction, a superfluity. Design . . . lets us see something superior to apparent reality [*la vérité apparente*]. . . . But what is this superior truth? It is sometimes the character of the object represented [*dessiné*], sometimes the character of the designer [*dessinateur*], and, in great art, it is precisely what we call style. [P. 531][19]

Given the extent to which Blanc finds it necessary to discuss the various types of "style," it is apparent that the generalized style (or the stylelessness) of the Greeks is not the rule but the exception within the diversity of the world's art. The word "style" itself was generally believed to have derived from the tool called the "stylus," and to signify the mark or physical imprint of the individual maker.[20] For Blanc, a particularized style would often be evident because the artist "imitates nature not precisely as nature itself exists, but as he himself exists . . . each artist impresses his personal character on his imitations . . . the temperament of the painter modifies the character of things . . . and nature is for him what he wants it to be" (pp. 19–20, 532). Thus, a fully accurate imitation or "faithful copy," if it were possible, would deny or falsify a major aspect of reality, the presence of the artist. In his scrupulous attempt to render reality, the artist would deny *himself*. Blanc recognizes that there must be degrees of imitative copying corresponding to a range of artistic styles: from those of a precise realism, to those of a pronounced particularity (styles of "character"), to those of grand generality ("absolute style"

---

19. "Dessin" is for Blanc both drawing and design; he notes that the old spelling of "dessin" was "dessein." The association of drawing with design, premeditation, and an intentional bringing into being is clearly related to the opposition of the technique of drawing to that of color. Generally, drawing was regarded as reflective, analytical and compositional; and color as emotional, expressive and organically whole.

20. Cf. Émile Deschanel, *Physiologie des écrivains et des artistes, ou essai de critique naturelle* (Paris: Hachette, 1864), p. 9.

or simply "style"—*le style* as opposed to *un style*). At both ends of the spectrum the mark of the individual artist becomes undetectable, for either the abundant *reality* of nature will have absorbed it in the way that a single hue may be absorbed into black, or the *ideality* of art will have rendered it invisible in the way that a pure light appears colorless. For Blanc, what lies between these two possibilities (the absolute real and the absolute ideal) is style itself, considered as the product of technical *choices*—indeed Blanc defines (and dismisses) extreme realism as "imitation without choice" (p. 18). Like Quatremère, Blanc conceives of an idealizing art as a process of invention or composition, a combination of elements: in painting, the artist must "choose, within the immense repertory of human forms, those that serve the best to translate his emotion or his thought" (p. 531). In the end, one arrives at a higher form of reality, not at falsity or mere repetitious convention, as some might argue:

> Those who, through love of the natural, defend themselves from the ideal as if from an enemy, and who would confine the artist to rigorous imitation [of nature], imagine no doubt that on one side lie truth and life, while on the other, convention and falsehood: this is a profound error. The ideal and the real have one and the same essence. The rough diamond and the polished diamond are both diamonds; the rough diamond is the real; the polished diamond is the ideal. [P. 21]

Polish (*poli*)—or refinement, or finish (*fini*)—becomes the evidence of technical choice and manipulation, the gradual accretion of style leading away from direct imitation (copying) toward an ultimate idealization; it is also the sign of intellectual activity and, more generally, the imprint of the human spirit striving for a divine perfection. Is there then something subhuman in a simple copying, a thoughtless animal-like "*singerie*"?—"the conceit of the copyist quite often imposes the name of creation [*création*] upon what is only a successful aping [*une heureuse singerie*]."[21] Certainly, mere copying was not regarded as a valuable artistic act, but was instead seen as meretricious, a prostitution of the self. Even when artists were commissioned to copy masterworks for educational purposes, they were not expected to suppress entirely their own personalities. When vari-

---

21. Jacques Nicolas Paillot de Montabert, *L'Artistaire, livre des principales initiations aux beaux-arts* (Paris: Johanneau, 1855), p. 180. Paillot's writings were often cited by Blanc.

ous artists produced paintings for the "Musée des Copies," one of
Blanc's major projects during his tenure as Director of Fine Arts, each
artist (according to a contemporary account) "in performing [his]
copy-work faithfully, [put] something of himself into the task of
assimilation."[22]

With the increased sensitivity to individual style, the prohibition against simple copying might be extended even to what had
traditionally been considered imitative *invention*. An original artist
should not create a "pastiche," a combination of images or stylistic
elements drawn from antecedent sources. Thus, Thoré saw fit to
question Manet's integrity when he recognized elements of Velasquez and Goya in the modern master's painting of the *Incident in the
Bull Ring* (1864); and in response to Thoré, Baudelaire defended Manet by claiming that such resemblances were fortuitous, not the
result of deliberate imitative pastiche, but of a coincidence of artistic
temperaments.[23] Manet himself, according to Émile Zola, denied
that he ever invented anything; Zola reports him to say:

> I can do nothing without nature. I do not know how to invent. As
> long as I wanted to paint according to the instruction I had received, I
> produced nothing of merit.[24]

If Manet does not invent, nor imitate the masters' techniques taught
in the schools, what does he do? A dramatic inversion of theoretical
principles is suggested by Manet's statement: perhaps this artist acts
as unimaginatively as an ape and has no "ideas" of his own; he
"copies."

Here, the issue does not turn upon what the art historian might
consider the true facts of Manet's case—his artistic education, his
borrowing of motifs from other artists, the social and historical commentary he revealed through his paintings, even his "philosophy."
Instead one encounters an ideological commitment to individuality
and modernity revealed through a rhetoric of artistic theory and tech-

22. Henri Delaborde, "Le Musée des Copies," *Revue des deux mondes* 105 (1 May
1873): 215.
23. Thoré, "Salon de 1864," 3, 98–100; Baudelaire, letter to Thoré, c. 20 June
1864, reprinted in Charles Baudelaire, *Oeuvres complètes, Correspondance générale,*
ed. Jacques Crépet, 18 vols. (Paris: L. Conard, 1948), 4, 275–77. See also my discussion
of the Thoré-Baudelaire exchange in "Miscreation," pp. 67–68.
24. Émile Zola, "Mon Salon" (1868), *Mon Salon, Manet, Écrits sur l'art,* ed. An-
toinette Ehrard (Paris: Garnier-Flammarion, 1970), p. 142.

nical procedure. Manet's own style was characterized by a lack of "polish" and "finish"; he emphasized those elements of technique— color and brushstroke—associated with instinct and spontaneous self-expression. He did not usually depend on contour or the complexities of a preconceived perspectival system.[25] Manet's style thus signified either a return-trip on the conventional artistic voyage from the real to the ideal, or, more accurately, a journey on which *one never departs from the station of origin.* Manet seemed neither to invent nor to compose, nor even to imagine, that is, to form the artistic "appearances" of reality which Quatremère would call "imitations" or "images." Instead Manet "copied," remaining absolutely faithful to the original. But what was his original, his model?

In one case at least, Zola served as model. In 1868 Manet painted Zola's portrait, and simultaneously, of course, the critic observed the artist at work. Soon afterward Zola described the process, stressing both the intense deliberateness and the lack of deliberation in Manet's act—Manet's copying was, if anything, direct:

> He had forgotten me, he no longer knew that I was there, he was copying me [*il me copiait*] as he would have copied any human animal whatever, with an attentiveness, an artistic awareness [*une conscience artistique*] that I have never seen elsewhere. ["Mon Salon", p. 141]

Manet does not seek out Zola's special character, his intellectual or spiritual qualities; he seems to concentrate on the surface appearance. He is making, or "copying," a portrait. Traditionally, portraits had indeed been called "copies," had been associated with a realistic manner of painting, and had been said (by Quatremère among others) to be inherently devoid of ideas.[26] But there is more significance to Zola's choice of the term "copy" in his description; Manet's "copying" becomes a characterization of his style or technical procedure, not a reference to the realistic nature of his subject

25. On the hierarchy of techniques, from linear composition to color and brushstroke (from the intellectual to the emotional), cf. the organizational structure of Blanc's *Grammaire* and see also Paillot de Montabert, pp. 119–20.

26. See, e.g., Johann Joachim Winckelmann, "Gedanken über die Nachahmung der griechischen Werke in der Malerei und Bildhauerkunst" (1755), *Winckelmanns Werke,* ed. Helmut Holtzhauer (Berlin: Aufbau-Verlag, 1969), p. 11; and Quatremère de Quincy, *Idéal,* p. 50. Cf. also Littré, *Dictionnaire,* entry for "copie," where one of the figurative senses of the word is given as "portrait."

matter. Actually, the "subject matter" of the Zola portrait is quite complexly presented, quite "composed." The painter depicts his critic surrounded by identifiable works of visual art and literature, signs of the mutual interests of the two men. Yet in his review Zola chose not to discuss these things. Despite Manet's insertion of references to the art of Spain and of Japan, Zola focused *his* attention on the painter's supposed attempt to remain *apart* from any artistic tradition. Manet is conceived of as creating a representation independent of all the various sequences of imitative works which form the various traditions. Consequently, his vision cannot be traced back to an *artistic* source. Manet's only source is his model in nature—and, of course, also his *self*.

Can the self be revealed in, or even influence, a copy? Zola could make "copying" seem compatible with "interpretation," "translation" or "expression." Copying would assure strict adherence to nature; it would eliminate the influence of other artists by obviating access to the works of art that migbt serve the more traditional painter as models for his own image of reality. While Zola denied to his mature naturalist painters any limiting sources in artistic tradition, he assumed that the self would give form to their work *even in the case of painting a direct copy*; for no conscious or sane man could negate the living presence of his own particular being. This point had been noted also by Quatremère and Blanc, but was not at all central to their arguments; for Zola it became the keystone. He defined the work of art as "a bit of nature seen through a temperament." "Temperament" was the product of individual physical constitution and caused the immediate vision of artists to vary accordingly.[27] Hence Zola always praised an artist for painting "ce qu'il voit." There could be no fixed reality in genuine art which must always be the product of human experience. No artist could see or render an invariant reality, nor could a rigid idealism have any relation to real experience or life. In the "copy," contrary to what Quatremère would argue, there

27. For Zola's definition of art, see his "Proudhon et Courbet" (1866) and "M. H. Taine, artiste" (1866), *Mes Haines* (Paris: Charpentier, 1879), pp. 25, 229. Cf. also Zola's letter to Valabrègue, 18 Aug, 1864, reprinted in Jean-Paul Bouillon, ed., *Émile Zola, le bon combat* (Paris: Hermann, 1974), pp. 297–303. For the definition of temperament, cf. Deschanel, p. 82: temperament is "the particular state of the physical constitution of each person, caused by the diverse proportion of elements which enter into the composition of his body."

would always be a difference; this difference, this *individual* identity, was not rooted in some external reality, but in a man:

> The artist places himself before nature . . . he copies it in interpreting it . . . he is more or less realistic in his own eyes; in a word . . . his mission is to render objects for us as he sees them [*tels qu'il les voit*], relying on such detail, creating anew. I will express my whole thought in saying that a work of art is a bit of nature [*création*] seen through a temperament . . .
>
> A work for me, is a man; I would find [*retrouver*] a temperament in this work, a particular, unique accent. ["M. H. Taine," pp. 229, 225]

Zola's remarks, just cited, appear in his essay of 1866 on Hippolyte Taine, the philosopher, psychologist, historian, and professor of aesthetics at the École des Beaux-Arts. Zola fell into Taine's sphere of influence, but resisted this academic master's teaching on certain issues. Although he admired Taine's scientism and his theory of genetic, environmental, and historical causes (*race, milieu,* and *moment*), Zola felt that Taine did not sufficiently stress the absolute individuality of the artist; his theory led to a definition of racial, national, geographical, or historical types, but not necessarily to *unique* artistic temperaments. Taine could adequately deal with broad stylistic differences between English and French literature or Flemish and Italian painting, but not so well perhaps with something analogous to what Zola would call Manet's "original language."[28]

Manet spoke this "language" in his painting, but how had he developed it, and how might he pass it on to others? Would Taine's amalgam of genetics, environment, and history provide a satisfactory explanation? Would even the history of *art* do so? Perhaps not. Zola

---

28. Zola, "Édouard Manet, étude biographique et critique," *Écrits,* p. 103, cf. "Mon Salon," p. 159: "The naturalists of talent . . . are personal interpreters; they translate truths in original languages, they remain profoundly truthful, all the while retaining their individuality." When Zola discusses Taine's concept of imitation, he reveals how distant he is from Quatremère de Quincy's careful distinction between "imitation" and "copy"; Zola uses "imiter" where "copier" would be more appropriate, and vice versa: "one cannot *imitate* the object in its reality; it suffices to *copy* it, in maintaining a certain relationship among its diverse proportions, a relationship that one modifies in order to bring out the essential character." See "M. H. Taine," p. 228 (emphasis added). Taine himself had referred to "l'imitation matérielle" and "l'imitation intelligente"; Hippolyte Taine, *Philosophie de l'art,* 2 vols. (Paris: Hachette, 1921; orig. ed., 1865–69), 1, 46.

defines Manet's style of "copying" in terms appropriate to Manet alone, and never defines it very precisely; nor does he analyze it with regard to the relation of parts to a whole ("Manet," pp. 100–01). Although the critic is not entirely consistent on this issue, one can conclude that for Zola, *in theory,* a closer analysis of Manet's language is an impossibility since (as Bouchitté, too, might claim) the genuinely new cannot be understood in terms of old and familiar elements—it exists only in its entirety. Manet does not "imitate" (in Quatremère's sense); he "copies." He does not analyze and reconstruct reality; on the contrary, he acts spontaneously and with immediacy, and, as Zola claims, "what we call composition does not exist for him" ("Manet," p. 102). Curiously, then, this painter who copies cannot be imitated by others; for Manet's "style" is not a style in the traditional sense of the application of artistic convention. Having no parts, it can be copied only in its entirety, and such a copy is not an imitation or a pastiche, but, as Quatremère would insist, another work identical to the original. Among copies, there are no differences (other than temporal or spatial displacement). A pastiche of Manet, *theoretically,* could not be recognized as such—variants or distortions of Manet's style would seem unrelated to his art since his style exists as a whole, or not at all.

Like the art of the classic, Manet's art is somehow without a particularity that one can adequately characterize; yet, unlike classic art, Manet's painting is anything but "impersonal," and it does nothing to encourage an academic tradition of idealization. Manet seems an aping realist who nevertheless has his own manner, one that remains steadfastly faithful not only to the nature it copies, but to the man it reveals. Such style will change as the man himself changes; and the artist will never fully comprehend his own style. As long as he adheres to direct, naive vision, he will continue to discover in his art his own originality; and he will never become alienated, divided among imitations of himself.

IV. THE SPONTANEOUS CLASSIC

If Quatremère, following Aristotle and the classical tradition of rhetoric, presents a theory of original imitation, Zola, following the French Romantics, offers a theory of original copying. It seems, *in practice,* not to have worked. Manet, according to critics and historians writing even before his death, gave rise not only to the "independent" school of the Impressionists, but to academic followers and endless numbers of "pasticheurs."[29] He became one of several individuals called the "father of modern art" and has been continually subjected to interpretation and imitation during the past century; one might even speak of a Manet "tradition".

Another candidate for "father of modern art" is Cézanne; and Cézanne, too, gave rise to a "tradition," apparently even before he was well-known, and at a time when he lived in relative isolation. From the start, admirers noted the striking originality of his style—he did not imitate others, nor resemble them; he was "strictly himself."[30] Yet Cézanne had "followers," especially among the Symbolist painters; these included Paul Gauguin and Maurice Denis. Denis, an influential critic as well as a painter of note, linked Cézanne simultaneously to Manet's spontaneity and to the classical tradition of the Greeks and their French reincarnation, Poussin. Denis called Cézanne "spontaneously   classical"   and   the   "Poussin   of Impressionism."[31]

One is frequently tempted—or perhaps compelled—after having either made or found a distinction, to bring forth a synthesizing term or a mediating concept, to transcend the distinction as soon as it is realized. Denis's theoretical writings abound in figures of synthesis, and the "spontaneous classic" may be the most powerful of them; it juxtaposes, and attempts to integrate, Quatremère's "imitation" and idealism with Zola's "copying" and realism. Quatremère admired classic Greek art and the tradition it generated, including the French classicism of Poussin; Zola praised Manet and the Impressionists, including Cézanne (although the early promise of Cézanne's art seemed to him unrealized). Denis joins Quatremère's idealism to Zola's realism—he would refer here to a union of (universal) "style"

29. See, e.g., Théodore Duret, "Les Peintres impressionnistes" (1878), *Critique d'avant-garde* (Paris: Charpentier, 1885), pp. 63–64; and Henry Houssaye, "Salon de 1882," *Revue des deux mondes*, 3rd per., 51 (1 June 1882): 561–63.

30. Georges Lecomte, "Paul Cézanne," *Revue de l'art* 1 (9 Dec. 1899): 85. On the Cézanne "tradition," cf. Félix Fénéon, "Paul Gauguin," *Le Chat noir*, 23 May 1891, reprinted in Joan Halperin, ed., *Félix Fénéon, Oeuvres plus que complètes*, 2 vols. (Geneva: Droz, 1970), 1, 192.

31. Maurice Denis, "Cézanne" (1907), *Théories, 1890–1910: Du Symbolisme et de Gauguin vers un nouvel ordre classique* (Paris: Rouart et Watelin, 1920; orig. ed., 1912), pp. 251, 260. All subsequent page references for Denis's various essays are to this volume unless otherwise noted.

and "nature"—when he suggests the possibility, realized in Cézanne, of a "classicism of Impressionism" ("Cézanne," p. 250). In its own time, Impressionism was generally regarded as an art of spontaneous expression, a finding of the self in the creation of a painting which recorded direct and naive vision; but this style was also often criticized for being "imitative," or merely "copying" nature as a photograph would.[32] . To a great extent, Denis and other Symbolist artists opposed the irregularity of Impressionism's extreme individuality and sought a return to "tradition." In 1890 Denis used the term *"traditionnisme"* as the antonym for *"impressionnisme"*—a "traditionnisme" would have origins in the classic art of the past, would have a systematic manner, and would speak to and for all mankind; in contrast, an "impressionnisme" would express only its particular author, who would also be its only fully competent interpreter.[33] The "spontaneous classic," however, would combine both tradition and individuality, as would a "Poussin of Impressionism," if such a character could be found.

Cézanne, of course, was Denis's first choice among modern "masters" to be emulated; he was both a product of Impressionism and its reformer, seen as one who, like Poussin, had turned away from pastiche and the imitation of the styles of others to return to origins. The "myth" of Poussin's return transfers meaning to the "myth" of Cézanne; for as Poussin returned to the classical antique, so Cézanne, modern classic himself, returned to nature; and, as it was often stated around 1905, Cézanne brought the moribund tradition of Poussin (Poussin's classicism) back to life by way of nature.[34] Now, according to this formula-

32. Charles Blanc was one among many who regarded the Impressionist enterprise as a trivial form of realist art; see his *Les Beaux-arts à l'exposition universelle de 1878* (Paris: Renouard, 1878), p. 272. On subjective expression in Impressionist painting, see my forthcoming book, *Cézanne and the End of Impressionism* (University of Chicago Press, 1984).

33. More specifically, Denis was opposing "Néo-Traditionnisme" to "Néo-Impressionnisme"; see his discussion of his choice of terms in his "L'Époque du Symbolisme," *Gazette des beaux-arts*, 6th per., 11 (Mar. 1934): 165.

34. Cf., e.g., Charles Camoin's statement: "[Cézanne] is profoundly classical, and he often repeats that he seeks only *to bring Poussin back to life by way of nature [vivifier Poussin sur nature]*"; Charles Morice, "Enquête sur les tendances actuelles des arts plastiques," *Mercure de France*, n.s., 56 (1 Aug. 1905): 353. "Sur nature" is perhaps more accurately translated as "on [the model of] nature." On the (mythical) link established between Cézanne and Poussin, see my "Seeing Cézanne," Critical Inquiry 4 (Summer 1978): 773, 788–89. For an extended discussion of this issue, see *Cézanne and the End of Impressionism*.

tion, who was copying what or whom, if indeed any imitation was involved at all?

   To answer this question requires a recapitulation of the understanding of classicism that has been developed thus far, as well as more information concerning the confluence of the myths of Poussin and Cézanne in the years around 1900. Quotations from Quatremère and Delacroix have established that the classic serves as a model for others who imitate not his personal style but his general technical system, the conventions established in his art. Furthermore, critics and theorists argued repeatedly that the classic artist himself imitates no one; he has no predecessors. This point was most often made in reference to the classic Greeks; Taine, for example, compared the Greeks to primitive peoples of all kinds and speculated that their advantage over the moderns was to have enjoyed "a new and *naturally spontaneous* civilization [une civilisation *prime-sautière* et nouvelle]," as opposed to one that had become elaborate and complex.[35] From Taine's sense of the history of Western civilization comes the notion that the classical style of the Greeks is not *part* of a tradition, but arises spontaneously in its wholeness; it is *entirely* original.

   Now Poussin, too, was a classic. Was he part of a tradition? Did he imitate aspects of the conventional art of his predecessors? According to legend he did not. Blanc's colleague Paul Mantz, in his review of Bouchitté's book on Poussin, provides a most interesting account of the French classic, one that sets, once again, the copy against the imitation. Mantz relates that Poussin went to Rome and admired the works of Raphael, but did not make the mistake of becoming another *part* of the Roman school; instead he returned to the antique origin, not to imitate it in its complexity and composition, but to *copy* it in its *wholeness*. The relevant passage (based on readily available biographical information) merits direct quotation; Mantz writes:

> Raphael and the Roman school attained beauty no doubt, but their ideal is derived from history; however pure it appears, their style is only an interpretation, a translation of the antique. It is thus neces-

   35. Taine, 2, 182 (emphasis added). On this theme, cf. also Quatremère de Quincy, *Idéal*, p. 103; and Denis Diderot, "Salon de 1767," *Salons*, ed. Jean Seznec and Jean Adhémar, 4 vols. (Oxford: Clarendon Press, 1957–67), 3, 61–62.

sary to return to the origins, to trace back to the source of the great
current which Greek and Latin art spread throughout the world; and
so we see Poussin studying antiquity, copying and measuring the
statues, and trying his skill at modeling [i.e., sculpting], in order to
take by surprise in its most secret mystery the splendor of ideal form
and living relief.

This vigorous return to antique art constitutes the better part of
Poussin's originality. . . .[36]

Mantz goes on to assure his reader that Poussin's absorption in ancient art did not deny the artist's own temperament; but the image he
provides of Poussin "copying and measuring" remains striking.
Granted that any study of measure and proportion entails analysis,
that analysis involves the relation of parts to a whole, and that such
relationship characterizes imitative invention. However, the significance of Mantz's account (and many similar ones) lies in the suggestion that Poussin's art seeks to approach as closely as possible that
of the ancients—to be identical to it. As a result, both the Greeks and
Poussin must belong to the same tradition. Yet one is not the imitation of the other, but rather the copy. As in the definition of "copy"
taken from the field of printing, the "copy" by Poussin is no different
from its original (even if the medium differs, as when a drawing is
made after a sculpted model). Poussin's copy and the antique original
share the same style or ideal. Hence the original may *also* be called
the "copy," the object that is copied—or, alternatively, all copies
may be described as *original*, as when (printed) copies of a book are
seen to be genuine presentations of an original (manuscript) text.
Consequently, classic art is *inimitable* in the sense that to imitate it
with a difference is to falsify it; the absolute and unmediated truth of
classic art demands copying, not imitation, and its copies are as complete, as original, as their historical antecedents. Classic art thus

36. Mantz, p. 41. Cf. Blanc, "Nicolas Poussin," *Histoire des peintres*, 1, p. 5: "Not
wanting to begin with the interpretation of someone else, [Poussin] went straight to
the [original] sources." In a variation of the Poussin "myth," Thomas Couture claimed
that Poussin "copied" nature; see his *Méthode et entretiens d'atelier* (Paris: L. Guérin,
1867), p. 247. The invariant elements of the Poussin story are the artist's rejection of
conventionalized imitation and his return to a legitimate source, *either* antique art *or*
nature (and sometimes both). Nearly all nineteenth-century French artists appropriated Poussin as a heroic ancestor, regardless of their position as to what constituted a
proper source—classic art, nature, or perhaps a combination of the two. In this context,
one must recall that for many theorists classic art and nature were one and the same.

seems to transcend or negate history and the passage of time. It seems always to arise spontaneously, as if it were the product of a primitive or prehistorical society, one without predecessor or precedent. Furthermore, classic art becomes an art of *identity* in several senses—not only because it can be associated with an intensity of personal experience, but because it denies stylistic or technical difference, and even denies the more significant forms of the "difference" of temporal and spatial displacement. Classic art knows no historical, chronological, or geographical limits.

And so Cézanne, the isolated artist often called a "primitive," can be *spontaneously* classical. He "brings Poussin back to life by way of nature" in a manner analogous to Poussin's revival of the ancients. When Denis wrote of Cézanne, he emphasized the uniqueness of this painter's style. Yet he also noted Cézanne's capacity to stir the imagination of all other artists, as if to bind them into a common tradition. If the earlier tradition of the Greeks and of Poussin had degenerated, Cézanne would revive it. One might describe the situation in terms of both a likeness and a difference: just as Poussin ignored artistic convention and "copied" classic *art,* so Cézanne (according to Denis) is absorbed in "copying" *nature.* Nature, not art, serves him as an origin or source; and, significantly, *his direct vision of nature is itself a classic one:*

> We have discerned classical spontaneity in [Cézanne's] sensation itself. . . . What others have sought and sometimes found in imitating the ancients . . . he discovers finally in himself. . . . He is so naturally a painter and so spontaneously classical [*spontanément classique*]!" ["Cézanne," pp. 254, 251][37]

Denis proceeds to explain that Cézanne's immediate personal vision of nature reveals the *conventions* of art that lesser spirits can understand only by way of academic study ("De Gauguin et de Van Gogh au classicisme" [1909], pp. 276–78). In other words, the spontaneous classic establishes his own style and, simultaneously, a style for all.

The nineteenth-century argument may be summarized: the most original "classics," indeed the truest ones, arise spontaneously;

---

37. Cf. Cézanne's other major Symbolist critic, Émile Bernard, who claimed that Cézanne had told him that "one must become classical again by way of nature [*classique par la nature*], that is, by way of sensation"; Bernard, "Paul Cézanne," *L'Occident* 6 (July 1904): 24.

the spontaneous classic speaks a universal artistic language, paints with a style that mediates with immediacy; and this eternal language does not evolve through any mediating process, whether academic training, emulative imitation, or even "copying and measuring the statues." To reiterate: this artistic language is present to the spontaneous classic *by nature*—both through his personal experience of nature, and by his own nature, his own self.[38]

Denis's concern for a modern classicism led him to compare many of his favored artists to Poussin; although Cézanne seemed the most appropriate candidate, Denis also linked Gauguin to the earlier classic master. Gauguin became for Denis "a kind of Poussin without classical culture" who studied primitive art instead of the classical antique ("L'Influence de Paul Gauguin" [1903], p. 171). Alluding to one of La Fontaine's "classic" fables, Gauguin himself once noted that he was not "Greek, [but] a savage, a wolf in the forest" (Letter to C. Morice, July 1901, Malingue, p. 300). And, as several "witness" accounts confirm, this "wolf" threatened to steal Cézanne's dearest possession, the origin of his art, his "petite sensation." Gauguin had shared some days painting with Cézanne during the summer of 1881, purchased several of his works in the following years, and was generally thought to have derived his simple and direct manner of brushwork from the older man. Cézanne himself, frequently described as reclusive and a bit paranoid, apparently complained bitterly about Gauguin's plagiarism.[39] As a modern artist deeply concerned with originality, Cézanne had cause to worry over his aggressive admirer, for it was commonly argued that the original must be inimitable. Thoughts such as the following (from an essay on Ingres by the critic and historian Ernest Chesneau) might have troubled any artist, and especially one touched by a fear of others:

38. A parallel to the argument which I have sketched here takes the form of stating that in the case of the classic (and also the primitive) artist, the "real" and the "ideal"—immediate vision and mediated style—are identical. Nineteenth-century artists and theorists commonly made this assertion, which the logic of their own beliefs clearly justified.

39. See Denis, "L'Influence de Paul Gauguin," p. 170; Gustave Geffroy (reporting a conversation with Cézanne of 1896), *Claude Monet, sa vie, son oeuvre*, 2 vols. (Paris: Crès, 1924), 2, 68; and Émile Bernard (reporting a conversation with Cézanne of 1904), "Souvenirs sur Paul Cézanne et lettres inédites," *Mercure de France*, n.s., 69 (1 Oct. 1907): 400.

We are now in a position to reply to this question: is M. Ingres an original painter? and to reply negatively. The final proof that we shall give is irrefutable. *True originality escapes imitation [La véritable originalité se dérobe à l'imitation].* No artist will succeed in deceiving us and making us regard as authentic an imitation of Michelangelo, of Correggio, of Rembrandt or of M. Eugène Delacroix. [But] every one of the pupils of M. Ingres is capable of simulating any work whatever of his professor to the point of our mistaking it [for the original].[40]

If the "pupil" Gauguin had indeed stolen something from his master Cézanne, it was his technical procedure. Was this tantamount to stealing Cézanne's *identity,* his own classic "sensation," his originality? Was Cézanne subject to the same victimization as Ingres?

In the case of most artists, the technique which defines the style seems also to indicate authorship; a pastiche of Goya and Velasquez, if Manet had ever made such a creature, would be identified with the two Spanish masters. To steal technique, as some claimed Manet had done, would be to appropriate an original identity and perhaps to alter and violate it. Cézanne, however, as a "spontaneous classic," exposed his identity but not any vulnerability; his technique was of a very peculiar sort. Denis wrote that this technique was so natural and spontaneous that one could not grasp it "without carrying away at the same time a little of the best" of the painter himself ("Cézanne," p. 261). *Cézanne would not lose anything in the transaction.* Denis indicates here that the painter's artistic identity is inviolable—it can be borne off by another, but at the other's risk, not Cézanne's. Theoretically, Cézanne's vision of nature is neither conventional nor an "image" in Quatremère's sense; it is not an appearance or an imitation of something else, but something that may exist only in its unique manifestation. If Gauguin should copy it successfully, he would not be the master of it—it would have mastered him. Rather than transform Cézanne, he would be transformed. He would simply become (another) Cézanne; for Cézanne, as a spontaneous classic, remains inimitable.

The conclusion has become as inescapable as the influence of the classic: Gauguin, in his dealings with Vollard, should not have been so worried about resembling his own followers, "those who resemble

40. Ernest Chesneau, "Ingres," *Les Chefs d'école* (Paris: Didier, 1862), p. 269 (emphasis added).

me, that is those who imitate me." Gauguin had his own spontaneity, his primitivism. He was (is) a classic. He could survive as an original who became the original copy for others. But the "anxiety of anticipation" caused the artist to see history as he saw himself—as a conniving and stealthy wolf. Gauguin had little faith in what the time of others might bring; so he wrote profusely to establish the permanent record of his artistic achievement *and its interpretation.*

If Gauguin was a classic, then he is in all of us. We are like Gauguin. Accordingly, we grow anxious over the fact that all people and all things are like one another: the emulative imitation, the deliberate misrepresentation, and even the aping copy—all may resemble the original with as little or as much identity and difference as it takes to displace the original('s) meaning. The vexing problem is that the final distinctions are not at all self-evident.

The Future-Past

LOUIS A. MACKENZIE, JR.

To the Brink: The Dialectic of Anxiety in the *Pensées*

> Satan exalted sat, by merit raised
> To that bad eminence; and, from despair
> Thus high uplifted beyond hope, aspires
> Beyond thus high, insatiate to pursue
> Vain war with Heaven . . .
> —Milton: *Paradise Lost*

> Man is a rope stretched between the animal and the Superman—a rope over an abyss.
> —Nietzsche: *Thus Spake Zarathustra*

> Le Temps est l'invitation à mourir, le moyen qui permet aux choses d'avouer en expirant leur néant dans le sein de leur Créateur.
> —Claudel: *Art poétique*

The *Pensées* are a terrorizing piece of writing: a fragmented structure disrupts and defies instinctive urges to excavate and contain the argument. This writing, by laying open its textuality—which in this case is a refusal to supply the very warp of textuality—tends to disorient the reader who in order to come to grips with the text must overcome and account for the shock of silent spaces marking the explosion of logic and order. Exploded also, then, is the comfort of reading directly from beginning to end with the firm footing that sequential writing allows. In the refuse of "well-made" discourse there remains a double confusion: 1. bewilderment, more or less pronounced, on the part of the reader; 2. a running together, a confusing of fragments, tonalities and techniques. And confusion—the very term Pascal will use to describe his style of writing[1]—is the

---

1. Pascal, *Oeuvres Complètes,* ed. Louis Lafuma (Paris: Seuil, 1963). "J'écrirai ici mes pensées sans ordre et non pas peut-être dans une confusion sans dessein" (532), ["I will write my thoughts here without order and not perhaps in an aimless confusion."] All subsequent numbers will refer to this edition. All translations, unless otherwise indicated, are my own.

agent of anxiety, if only in the restricted sense of uncertainty over the way things (and apologies) are to end. While Pascal seems to exploit such textually induced uncertainty in order to sensitize his reader to the larger design of the project, it is in that larger design that the problematics of anxiety are most forcefully manifest. Indeed, anxiety seems to hold a crucial position in the philosophical and psychological thrust of the *Pensées* and any effort at evaluating that thrust will benefit from an appreciation of its complexity.

Choking; suffocation; angina: etymological resonances lurking below the surface of the word are—as anxiety itself—easily indicated and reduced. Such is the security language seems to offer. The actual phenomenon is not cornered so handily. Indeed, anxiety is characterized by an essential resistance to such localization. With distinctly Pascalian intonation, Daniel Le Roy suggests that this elusiveness haunts the kind of vague yet profound questions anxiety—or more precisely, anguish, which is what he calls anxiety, come to consciousness of itself—tends to elicit:

> Anguish cropping up only in idleness and in the absence of urgent disquietude, if I turn my questioning towards the world and my worries, I cannot ascertain if my present emotional state has been provoked by this thing any more than by that thing; neither of them seems to justify my distress, none of my customary preoccupations can be blamed, such that my questioning, leaving the arena of daily cares takes the shape of vague generalizations such as: "What's the use of it all?" "What am I?" "What should I do; to what end?"[2]

Significant here is the seamless slide from the psychological to the metaphysical, from everyday cares to everyman's questions of self-identity and self-worth. In his anxious condition—Pascal will refer to it as *inquiétude*[3]—man faces the void as he senses his own loss and deprivation.

From another perspective, Kierkegaard complicates this confrontation with nothingness by linking dread (*angst*) not to loss of innocence, but with innocence itself: "In this state there is peace and repose; but at the same time there is something different, which is

---

2. Daniel Le Roy, *Mythologie de l'Anxiété* (Paris: J. Corti, 1956), p. 14.
3. (24), "Condition de l'homme. Inconstance, ennui, inquiétude." ["Man's condition. Inconstancy, boredom, anxiety."]

not dissension and strife, for there is nothing to strive with. What is it then? Nothing. But what effect does nothing produce? It begets dread. This is the profound secret of innocence, that at the same time it is dread."[4] Innocence, which for Kierkegaard is coextensive with ignorance, generates dread as a yearning—for freedom, for knowledge, for a condition which does not exist in the present and which can, therefore, "make itself felt only negatively as a kind of lack or insufficiency."[5] Such yearning goes by the name of anticipation, a point upon which Kierkegaard is linguistically sensitive: "A precise and correct linguistic usage associates therefore dread and the future. It is true that one is sometimes said to be in dread of the past, and this seems to be a contradiction. Nevertheless, upon closer inspection it appears that this manner of speaking points in one way or another to the future. The past of which I am supposed to be in dread must stand in a relation of possibility to me. If I am in dread of a past misfortune, this is not in so far as it is past, but in so far as it may be repeated, i.e., become future."[6] Anxiety and anticipation are thus coupled in a way that destabilizes normal conceptions of time and space. Past has yet to come; fact may be loosened from its moorings in a personal history to become phantasms of the future.

Finally, the name of Freud can be introduced into these preliminary remarks. For him, anxiety is a recurrent response to a particular kind of danger, namely, a danger which recalls the "primal anxiety of birth."[7] It is at the moment of birth that one feels for the first time a profound and unanticipated sense of loss and separation as the warmth and security of dependance are shattered and replaced by the shock of helplessness and seeming abandon.

Anxiety as delimited from etymological, philosophical and psychoanalytical positions is then a fluid yet consistent term which embraces physical and metaphysical considerations. The immediate task is to assess the uses, both explicit and figurative, that Pascal makes of these considerations.

4. Søren Kierkegaard, *The Concept of Dread*, trans. Walter Lowrie (Princeton: Princeton U. Press, 1944), p. 38.

5. Ronald Grimsley, *Søren Kierkegaard: a Biographical Introduction* (New York: Scribner, 1973), p. 62.

6. Kierkegaard, p. 82.

7. Sigmund Freud, *Inhibitions, Symptoms and Anxiety*, trans. Alix Strachey (New York: Norton, 1959), p. 63.

With his frequent evocations of the *néant*, the abyss, the void, Pascal would take his reader to the edge of unfathomable darkness, to the brink of oblivion. The image of man teetering and groping on the frontier of the darkest darkness—or to use Nietzsche's terms, the loneliest loneliness—is an especially forceful one as it exploits primitive fears of being swallowed up:

> Quand je considère la petite durée de ma vie absorbée dans l'éternité précédante et suivante—*memoria hospitis unuis diei praetereuntis*—le petit espace que je remplis et même que je vois abîmé dans l'infinie immensité des espaces que j'ignore et qui m'ignorent, je m'effraye et m'étonne de me voir ici plutôt que là, car il n'y a point de raison pourquoi ici plutôt que là, pourquoi à présent plutôt que lors. Qui m'y a mis? Par l'ordre et la conduite de qui ce lieu et ce temps a(-t-)il été destiné à moi?[8]

In this passage Pascal isolates man in time and in ignorance. A lifetime, which implies the memory of a past and the promise of a future is swallowed up by a limitless past and future. The lie of life is thus revealed: appearances to the contrary, life is not a plenitude, nor is it simply imprisoned in eternity. It is, rather, lost without a trace in the fabric of the infinite. Life as place ("le petit espace que je remplis") is

8. (68): "When I consider the short duration of my life absorbed into the eternity which precedes and follows it—*the memory of a guest lodged for a single day*—the small space I occupy and even which I see thrown into the abyss of the infinite immensity of spaces of which I know nothing and which know nothing of me, I become frightened and astonished to see myself here rather than there; for there is no reason why I should be here rather than there; why now rather than then. Who put me here? By whose order and action were this place and this time destined for me?"
    It is, I think, prudent to grapple early on with the chronic and nettlesome matters of voice and viewpoint in the *Pensées*. We recognize from the opening moments of the *papiers classés* as well as from the subsequent indications in typology and punctuation that Pascal planned to use dialogue as an essential feature of the *Apology*. He was going to provide a voice for the positions of his libertine, worldly audience for whom the *Apology* was in principle intended. The import of this on analyses of the *Pensées* is clear: recuperation of the argument is problematized (further) when one is not sure who is speaking, apologist or libertine. Jean-Jacques Demorest is especially heated on this point when he accuses Valéry of never even considering the possibility of a libertine voice behind the famous "le silence éternel de ces espaces infinis m'effraie" ("Pascal's Sophistry and the Sin of Poesy," *Studies in Seventeenth-century French Literature* [Ithaca, N.Y.: Cornell Univ. Press, 1966]). My own feeling on this matter is that doubts, fears, anxieties—though unexpressed—must ricochet and echo even in the most fervent believer, that uncertainty over matters metaphysical and eschatalogical is an essential troubling price the intellectually aware person must pay; and while I recognize a place for critical discrimination between the voices of libertine and believer, I also feel that expression of terror and feelings of insignificance before the void must also express Pascal's own, plainly human, preoccupations.

likewise lost, thrown into the abyss of infinite spaces. The tension of this loss is amplified by a circuit of ignorance, of neither knowing nor being known. It is this ignorance which is perhaps most troubling: the mysteries of the eternal and infinite spaces being ultimately impenetrable, the questioning must—almost by default—refer back to the self. "Why am I here as opposed to there? Whence do I come? By whose design?" Pascal does not provide an answer here; he opts to leave the questions hanging, taunting and thus conserving their power of erosion. They eat away at the questioner as they keep him in a state of anxious wonderment. This idea of erosion is refined in another fragment where the speaker sees himself surrounded on all sides by infinities "qui [l']enferment comme un atome et comme une ombre qui ne dure qu'un instant sans retour."[9] The erosive feature of the speaker's vision figures in the movement from atom to shadow, from physical presence, minimal though it may be, to a disembodied, shadowy state which threatens, if not predicts, total disappearance.

The threat of falling—as the libertine fears into the *néant* or into the hands of an irritated God—is all the more troublesome to the extent that man is drawn *instinctively* towards the edge, towards that place where he must confront the very questions which will torment him and bring on his anxiety. In Pascal's thought, this instinct is a sickness ("la maladie principale de l'homme" [Lafuma 744]) which goes by the name of *curiosité inquiète,* an anxious curiosity which is more painful than error itself: "il ne lui est pas si mauvais d'être dans l'erreur que dans cette curiosité inutile" [it is not as unpleasant to be in error as to be (prey) to this useless curiosity (Lafuma 744)]. The special character of this pain may be defined in two ways. First, by exploiting the etymological resonance of the term curious—*cura* denoting among other things anxiety—we are able to propose something like anxious anxiety (*curiosité inquiète*). This radical formulation suggests an anxiety which is self-generating, a yearning which arrives only at yearning. And if, as Kierkegaard is to assert, yearning is dread, a masochistic feature of this curiosity starts to emerge: man desires that which he fears most.[10] At this point, the thing which is feared and desired may in fact be the answers to the questions, the resolution to the curiosity, in fine, an end to anxiety:

9. (427): "[I see only infinities on all sides] which hem me in like an atom or a shadow which lasts only an instant never to return."

10. "In dread there is the egoistic infinity of possibility, which does not tempt like a definite choice, but alarms and fascinates with its sweet anxiety" (Kierkegaard, p. 55).

"J'ai dit souvent que tout le malheur des hommes vient d'une seule chose, qui est de ne savoir pas demeurer en repos dans une chambre. . . . Ils ne savent pas que ce n'est que la chasse et non la prise qu'ils recherchent."[11]

A second way of defining the particular character of this painful curiosity may be effected by equating *curiosité inquiète* and *curiosité inutile*—something Pascal's text seems to authorize. We can then factor out the two adjectives and derive a second equation in which *inquiète* (anxious) is equivalent to *inutile* (useless). Now, the uselessness of anxiety is not frivolity; it is, rather, a tragic pointlessness in that it never comes to resolution, it never terminates in an object. Indeed, Freud stresses in his own delimiting of the term that unlike fear, which has a transitive quality—it attaches itself to a specific object—anxiety is marked by indefiniteness and incompletion. "Anxiety has an unmistakable relation to expectation: it is anxiety about something. It has a quality of indefiniteness and lacks an object. In precise speech we use the word "fear" rather than anxiety if it has found an object."[12]

The anxiety-ridden urge toward anxiety is then a circular entrapment which advertises a basic impotence:

> Nous souhaitons la vérité et ne trouvons en nous qu'incertitude.
> Nous recherchons le bonheur et ne trouvons que misère et mort.
> Nous sommes incapables de ne pas souhaiter la vérité et le bonheur et sommes incapables ni de certitude ni de bonheur.[13]

In other words, a sense of deficiency, of lacking truth and happiness generates a desire to rectify that deficiency; desire then prompts a search which arrives only at uncertainty and unhappiness, the realization of which generates desire—and so on. The consequence of this circular, pointless activity may be expressed as dizziness, a condition linked explicitly with anxiety: "One may liken dread to dizzi-

---

11. (136): "I have often said that all of man's unhappiness comes from a single thing, which is not knowing how to stay quietly in a room. . . . They do not know that it is only the hunt and not the catch that they are after."

12. Freud, p. 91.

13. (401): "We desire truth and find in ourselves only uncertainty.

We search for happiness and find only misery and death.

We are incapable of not wanting truth and happiness and are incapable either of certainty or happiness."

ness. He whose eye chances to look down into the yawning abyss becomes dizzy. But the reason for it is just as much his eye as it is the precipice."[14] And although terms of dizziness do not appear in the *Pensées*, one does nonetheless find frequent indications of this sensation both on the level of style and discourse. An especially vivid example, one in which the reader not only reads, but comes to experience through a stylistic pirouette, a loss of equilibrium, appears in the first series of unclassified papers: "Les hommes sont si nécessairement fous que ce serait être fou par un autre tour de folie de n'être pas fou."[15] In a manner of speaking, this text absorbs the reader. On the one hand, the persistent and vertiginous turning on the notion of folly challenges his interpretive agility; on the other, it locks him into a circuit of craziness from which reprieve is not forthcoming—even for reasons of sanity. The phatic and poetic force of this fragment is enhanced further by its phonological coherence: the spectacular recurrence of *s* and *f* complement the notion of an enclosed system, of a redundant, chronic condition of folly.[16]

The most effective expression of this condition of inescapable craziness is therefore the paradox, i.e., the rhetorical formulation which by definition problematizes "good sense" and which therefore destabilizes the firm footing of simple and conclusive modes of thinking. It is then no surprise that this same destabilization would touch on the already difficult matters of metaphysics and theology: "Incompréhensible que Dieu soit et incompréhensible qu'il ne soit pas, que l'âme soit avec le corps, que nous n'ayons point d'âme, que le

14. Kierkegaard, p. 55.
15. (412): "Men are so necessarily crazy that not to be crazy would be to be crazy by another turn of craziness."
16. A more experimental reading would have these consonants imitating the sound of a pair of bellows—it is from the Latin *follis* that we derive *folie*. This experiment would then lead us to speculate on the ways in which the *Pensées* enflame the embers of anxiety in the reader. In the same vein, one might be tempted to hear in the phonetic repetition the labored breathing implied in the etymological and etiological senses of anxiety: "The clearest and most frequent sensations representative of anxiety are those connected with the respiratory organs and with the heart" (Freud, p. 58). Finally, and on a somewhat less speculative plane, there is another analysis which may be confected from the etymological heritage of *folie: follis* can simply indicate a bag full of air, that is to say, something which in giving the appearance of fullness, seems ripe for puncture, for deflation; and the *Pensées* are in a very strong sense a text which would deflate, which would explode the self-sufficiency and self-containment that inflated valuations of reason and natural powers of judgment tend to produce in man.

monde soit créé, qu'il ne soit pas, etc., que le péché originel soit et qu'il ne soit pas."[17] On these issues which concern him directly and profoundly,[18] man is caught up in and set to spinning by a play of opposing valences, e.g., God must exist, God cannot exist; there must be original sin, there can be no original sin. The very knowledge he needs flees and taunts him: "C'est une chose horrible de sentir s'écouler tout ce qu'on possède."[19] *S'écouler*—and again the repetition of *s*: it all becomes fluid and viscous; the grounding erodes and offers no foundation in any truth other than the realization of a loss of truth. In his consideration of the principal strengths of Pyrrhonism, Pascal highlights this awareness when he asserts that ". . . nous sentons une image de la vérité et ne possédons que le mensonge. Incapables d'ignorer absolument et de savoir certainement, tant il est manifeste que nous avons été dans un degré de perfection dont nous sommes malheureusement déchus."[20] The first part of this declaration operates as a sequence of approximations: *sentir*, a physical, sensual reaction which has not yet penetrated to the level of cognition; *image*, an analogue at least once removed from reality; *mensonge*, an anagrammatical approximation of "sentons" and "image," and from that perspective as well as from the sense of the term, a step further removed from truth. In the second statement, Pascal begins to give ignorance, approximation and un-truth positive values. The mechanism for this transformation is memory, or more precisely, something preliminary to memory which makes itself felt in the intellect ("tant il est manifeste que nous avons été . . ."). At this

17. (809): "Incomprehensible that God should exist and incomprehensible that he should not; that the soul should be joined to the body, that we should have no soul; that the world should be created, that it should not, etc; that there should be original sin, that there should not be."

18. (427): "L'immortalité de l'âme est une chose qui nous importe si fort, qui nous touche si profondément, qu'il faut avoir perdu tout sentiment pour être dans l'indifférence de savoir ce qui en est. . . .

Ainsi notre premier intérêt et notre premier devoir est de nous éclaircir sur ce sujet, d'où dépend toute notre conduite." ["The immortality of the soul is something which is of such great importance to us, which touches us so deeply, that one would have had to lose all feeling not to care about knowing what it is all about. . . . Thus our primary interest and our first duty is to become enlightened on this subject, upon which all our actions depend."]

19. (757): "It is a horrifying thing to feel everything one possesses flowing away."

20. (131): "We sense an image of the truth and possess only falsehood. [We are] incapable of absolute ignorance and of certain knowledge, so obvious is it that we were once at a level of perfection from which we have unhappily fallen."

point, the middle ground between ignorance and knowledge, between stasis and movement—in short, that place of yearning and anxiety—is glossed in terms of logic. The Fall is accepted as a manifestly intellectual fact, i.e., as universally and scientifically valid.

In another place, Pascal will intensify the apprehension of paradise lost, which he frames in terms of a shout: "Qu'est-ce donc nous crie cette avidité et cette impuissance sinon qu'il y a eu autrefois dans l'homme un véritable bonheur dont il ne lui reste maintenant que la marque et la trace toute vide."[21] Once again the polarities of yearning (avidité) and impotence tug simultaneously—something which may be underscored by the singular verb "crie." The frustration of yearning and the arrival at nothingness is put into even sharper relief by the phonological reduction of avidité into vide, which stands as the weak and therefore all the more mocking echo and reminder of that appetite for happiness. Indeed, it is the very insufficiency of the echo—"la marque et la trace toute vide"—which constitutes and sustains the irony and the terror of such aspiration; and it is this very terror and irony that Pascal seems determined to exploit. The void must be felt. One must stand at its lip in order to sense loss not only as part of history (as original and subsequent sin) but also, and more menacingly, as a future, as an eternity. It is as if Pascal, in the role of some prototherapist, is to bring his "patient" back into contact with the trauma which is at the root of his sickness, a sickness already diagnosed as curiosité inquiète or anxious yearning.

In one of several fascinating observations on his own writing, Pascal valorizes the mnemonic function and advantage of this contact with oblivion: "En écrivant ma pensée elle m'échappe quelquefois; mais cela me fait souvenir de ma faiblesse que j'oublie à toute heure, ce qui m'instruit autant que ma pensée oubliée, car je ne tiens qu' à connaître mon néant."[22] The yearning (tenir à means to be anxious for, to valorize and also retains connotations of possession) and the thing yearned for do not diverge. The essential objective of

21. (148): "What then does this yearning and this impotence shout out to us if not that there was once in man a true happiness of which there now remains only the stamp and wholly empty trace?"
22. (656): "In writing down my thought it sometimes escapes me; but that makes me remember my weakness, something I am always forgetting, and that is as instructive as my forgotten thought, for the only thing I care about is knowing my own nothingness."

Pascalian anxiety is anxiety, a dread of and an impulse towards absorption by what we have been calling the *néant*, what we will
eventually have to call God. The coextensiveness of the yearning and
the thing yearned for can be highlighted in an analysis of the verb
connaître, an analysis in which I take the liberty of reversing the
elements of Paul Claudel's equation: "Co-naître, pour tout, c'est
naître. Toute connaissance est une naissance."[23] One is then
tempted to read in Pascal's single-minded resolve to "connaître son
néant," a concommitant faith in the renascent character of such
knowledge. By acceding to the knowledge of one's fundamental lack
of knowledge, by letting oneself fall into an abyss of personal oblivion—in short, by being born (again) in that place of negation—man
will be able to survive and transcend his anxious condition. And if, to
appropriate Freud's assertion that anxiety is intimately associated
with memories of traumatic, violent birth, it is possible to propose
that rebirth in Pascal may be more precisely termed pre-birth. In a
historical as well as moral context this pre-birth would be that condition of harmonious nurture and coexistence with the Divine, which
preceded the "birth," i.e., the violent expulsion from the womb-
garden onto the human scene—a scene defined in terms of a longing
for a once and future past. In fine, the issue for Pascal is one of
conversion, of converting anxiety as misery and nothingness into
plenitude and repose, the repose Augustine anticipates for an anxious
heart (*cor inquietum*). This conversion is, in the end, a self-inflicted
and immortal wound; it is a leap into self-annihilation, a leap of
faith.[24]

23. "To know [to be born with] is in all things to be born. All knowledge is a
birth." Paul Claudel, *Art poétique* [Paris: Mercure de France, 1915], p. 62.
24. (378): "La conversion véritable consiste à s'anéantir devant cet être universel
qu'on a irrité tant de fois et qui peut vous perdre légitimement à toute heure. . . ."
["true conversion consists in annihilating oneself before that universal being that one
has irritated so many times and who can legitimately destroy you at any time. . . ."]

PATRICK COLEMAN

Rousseau and Preromanticism: Anticipation and *Oeuvre*

"Is it possible to write literary history, that is, to write that which will be both literary and a history?" In the last decade, new and fruitful efforts have been made to answer René Wellek's question of a generation ago.[1] One is the theory of *Rezeptionsgeschichte* developed by Hans Robert Jauss, who establishes a dialectical relationship between the response the work demands of its readers and the reactions it actually provokes. In so doing, Jauss tries to account for the enduring "presence" of art while opening the work onto the past and future of the culture. Another is the genealogy of poetic influence proposed by Harold Bloom, where "influence" no longer designates an external relation between authors—a matter of allusions, commonplaces, and conventions—but an inner determinant of the poem itself as it emerges from a struggle with the burden of the past.[2] To speak of "anticipation" and its anxieties is to adopt a metaphor that combines elements from both these perspectives in a particular way, in order to do justice to certain features of the French tradition. The choice of an appropriate metaphor is important. If there is to be a renewal of French literary history, that much-maligned discipline, then its myths and metaphors, so often decried by "rigorous" contemporary critics, need to be addressed on their own level for the dimensions of the task to be fully understood. The following remarks are intended as a preliminary exercise in this direction.

1. René Wellek and Austin Warren, *Theory of Literature,* third edition (New York: Harcourt, Brace, and World, 1962), p. 52.
2. Hans Robert Jauss, "Literaturgeschichte als Provokation der Literaturwissenschaft" (1967), in *Literatur als Provokation* (Frankfurt: Suhrkamp, 1970); Harold Bloom, *The Anxiety of Influence* (New York: Oxford, 1973).

Of the great French writers, Rousseau is preeminently the figure of anticipation. A commonplace of literary history is the story of how themes, moods, poses even, and literary devices we associate with the Romantic period find early expression in Rousseau's writing. Perhaps no other French author of the first rank is famous as much for what he initiated as for what he accomplished. As a result, the actual impact of his works has often been distorted. On the other hand, Rousseau himself encouraged such an emphasis on this part of his activity. Especially towards the end of his life, he speaks of his writing career as determined by the anticipatory movement of his imagination. In the third of his *Rêveries*, the solitary walker recounts how

> thrown into the whirlpool of life while still a child, I learned from early experience that I was not made for this world, and that in it I would never attain the state to which my heart aspired. Ceasing therefore to seek among men the happiness which I felt I could never find there, my ardent imagination learned to leap over the boundaries of a life which was hardly yet begun, as if it were flying over an alien land in search of a fixed and stable resting-place.[3]

Coming from a poet, the statement would not be exceptional in itself, were it an explanation of what led him to write. In Rousseau's case, however, it is as much a characterization of the writer as of the man. He was proud of his *Discours* and of *Emile*, but never did he possess that confidence in the stability of his *oeuvre* which we find even in anxious poets like Rimbaud. Rousseau's autobiographical writing, initially undertaken to justify his works, ultimately lends support to the view that the author's most enduring legacy is to be found in the very movement of anticipation itself, of which the work is less the product than the expression. Or even the consecration, for Rousseau would like to consider his expressions of anticipation as more than proof of his good faith: as themselves a contribution to culture, as a "good work" in the practical sense of the term. Although I shall not explore the question here, the special quality of Rousseau's political thought might also be linked to the theme of anticipation. Rousseau's theory of legitimacy makes anticipation a source of political right, a key factor in the reconstruction of legitimacy.

In this essay, I would like to examine two aspects of the anxiety

3. Jean-Jacques Rousseau, *The Rêveries of the Solitary Walker*, trans. Peter France (Harmondsworth: Penguin, 1978), p. 48.

of anticipation as it affects the "placing" of Rousseau in the French canon. The first is the controversy over the historical period to which he is often, if uneasily, assigned. "Preromanticism" has become something of an embarrassment to literary historians because of its nakedly anticipatory, teleological character. If, as Claudio Guillén has said, "a system of periodization is a *criticism* of becoming,"[4] an attempt to abstract from the flow of history structures of norms or styles of thought endowed, like works of art, with their own at least relative autonomy, then Preromanticism as a period label is a contradiction in terms. It is as much of a scandal as the idea that an artwork could be defined in terms of works not yet produced—even though, of course, we often speak in just this way, just as we isolate historical periods only to show how one leads into the next. But if our definition of literary periods is to be derived from the study of particular works before they can be used to define a work's place in a series,[5] then we should try to connect the historical difficulty of Preromanticism with the surprising ease with which we accept the anticipatory interpretation of Rousseau's writing. The second part of the essay offers a few reflections on Rousseau as a preromantic author.

I.

A few years ago, a collection of articles appeared in France under the title *Le Préromantisme: hypothèque ou hypothèse?*[6] What perplexed the contributors was that although from a theoretical point of view no defense could be found for "préromantisme" as a period term, its usefulness could not be denied, especially for a study of French historiography. In other European literatures it was possible to locate images and themes one could call preromantic, but only in France did

---

4. Claudio Guillén, "Second Thoughts on Literary Periods," in *Literature as System* (Princeton: Princeton University Press, 1971), p. 437.

5. Wellek and Warren, p. 257.

6. *Le Préromantisme: hypothèque ou hypothèse?*, ed. Paul Viallaneix (Paris: Klincksieck, 1975), from a colloquium held in Clermont-Ferrand in 1972. See in particular the essays by José-Louis Diaz, Roger Fayolle, Françoise Gaillard, and the editor. Unfortunately, they make no mention of the important earlier discussions by Hugo Friedrich, in his book *Das anti-romantische Denken im modernen Frankreich: sein System und seine Herkunft* (Munich: Heubner, 1935) and his article "Der Epochebegriff im Lichte der französischen Préromantisme-Forschung," *Neue Jahrbücher für Wissenschaft und Jugendbildung* 10 (1934), 124–40.

the pursuit of forerunners lead to the imposition of a term designating a specific Preromantic period, as if there were such a style or movement warranting its own distinct label. The term did have its analogue in "préclassicisme," invented to describe certain aspects of the earlier seventeenth century. Yet "préclassicisme" enjoyed only a brief vogue, and although the objections to its use applied equally to "préromantisme"—the difficulty of assigning limits to the period, an all-too-neat teleology, the exclusion of many, perhaps most of the writers active at the time—the word is still with us. Despite numerous attacks from Enlightenment scholars angry at the "theft" of some of their writers or themes,[7] and the desire of *dix-neuvièmistes* to define their turf, it has not gone away. The very reference to the notion as an "hypothesis" in a symposium dominated by critics skeptical of the viability of any concept of periodization suggests that something of value might come from giving it a closer look.

Préromantisme is a peculiarly French problem because in France Romanticism itself was for a long time the focus of not only literary but political and ideological conflict. Throughout the late nineteenth and early twentieth centuries, polemicists of the Right denounced it as the product of the Revolution, and as the symbol of all revolts against authority. Romanticism was not just another phase of the national spirit, it was a radical break with tradition, with *l'esprit français*. It was a foreign influence corrupting the purity of French civilization, the only properly universal culture.[8]

So powerful was the force of this critique that the supporters of Romanticism, as well as those who merely wished to give it *droit de cité*, adopted some of their opponents' assumptions in their own interpretations of the movement. They continued to view Romanticism in terms of a historical consciousness unmodified by what might be called "poetic" considerations. Their replies took two forms, depending on whether they understood Romanticism as an epochal event or not. Some, agreeing with the idea that Romanticism

---

7. See, for example, Peter Gay, *The Party of Humanity* (New York: Knopf, 1964), p. 253–54.

8. "Most of the authors who have written since 1800 . . . have boldly wreaked havoc in areas of French literature" (Frédéric Godefroy); "However high the Lamartines, the Mussets, and the Hugos might have risen, they are not and will never be classics: too far removed from the age of the language's perfection, they are too deeply marked by foreign literatures" (Brunetière). Cited in *Le Préromantisme*, pp. 41, 43.

was an extension of the Revolution, and defining it summarily in such phrases as "jeunesse et liberté," emphasized the doctrinal aspects of the movement, its schools and *cénacles*, celebrating where others deplored the victory of the "cause." Others, like Daniel Mornet and André Monglond,[9] tried to downplay the originality of the Romantics by tracing the origins of the new sensibility to a host of eighteenth-century sources. In Mornet, the representative of the new Sorbonne's more "objective" approach to literary history, it was a matter of asserting the continuity of things, of accepting as "facts" to be accounted for and ordering the whole variety of literary expression. Monglond's concern went deeper. He sought to show a continuity of feeling between the Romantics and isolated men and women of the *ancien régime* as a way of escaping the political question altogether. The melancholy yearnings and inchoate *rêveries* of tender souls in the French provinces could not be attributed to social discontents alone or to the turbulence of individualistic genius. Romanticism for Monglond had its roots in a deep existential crisis which was almost religious in character.

In either case, *préromantisme* did not name a school, or describe what could be called an artistic style except for certain minor, that is, nonepochal works.[10] Some critics objected to the substantive *préromantisme* as suggesting too much coherence where there were only disparate phenomena: better to speak of preromantic ideas or moods, or, as Monglond did in one of his books, of preromantic lives. The fact that one could assign no definite temporal boundaries to Preromanticism or coherence to its poetic expression became an advantage in a way: Romanticism seemed all the more rooted in French soil.

Préromantisme served, in other words, to soften the impact of Romanticism. The latter found its place in French literary history by losing its event-character and gaining an aura of permanence. The ultimate stage of this development is to place Romanticism alongside Classicism as two poles of an eternal dialectic between mind and heart. At this point history becomes nature, the supposed rhythm of

9. Daniel Mornet, *Le Romantisme au XVIIIe siècle* (Paris: Hachette, 1912); André Monglond, *Le Préromantisme français* (Grenoble: Arthaud, 1930), and *Vies préromantiques* (Paris: éditions des presses françaises, 1925).

10. Monglond's work of 1930 does discuss full-fledged novelists like Prévost, but concentrates on letter writers, diarists and other *minores* as more characteristic of the period.

life. This paradoxical result should not surprise us, though, for in French eyes Classicism was until very recently not considered a historical period at all in the modern "historicist" sense.[11] It was an eternal moment on a par with the golden ages of Greek and Roman art. To rival it, Romanticism would have to become timeless too, but since it is so obviously linked to change and dislocation, it needs the mediating role of *préromantisme* to minimize its disruptive force.

But what is it about Preromanticism, if we can speak of it substantively for a moment, that allows it to play such a role? Granted that it is a convenient fiction, what is the tenor of that fiction? Monglond touches on it when he speaks of the period as manifesting a poetic experience without poems.[12] It is the *felt absence and impossibility* of a poetic *work* that defines the age. Nothing could be more curious than a period defined by a lack of achievement, and yet nothing more instructive for a meditation on literary history. One could say it was just this marked absence of the disruptive force characteristic of the fully achieved work that provides the key to the historical importance of Preromanticism.

Here I would part company with the interpretation offered by the speakers at the symposium. For them, the campaign against Romanticism has nothing to do with art as such. The *récuperation* of the movement, like its banishment, is an ideological process reflecting a political crisis. *Préromantisme* is nothing in itself, and nothing to a strictly literary history. But it is possible on the one hand to trace some of the anxiety over the power of Romanticism to a widespread literary phenomenon of the later nineteenth century, which finds its late echo in Monglond's fascination with the unproductive disquiet of the preromantics. Where Romanticism represented strenuous ac-

11. "For a Frenchman, there are not two classical periods [antiquités], but three: the Greek, the Roman, and the French of the seventeenth century. This chain of continuity was lived by the artists of the seventeenth century; but even when Romanticism came along to break it, it was still maintained by the critics," Albert Thibaudet, *La Physiologie de la critique*, cited in Ernst Robert Curtius, *Gesammelte Aufsätze zur romanischen Philologie* (Bern and Munich: Francke, 1960), p. 20.

12. Monglond, *Le Préromantisme français* I, 171–72. For a somewhat analogous view of late eighteenth-century English literature as process and mood rather than product, see Northrop Frye, "Toward Defining an Age of Sensibility," in *Fables of Identity: Studies in Poetic Mythology* (New York: Harcourt, Brace, and World, 1963), pp. 130–37.

tivity, an effort of the will, writers like Gide who are quite removed from the political fray can be seen to echo Barrès's laments about the loss of energy or heroism in French culture. Without appealing to the oddly powerful transformation of this complaint in Mallarmé or Rimbaud, we can find in Gide's *Paludes* ("Marshlands") a symptomatic indication of what I mean. *Paludes* is hardly a "work" at all, and yet Claudel called it, just for that reason, "the most complete document we have on that curious atmosphere of suffocation and stagnation we breathed from 1885 to 1890."[13]

These were the very years of the antiromantic campaign, and it would be tempting to pursue the connection between the literary and ideological debates of the time as parallel instances of an "anxiety of influence" with respect to Romanticism. Some of the right wing critics who denounced the movement were, as René Wellek reminds us, avid readers of at least some of the Romantic poets.[14] The portrait of a preromantic age when some of the same lassitude and diffuse expectation was apparently predominant could be taken as a cultural defense mechanism, more subtle in its implications than a bare denial of Romanticism's legitimacy. But to do so would only perpetuate the negative image of *préromantisme*. More interesting would be to read the weakness it names as inaugurating a trend in the poetic creation of the nineteenth century as well as in criticism. The lack of poetic works that characterizes Preromanticism becomes what Michel Foucault has called an *absence d'oeuvre* within the great poetic achievements of the Romantic and post-Romantic periods.[15] What was a cultural condition is internalized as part of the poetic process becoming an anticipation and postponement of the poem's status as a finished "work," a poetic theme whose reflection in turn affects the idea of the poet's possible contribution to society—his work in the cultural sense. If, as has been suggested, we read nineteenth-century French poetry prospectively, it may derive from our

13. Paul Claudel, letter to Gide of 12 May 1900, cited in André Gide, *Romans* (Paris: Gallimard, 1958), p. 1473.

14. René Wellek, "French 'Classicist' Criticism in the Twentieth Century," *Yale French Studies* 38 (1967), 47–71.

15. Michel Foucault, *Histoire de la folie à l'âge classique*, second edition (Paris: Gallimard, 1972), pp. 179–80. The notion has been fruitfully extended to the interpretations of a number of texts by Shoshana Felman, *La Folie et la chose littéraire* (Paris: Seuil, 1978).

perception of this internal feature of the poems: it is not always easy to distinguish incompletion from incompleteness.

Another, related reason for this kind of reading is proposed by Harold Bloom. It is the absence of any "blocking" precursor among the French poets whose work seems to preempt the future and require his successors to define themselves against the strength of the earlier one.[16] The rage against Romanticism in some quarters might have come from the absence of any stimulation—and thus justification—of the latecomer's own assertiveness. In reaching to the "weakness" of the past, the latecomer finds no cover under which to pursue his achievement, and so denounces the paralyzing power of that "weakness." This might help to explain how Romanticism could in France be denounced as soft and decadent, and at the same time as capable of sapping the strongest of institutions. We should not, moreover, confuse the doctrinal force of French Romanticism with the strength of its poetic example, just as we should not misinterpret the Enlightenment's optimistic work as a sign of poetic confidence. As Monglond shows, the optimism of the *philosophes* did nothing to relieve the preromantics' sense that men's artistic capacity had atrophied.

This brings us back to Rousseau, that ambiguous figure of power and uncertainty on the threshold of Romanticism. Perhaps he would not have been so vilified in the century after his death had his achievement been more unequivocal, had he been perceived, whatever his ideas, as the author of fully finished poetic works in whose shadow it was possible to grow and whose influence one could eventually and creatively overthrow. Preromanticism has often been seen as the age of Rousseau; its fragility as a historical category should perhaps be related to the problematic status of Jean-Jacques' works. Not that these were ever viewed as negligible. On the contrary, they have always been felt to concentrate within themselves a whole mode of feeling; and their political influence was immense. But *as works* they did not, despite—perhaps because of—their author's self-dramatization, clear a space for themselves in a way that would "contain" the transgressions of later writers and so contribute to the edifice of culture. For it was obvious that Rousseau's own transgressive action in writing was hedged about by a fundamental ambivalence.

16. Harold Bloom, "The Breaking of Form," in *Deconstruction and Criticism*, ed. Geoffrey Hartman (New York: Seabury Press, 1979), p. 13.

II.

Rousseau is uncompromising in his rejection of modern society, but always uncomfortable about the violent, transgressive aspect of his enterprise. But if society was as corrupt as he claimed, then how could his criticism of it be aggressive, especially as a thorough critique was, he felt, the first step in restoring authentic values? Oddly enough, what causes Rousseau most anxiety is not his polemical ardor but his effort to provide consolation afterwards and help to his beleaguered contemporaries. We need only to compare the confident way he offers his *Discours sur l'inégalité* to the world with the distanced, diffident presentation of *Julie* and *Emile*. It seems as if the work of reparation is fraught with more danger than the destruction of long-cherished illusions. In assisting in the latter, however, Rousseau is only following an already established mode of discourse, since modern culture is essentially a critical culture. On the other hand, despite the numerous references to Fabricius, Cato, and Socrates, Rousseau feels that his positive work lacks authority. He worries that to his intended audience he must appear as a dangerous innovator, substituting a chimerical imagination for the palpable reality of scientific achievement and material progress. He may appeal to the authority of nature, but realizes that nature does not sanction the act of writing itself except perhaps as the simple expression of feeling (the *cri de la nature*). Writing as work, however, as the fashioning of a finished product or monument is a mediated, cultural process whose only justification lies in its effect, whether it helps or not to forestall the negative impact of historical decline. But this effect cannot be predicted, only anticipated. Like the Legislator of the *Contrat social* (I,7), Rousseau must "work in one age and enjoy in another" the fruits of his labor—if the verdict of posterity is favorable.

Here Rousseau hesitates. How can his work at once be an instrument of change while containing the process of change? Only if it acts as an obstacle as well as a spur to action. But in that case, Rousseau fears, his "constructive" writing will not be as purely or as simply helpful as his criticism was devastating. The very ease and spontaneity with which he began his career, untrammelled (as he felt) by any anxious influences; the immediacy of eloquence which seems to bracket the whole question of the author's authority: these made it hard for Rousseau to contemplate without anxiety the completion and reception of his work. The formlessness of the conspiracy he imagined in his paranoid moments to be directed against the realization of his hopeful projects is a function of his own freedom from a formative struggle against literary—as well as personal—ancestors. The fulfillment of his enterprise appears all the more to be an act of aggression in that it is Rousseau's first real confrontation with others. Finishing the work, giving to his writing the status, the irreducibility of an *oeuvre* cannot constitute for Rousseau the sign of his reparative contribution to culture because the act of criticism which preceded it did not involve a difficulty to be consciously and aggressively overcome. As Rousseau experiences it, the second gesture is his first proper initiative or act of will—and thus the locus of his anxiety.

Rousseau develops a number of strategies to deal with the anxiety of anticipation, that is, with the trepidation before completion and reception of his work. Rather than give his writing its autonomy, he sometimes focuses on the circumstances from which it emerged. By identifying and thereby "preserving" the objects, persons, and places that made him what he is, the author of the *Confessions* or of the childhood scenes in the *Lettre à d'Alembert* mitigates the unsettling power of his activity. Or, taking an opposite tack, by subsuming all his impulses under the category of a generalized, ambient *sentiment* Rousseau hopes to contain his critical assertions within the *rayonnement* of a beneficent because unwillful influence.

Yet at this point a wider anxiety makes itself felt. It is one thing to worry about the effects of one's actions, to dread the isolation and vulnerability that comes from making room for oneself on the world's stage. What is done is done. But to seek comfort in the notion that one has not actually "done" anything but only expressed the purest of feelings or named the most innocent of objects—this means that the slightest gesture on one's part, including the gesture of defense against the aggression that, denied and split off, returns to haunt the self, is suddenly charged with guilt.[17] What is worse, there is little prospect for relief from this guilt, for only if one could point to

---

17. This insight is developed in Pierre-Paul Clément's scrupulous *Jean-Jacques Rousseau: de l'éros coupable à l'éros glorieux* (Neuchatel: La Baconnière, 1976), which stops short, however, of an interpretation of the works themselves.

some accomplishment, to some work whose reparative character may compensate for the violent assumption of initiative, could one hope for a fair judgment based on the preponderance of the evidence.

Rousseau's very attempt to defuse judgment by diffusing his literary action prevents him, ironically, from taking this way out. On the other hand, if by some special dispensation or by the operation of the historical trope Rousseau invokes in the *Contrat social*, the effect could become the cause,[18] the author might yet be vindicated. If the work, in other words, were in some sense already there to redeem *in advance* the disruptive effect of taking up the pen, then Rousseau could consent to becoming the agent of his *oeuvre*.

This is Pygmalion's dream in Rousseau's little play of that name, written in 1762. The artist's statue cannot fail to remind us of Rousseau's Julie and to appear as a reflection on the just-completed novel, which perhaps because it is so clearly a fiction is the book Rousseau is most willing to view as a work in its own right. We know how the story of Julie, her lover, and her friend enchanted its author by its consoling power even before he began to write it, and how the scourge of art, Jean-Jacques, felt no guilt as the novel flowed from his pen. But by an ironic twist, just because Rousseau experiences the autonomous and irreducible reality of the work, he cannot feel himself to be its author. Such is the embarrassed message of the second preface he added to the novel after the book had been warmly welcomed by the public.[19] Once the effect has become the cause, the erstwhile agent becomes superfluous. *Pygmalion* is the story of an author trying, and failing, to catch up with his work. Anticipation, which has been turned against anxiety, has only reinforced it.

There is another avenue to be explored. What Rousseau can recover and make his own is what he calls the "*sentiment de l'existence.*" This sense of his being is not, however, simply an empirical *donnée.* To experience it, Rousseau suggests in those lyrical pages he devotes to it and which are one of his greatest gifts, is in itself an exemplary achievement, requiring a laborious askesis from the vale of modern life. Yet even before the feeling is recovered, Rousseau is convinced of its availability, and so strong is his conviction that

18. *Contrat social*, bk. 2, ch. 7.
19. See Paul de Man, *Allegories of Reading* (New Haven: Yale University Press, 1979), pp. 199 ff., for a discussion on somewhat different lines.

conveying it can be viewed as a positive contribution on his part—
one for which Rousseau can claim credit. He could then, perhaps,
give up worrying about the reception of his writing.

We find the most successful expression of the *sentiment de l'existence*, however, where Rousseau has abandoned not the anxiety but
the hope of being understood: in the *Rêveries*. One might understand
this circumstance as a confirmation of our own contemporary idea—
one we derive, in part, from Rousseau himself—that such a sacrifice
lies at the heart of all artistic communication. The anxiety of anticipation would thus never be something one could resolve; one could
only transcend it. The answer would be the disappearance of the
question.

We should not be too quickly satisfied with this conclusion,
which might indeed apply to the process of writing in general, but not
to the problem of the work. The latter cannot be transcended unless
we do believe, with Roland Barthes, that it is a false problem.[20] If we
take it to be real one, and from a literary-historical point of view I
think we must, then we must look for evidence that Rousseau's
anxiety of anticipation is indeed "worked through" in the act of
writing. Otherwise we return to the helpless perplexity of *Julie's*
"editor," which is no serenely metacritical metaphor but itself a
source of renewed concern.

If Rousseau can do nothing with his book, perhaps something
more could be done in the domain of the self, that self which appeared
as a spontaneous fount of langùage before the anxiety set in and
became an obstacle to the channelling of utterance into a work. In a
sense, one might call this self Rousseau's problematic precursor, a
blocking antecedent who must be overcome if the author is to accomplish anything, and his anxiety (which is tied to the end product and
its reception rather than to the inception of the work) finally be
contained. We have an indication that Rousseau does turn against
himself in the motto he adopts: *vitam impendere vero*, "to stake
one's life on the truth." It is often forgotten that this phrase appears
for the first time only in 1758, *after* Rousseau has completed his
critical mission and when, paradoxically, he is meditating on the

20. Roland Barthes, "De l'oeuvre au texte," *Revue d'esthétique* 24 (1971),
225–32.

helpfulness of the fiction he has just written.[21] The motto does not proclaim the narcissistic integrity of Rousseau's self-image. Rather, it is directed against the idea of the self and the whole ethic of self-expression associated with it. It is assertive insofar as it marks Rousseau's attempt at a self-overcoming. It is meant seriously, for Rousseau in a sense must anticipate his own death in order to turn his works into an *oeuvre*.

Now in a way Rousseau never ceases contemplating his death, real or symbolic. In his anxiety over the reception of his books he tries to defend himself against a hostile world by anticipating the public's reaction and inflicting the blow before it comes. Thus his repeated declaration of exhaustion in his prefaces, and the pretense that we will be reading him "posthumously." "Reader, if you receive this last work with indulgence, you will be welcoming my shade, for, as for me, I am no more."[22] We read this at the opening of the same work in which Rousseau announces the motto of his present and his future work. The very juxtaposition of this swan song with the inauguration of a new relationship with his readers via "the truth" suggests that Rousseau's is more than a defensive move, that it is the beginning of a new phase. Or rather, it is the sign that, as Margaret Ferguson has shown, defense in literature is not always evasion but can be part of a productive confrontation with the poetic enterprise.[23] By "killing" himself before others get to him, Rousseau gives himself the opportunity he has lacked hitherto: the chance to undertake the work of mourning (*Trauerarbeit*, Freud calls it) which turns defensiveness into contact with reality, denial into an active negation, and opens up a space for an externally oriented work as well.

The absence of a blocking but nourishing precursor made it difficult for Rousseau to channel and contain his aggressive impulses. We might add that Rousseau's predicament has a wide cultural reso-

21. In the *Lettre à d'Alembert*. The motto appears in a footnote appended to a passage on dancing lifted verbatim from *Julie* and made the subject of a defiant identification with the extravagance of its apparent message. See the translation by Allan Bloom, *Politics and the Arts: Letter to M. d'Alembert on the Theatre* (1960; rpt. Ithaca: Cornell University Press, 1968), p. 132.

22. *Letter to d'Alembert*, p. 7.

23. Margaret Ferguson, "Border Territories of Defense: Freud and Defenses of Poetry," in *Psychiatry and the Humanities*, ed. Joseph H. Smith, vol. 4 (New Haven: Yale University Press, 1980).

nance, Rousseau being, as Erich Auerbach has suggested, the first European man of note who although "constitutionally" a Christian in background and temperament, nevertheless did not find in the Christian scheme of sin and redemption either an answer to his questions or a pattern to be translated into secular terms.[24] Thus there was for him no preestablished context within which his struggle and his detachment from early ties could be worked out. In mourning, we detach ourselves from the beloved obstacle to our imaginative survival by working through the anxious fantasy that we have contributed to its (necessary) death by our own murderous impulses, of whose reality we become more painfully aware on such occasions. Despite the early death of his mother and the disappearance of his brother, to name only two of the incidents related in the *Confessions* with a somewhat rhetorical pathos, Rousseau was for a long time a stranger to the process of mourning we expect to find more prominent in such a man. And such a writer: without going into a comparison between Rousseau's attitude toward the "lost" state of nature and that of his predecessors, I would cite Rousseau's novel as a prime example of deferred confrontation with the reality as opposed to the rhetoric of loss. Only late in *Julie* do we find what we looked for much earlier, and even then it is presented as part of the hero Saint-Preux's nightmare. "If only she were dead! I dared to cry out in a transport of rage; yes, I would be less unhappy: I would be able to give myself over to my sorrows. . . . But she lives; she is happy! . . . she lives, and her life is my death."[25]

More frustrating than anything else, more anxiogenic, is the impossibility of mourning what one can no longer possess but what one is as yet unable to give up lest everything else seem to go with it, swept away by the force of one's destructive desires. In a pattern reminiscent of one we have earlier mentioned, it would appear that for Saint-Preux Julie would first have to really die for him to give her up and acknowledge that in doing so he "consents" to "kill" her in his mind. This is in fact what happens. Instead of having Saint-Preux and Julie, the star-crossed lovers, drown together in the lake (as was the original plan so far as we can make it out), Rousseau has Julie live

24. Erich Auerbach, "Über den historischen Ort Rousseaus," *Gesammelte Aufsätze zur romanischen Philologie* (Bern and Munich: Francke, 1967), pp. 291–95.
25. *Julie, ou la nouvelle Héloïse,* Part 5, letter 9. Pléiade edition, p. 615.

long enough to allow Saint-Preux's awareness of what is at stake to come to the surface. There is still a degree of ambiguity: either Rousseau keeps the novel going because of his inability to part from his creation, as in the story of *Pygmalion*, or else he needs to make her real enough (by having her elicit contradictory feelings in the other characters) so that something is created that could in fact be mourned as a real loss, because invested with all, not just part of, the spectrum of human feeling. In these terms, Julie's necessary "first" or anticipated death from the creator's point of view is equivalent to her realization as a character in the literary work out of the idealized image in which she first appeared to him. I think it arguable, at least, that in *Julie* the "effect" did become—painfully—the "cause" despite the ironic and helpless distance with which the author contemplates the work after it was accomplished.

To say more than this would require a detailed interpretation of the novel I cannot provide here. I would suggest however, that Rousseau's treatment of Julie can be taken as a metaphor for his confrontation with himself throughout his effort to establish a secure reception for his writing. Rousseau sets himself up as the object of his own belated attempt to mourn something of value, something that acquires the essential part of its value when it becomes an object one can accept wanting to destroy. And one can accept that desire if one feels that the object's enduring "presence" to the mind will ultimately be enhanced in the process. Rousseau's presumption, if we can call it that, is to feel that only his own self can be meaningfully sacrificed in this fashion. The difficulty of his creative work lies in the necessity to establish his worthiness while at the same time proving it by allowing it to be impugned.

All this may seem a rather perverse way of going about the task of poetic creation. But the perversity is not, or not only, Rousseau's. Apart from its general affinity with the classical ideal of *la difficulté vaincue* as an essential characteristic of the literary work, the process of conjuring up an object to be lost and mourned is perhaps the only possible response to the dilemma of the "preromantic" writer. I referred in passing to the possible connection between Rousseau's lack of a blocking precursor and the Christian world-view's loss of reality in Rousseau's time. Not its active negation by the writers of the Enlightenment, but its simple fading away with all its structures of thought intact.[26] One could say that the preromantics among the late eighteenth-century writers were those who experienced this fading away in all its force, as it were. The preromantic paralysis, its *absence d'oeuvre*, might be traced to its inability to follow Rousseau's example and produce an obstacle worth overcoming, one whose "death" could be mourned. The void we find in the prose of Senancour, say, or often in Constant, is not pure nothingness, the absence of something that should have been there, and that still could be. The process of secularization has gone forward imperceptibly to the point where Pascal's anxieties, still so vividly present to a mind like Voltaire's, formed in the early part of the century, are no longer paradigmatic. Rather, what is missing is the sense of a former presence that could be felt as having been there and whose passing could be experienced. Failing that experience, the writer is condemned to passivity himself.

Later, in the full flush of Romanticism, efforts will be made to recreate such a presence, or at least such a feeling. Still later, the impossibility of doing so is itself thematized as the ironic subject of a different kind of poetry. But if Rousseau becomes a force to be reckoned with in later generations, a precursor in his own right, it is not only because of the spontaneous expressions of anticipation we find in passages like the one quoted from the third *Rêverie*. It is also because, by anticipating his own death in its reality, the death of the natural and representative man, Rousseau filled the void left by the fading of the old order long enough and vividly enough to make the active experience and working-through of its disappearance possible for himself and a challenge to his successors. To this extent, his writings can in retrospect be accorded the status of an *oeuvre*.

26. See Bernard Groethuysen, *Les Origines de l'esprit bourgeois en France* (Paris: Gallimard, 1927), for a detailed description of transformation.

MARY ANN CAWS

Winging It, or Catching Up with Kierkegaard and Some Swans

> Repetition and recollection are the same movement, only in opposite directions; for what is recollected has been, is repeated backwards, whereas repetition properly so called is collected forwards.
> —Søren Kierkegaard (Constantine Constantius) *Repetition*[1]

A. REPETITIOUS PRELUDE

Fearing—perhaps with some reason—a misapprehension of his thought, Søren Kierkegaard wrote to Professor J. L. Heiberg a much revised and finally open letter under the title "A Little Plea, by Constantine Constantius, author of *Repetition*," and then rewrote it as a letter to the "real reader" of *Repetition*. Here Kierkegaard best defines both the anxiety of repeating and the kind of forward framing that gives its thrust and its edge to some of our loftier poetic flights, paradoxically free and yet already repetitious. For the concept Repetition, applied to freedom, there are three major steps to pass through, ironic and resonant at once. Freedom defined as pleasure fears repetition, as if it were displeasure; a shrewder or level-two freedom tries to see new sides of the concept, but again despairs, as the sides are perhaps alternating (*Either/Or*, for example), but not infinite. In its highest form, freedom seeks repetition, and, fearing change in a world of change, asks anxiously if repetition is possible? "Freedom itself is now repetition" (*R*, xvii). Motion—including a vertical one—is implied, for from one step to the next, "the transition is a becoming" (*R*, xxviii). The following essay might be considered an attempt at transition as a forwards repetition of a few motives, partially in flight.

In a footnote for *The Concept of Dread*, Kierkegaard as Vigilius Haufniensis refers to his own *Fear and Trembling* under the name Johannes de Silentio and to the positive feeling expressed there: "Behold all things have become new!" He compares this to the negative

---

1. Constantin Constantius (Søren Kierkegaard), *Repetition* (*R* in text), ed. Walter Lowrie (Princeton: Princeton University Press, 1946), pp. 3–4.

feeling of repetition, discussing *Repetition* as the whimsical book "its author meant it to be," where what he has discovered he has hidden in the form of jest. Then, he adds, "the problem is to transform repetition into something inward, into the proper task of freedom, as to whether, while everything changes, it can actually realize repetition" (quoted in preface to *R*, p. xxxiv).

Now the question as to how we ourselves read S. K. reading Søren Kierkegaard as Constantine Constantius read by Kierkegaard-Constantius as Virgilius Haufniensis opens a major chapter in the history of irony, but also in that of the reading of repetitions and specifically, the repeats of images of reading. If I pick one of the most flighty of the latter and divest it of some weighty readings, it may be to give it back its freedom, even as it takes its wing from one author and period to the next, from symbolism to what we think of as contemporary poetry: it will undergo a translation-in-air, wherein the reading, like the victim, will be caught up.

B. BAUDELAIRE'S OWN BIRD

Baudelaire's tragic rendering of the bird-in-exile, whether the albatross on shipdeck, unsuited to the boards and to the play as well, or the swan in the poem by the same name, marks a double exile for the bird. He is condemned to being out of society and here, out of the protective cage or coding of the exile also. In his rough voyage, he is forced to drag his feathers in unesthetic soil, by the dry bed of a stream, bathing his plumes in the dust for want of water. The turn to dust revivifies, paradoxically, the reading which might otherwise find the great Mourning for Those Who Have Lost Everything a romantic banality rather than the moving image it should, presumably, be. "Behold all things are new," indeed.

That this image should work up to the color of mystery and the level of legend through loss and want is a matching mystery: "Je vois ce malheureux, mythe étrange et fatal"[2] and, a few lines later: "Je pense à mon grand cygne, avec ses gestes fous" All four adjectives are of the same sort—undefining, large, subjective, singular—"strange, fatal, great, mad." The wingspan stretches out to all of them at once, inclusive of what is to come and yet remains odd.

2. Charles Baudelaire, "Le Cygne," in *Les Fleurs du mal* (Paris: Gallimard, ed. Pléiade, 1975) I, p. 85.

The myth will hover over a flock of opposite swans in flight, potential or actual, and at rest, from Valéry's silky swans whose half-luminous plumes graze against the reeds in the lunar opalescence of his "Féerie"[3] to Mann's menacing and rearing Black Swan, signaling, signing and designing, in the novel blackened by his name. His sign might be that of a terrifying ambiguity, as the cancerous malady is wrongly interpreted as the sign of youth itself, writ large in the red of blood and passion and in the black of death itself.

But these are no stranger birds than the greatest and oddest of them all, Mallarmé's sonneted and much trumpeted swan.

C. MALLARMÉ'S SIGNS AND LEDA'S SITUATION

Two of Mallarmé's figures in situation—the swan on that lake frozen white[4] and the thoughtful and fated hero called by the name Igitur which is not properly one—furnish a fateful shelter for a multiplicity of subsequent texts. His involvement in that celebrated embrace of swan and sign, "cygne" and "signe," and in that room of Igitur's, less double than that of Baudelaire but no simpler for all that, have so marked our own present and future reading and writing that the two signs, directing us to lake and room, remain intact. The grip in which they hold us, tight as it is, may be unpacked in its thrust forward.

Nothing so perfectly indicates the seduction of some of the many future encounters under this first and frozen wingspan as Yeats' swanning of Leda, which obliges us to a re-reading of Mallarmé. Yeats' own presentation of the damsel and the beast is modestly and strikingly framed by the simple two dots of a colon at the incipit of the text, catching the eye no less surely than the swan catches Leda. This blow—aimed also at us—is thus isolated as by two precursor signals of destiny from its result which is this very seductive poem of creation and engendering.[5]

LEDA AND THE SWAN

A sudden blow: the great wings beating still
Above the staggering girl, her thighs caressed

---

3. Paul Valéry, "Féerie," in *Poèmes* (Paris: *Poésie*/Gallimard, 1976), p. 8.

4. Stéphane Mallarmé, "Sonnet," ("Le vierge, le vivace et le bel aujourd'hui . . .") in *Oeuvres complètes* (Paris: Gallimard, Ed. Pléiade, 1945), p. 67.

5. William Butler Yeats, "Leda and the Swan," in *The Norton Anthology of Poetry*, ed. Allison, etc., rev. ed. (New York: Norton, 1975), p. 926.

By the dark webs, her nape caught in his bill,
He holds her helpless breast upon his breast.

How can those terrified vague fingers push
The feathered glory from her loosening thighs?
And how can body, laid in that white rush,
But feel the strange heart beating where it lies?

A shudder in the loins engenders there
The broken wall, the burning roof and tower
And Agamemnon dead.
                            Being so caught up,
So mastered by the brute blood of the air,
Did she put on his knowledge with his power
Before the indifferent beak could let her drop?

LEDA

Le heurt d'un vent. De grandes ailes battent
Encore sur la fille chancelante, dont les cuisses
Sont frôlées par les palmes noires, dont la nuque
Est captive du bec. Et sa poitrine
Sous sa poitrine à lui est sans recours.

Comment ces vagues doigts terrifiés pourraient-ils
Des cuisses affaiblies repousser tant de gloire?
Comment un corps, sous cette ruée blanche,
Ne sentirait-il pas battre l'étrange coeur?   ·

Un frisson dans les reins engendre là
Le mur brisé, la tour et la voûte qui brûlent
Et Agamemnon mort.
                            Elle emportée,
Elle écrasée par le sang brut de l'air,
Prit-elle son savoir avec sa force
Avant qu'indifférent le bec l'eut laissé choir?
        (translation, Yves Bonnefoy)

When once the beat is given, the beating of wings continues, taken in
the paradox of the "still," as if the arrest of the stilled beak were to
preserve its ambivalent erotic violence. Behind the tender and ardent
monster Zeus becomes or is taken in by, there is to be read the profile
of another more modest beast, some Mallarmean spider whose web
leaves its trace upon the webbed feet of the swan, and like the verb
that is literally caught in suspense, it is "caught up," taken into the

web of the scene as of the text. A great palpitation quivers through the tissue, intensified by the strangeness of the receptive couch or the bed of the body as reader of the heart; the echoes, in repeating, frame the spectacle in sound and sight:

> *beating* still . . . strange heart *beating*
> body *laid* . . . where it *lies*

All this linguistic palpitation and its ardent reception enable the engendering of the future in the immobile time of myth, which is "caught up" or taken in by the canvas of the gaze.

The *arrest* of the moment is once again signaled by the typography, where the pause or blank space in the text after the announcement of Agammemnon's death, impels a stop as the colon after the blow. The space marks the shiver of conception, the tiny difference between death and life, between the warlike violence of the shattered wall, and its result, the engendering of being:

> And Agammemnon dead.
>
> Being so caught up

The play is double, between the verb "being" and the adjective that precedes it; an ambivalence signaled by this arrest, on the larger scale, of death, rendered formally by the period and by the displacement down to the line below.

Between the high—caught up—and the low point—Leda's abandonment by the beast, we read the tragedy of the fall of a passion as celestial as it is animal, a passion which has engendered this text, whose reception is inscribed in its very center.

But Leda hatched two eggs. In making his own portrait of Yeats' Leda, Bonnefoy called a wind to life:[6] this "blow" of Yeats initiating the poem and this beating in the air have engendered a breath of life, where the beating wings or "ailes" are absorbed in the simple pronoun: "Elle." Bonnefoy concentrates all his energy on that double wing, after the death of love, after the pause where the heroic *Elle* is engendered:

> Elle emportée,
>
> Elle écrasée

6. Yves Bonnefoy, "Leda," in *Argile* no. 1, 1976.

The wing takes all the room in his portrait, to such a point that the swan disappears entirely from the reading it engenders, from the title which it justifies. He unsigns Leda, or *unswans* her in pointing her out (*la désigne* or *la dé-cygne*) so that the engendering calls on some other wing of a bird still white. He may have leapt from this bed of reading, white as snow and from this white sheet toward another swan in a frozen lake, not just backwards towards another poem, but forwards to the reverse or mirror image of some future icy canvas wherein to be caught up, some painting white on white, upon the feathers of some bird and plume, or upon the sheets of a tomb as the oxymoronic cradle of the penned text. From the fecund womb and the devouring bird, the swan-sign of Mallarmé, silenced as he said, in its colors of a bygone time, brushes with a feather more alive than its subjects gone pale by de-sign. For Mallarmé's constellation written white on black in reverse upon the sky frames this other picture where the idea of writing unfolds among the contours of the feather-bed: here, in the reader's anxious obsession, the figure of Leda may now intrude, introducing her lover, as legend would have it, into the very highest room of her palace, oval shaped and thus called *ovum* by the Lacedemonians, providing, says Eluard, the fiction of the egg.

In Bonnefoy's rendering, the swan seems born from Leda. So too the translation of myth into poem, and of poem into poem has kept all the figures caught up in the air and inspired with new breaths of life. According to Yeats, the encounter between Leda and the swan is a second annunciation, in the world of myth: Bonnefoy's ardent contemplation dispenses with the nominal agent "swan" in order to inscribe the entire double portrait under a circumspect title, engendering an obsession, hatched in the night of some Idumée, providing a gift.[7] The myth of Leda is not, after all, to be dropped; the contagious and catastrophic fall of her fate still catches up the reader, translated into the winged air.

D. NERUDA'S TURN

Give or take a Spanish swan or two, Neruda's swans of "El Lago de los cisnes"[8] cast yet another light on these readings now near their close.

7. Bonnefoy, Ibid.
8. Pablo Neruda, "El Lago de los cisnes," in *A New Decade: Poems* 1958–1967, translated by Ben Belitt and Alastair Reid (New York: Grove Press, 1969), pp. 186–87.

Heaviness in name and sight and feeling preside over the initial place of claustration:

> Lago Budi, sombrio, pesada piedra oscura,
> agua entre grandes bosques insepulta

> Lake Budi, lackluster, the dark, weighted stone,
> forest on forest, with unburied water between

until the sudden switch to the jewelled compacity and the terrified flight, baroque in red and white and black, from the brilliant and static equivalence of the waters:

> el lago, el agua dura y escondida,
> compacta luz, alhaja del anillo terrestre.
> Un vuelo blanco y negro: los cisnes ahuyentaron
> largos cuellos nocturnos, patas de cuero rojo,
> y la nieve serene volando sobre el mundo.

> Oh vuelo desde el agua equivalente . . .

> the hard, hidden water was there, the lake
> compact in a dazzle, the terrestrial ring with its jewel.
> A black-and-white panic in air, the swans going up
> on feet of red leather, their stretched necks nocturnal,
> a halcyon snow soaring over the whole of a world.

> Oh flight from the water's equivalence . . .

The same oxymoronic tension (sombrio/luz), recreated in the colorful flight, is replayed in the air, where the motionless beating is hurtled apart by a savage unrest and the barbarous wings until the turn to order and to absence:

> y luego alas salvajes que desde el torbellino
> se hicieron orden, vuelo, magnitud sacudída,
> y luego ausencia, un temblor blanco en el vacio.

> then barbarous wings in the whirlwind
> turning all into order, tremulous magnitude, flying;
> last of all, silence: a white perturbation of vacancy.

The swans and signs are no longer stuck in the ice, now deserted of any trace, entirely vacant. While this last projection leads to the loss of swan and trace for the benefit of a tremor and a great void, it might be time to reassert the barbaric freedom of the continued flight in the face of that strange re-ordering of the birds to be read neatly in the sky, to repeat those disordered flapping wings, against the calm equivalence.

Thus the scriptorial struggle about the swan, to be repeated somewhere else, leaving only this trace of a former wing, only a potential tremor again in the most enduring swan song of them all, by Mallarmé's own frozen dazzle. It is in that we must dip our plumes in order to write. We too are caught up in the anxiously repetitious pleasure to choose between the repeated flap of wings and a unique flight, between order and disorder, between dive and soaring, between bird and sign, having the freedom to play it all over, as the swanspan permits.

RICHARD KLEIN

Under "Pragmatic" Paradoxes

Jonathan Culler writes,

"A sign," writes Umberto Eco in *A Theory of Semiotics*, is "everything which can be taken as significantly substituting for something else. Semiotics is in principle the discipline studying everything that can be used in order to lie. If something cannot be used to tell a lie, conversely it cannot be used to tell the truth" (p. 7). *The bat is on my hat* would not be a signifying sequence if it were not possible to utter it falsely. Similarly, *I now pronounce you man and wife* is not a performative unless it is possible for it to misfire, to be used in inappropriate cicumstances and without the effect of performing a marriage.[1]

Culler is making powerful use of Eco's troubling theory of lie in order to explain by analogy the seemingly "unusual" move with which J. L. Austin, in *How To Do Things With Words*, inaugurates the scientific study of performative speech acts on the basis of the principle of misfire.[2] What is disturbing about Eco's argument is concealed in its transitions. He begins with what has become the self-evident notion that *substitution* is the condition of the possibility of meaning, even of the least significance; he names the allusive transfer or carrying across (the trans-port or *meta-phorein*) of some relation or ratio from one term to another (*allo-(a)gorein*) or of one term

1. *On Deconstruction* (Boston: Routledge & Kegan Paul, 1982), p. 114.
2. The powerful synthetic understanding which has organized *On Deconstruction* has performed an incalculable service to critical practitioners, who will find most of their unspoken implicit assumptions meticulously and clearly displayed. By making those premises visible Culler not only clarifies a great deal of recent practice but lays the ground for new work proceeding in new directions on the basis of its now more certain grasp on where it came from. All page references will henceforth be given in the text.

put in the place of (replacing) another, within a finite system of differentially organized elements. That notion serves to account for the undeniable empirical fact that from any word in the dictionary one can trace a referential path across to any other. It also explains the corollary experience that a new term can always be found to extend the blessings of denotation, of significant indication and referential nomination, to every new discovery or invention, to any experiential fact which as yet has no name but can always find one, like *gluon*, whose definition can always be expressed by the synonomous substitution of other terms.

Eco next proceeds to assimilate the science of semiotics to the study of whatever can be used (instrumentally) in order to tell a lie. That would include not only words, of course, but, for example, gestures, acts, or artefacts—not however, we are accustomed to think, rocks and stones and trees (unless as a function of their context they are used to index other signs or themselves). With perhaps unwitting surreptitiousness, Eco here is substituting for the notion of the metonymic substitution of signifying terms (along a chain of equivalences) a quite different sense of putting in place of: the duplicitous, metaphoric substitution of one identity or role for another in the mimetic act of doubling that makes possible specular illusions and deceptions. The movement of one and two, of carrying across from one to another, no longer is interpreted as the purely mechanical trans-portation between terms, but becomes, in mimetic duplicity, conflictually charged with the pathos of trans-gression.

In the next sentence, Eco makes the move from lie to truth, thereby accomplishing the transition from the first kind of mechanical linguistic substitution to the condition of producing truthful statements that affirm a positive state of affairs. In order to make this connection, which allows semiotics to be the master of meaning, Eco must pass through the lie and make truth result from its converse. "If something cannot be used to tell a lie, conversely it cannot be used to tell the truth." But the symmetrical, dialectical obverse of truth is not necessarily, not usually lie, but error. Error is the movement of wandering away from the path of truth, at the risk of a perpetual detour like the all but endless work in progress of signifying substitution that menaces the scientific project of Bouvard and Pécuchet or the aesthetic one of *Finnegan's Wake*. It is in no ordinary sense that we believe that telling a lie will stop the movement of detour, will suffice to interrupt the progress of substitution and give rise to the affirmation of positively true statements, like those within a science of semiotics. Although from a Nietzchean standpoint one could argue, no doubt, that every founding principle of a science is a heuristically necessary lie, nevertheless it is possible to think of founding a science of signs on the basis of lying? Does its concept presuppose the sign or does it precede and underlie the science of signs?

What is a lie?

"If something cannot be used to tell a lie, conversely it cannot be used to tell the truth." This principial statement ought itself to be able to be studied semiotically, that is, used to tell a lie. If it could not, it would have the paradoxical consequence that the proposition which defines the scientific discipline of semiotics could not itself be analyzed according to the principle which it enunciates. If, conversely, we imagine that we might therefore use this proposition as a lie, what then would be the logical consequences of that use? Suppose Eco were to confess: "Yes, I am lying about lying being the condition of positive statements of fact." In that form, the form of the *pseudo-menon*,[3] it is easy to show that if he is lying he is telling the truth and if the truth then lying.

More seriously, were we to imagine that the statement itself could be used to tell a lie, the lie would authorize our drawing one of two possible conclusions: Either that something which cannot be used to tell a lie actually *can* tell the truth, or conversely that something which can be used to tell a lie *cannot* be used to tell the truth. In the first case, if the statement could be used to lie, it would lead to the conclusion that semiotics, obliged to study lies, would be obliged to neglect all the meaningfully true statements which cannot be used to lie, or in the second case it would be compelled to acknowledge that the object of its study, namely lies, has no bearing at all on the nature of truthful assertions. In either case, the logical conclusion which follows from using the underlying principle of semiotics in order to tell a lie renders impossible the task of erecting a scientific study of

3. The paradox is an old story: Eubulides, the Megarian sixth-century B.C. Greek philosopher and successor to Euclid, invented the paradox of the liar. In this paradox Epimenides, the Cretan, says, "All Cretans are liars." If he is telling the truth he is lying; and if he is lying he is telling the truth. In the simpler form, "I am lying," this paradox was known to the ancients as the *pseudomenon*. Patric Hughes and George Brecht, *Vicious Circles and Infinity, An Anthology of Paradoxes* (Middlesex, England: Penguin Books, 1978).

signs on the basis of that principle. It appears that Eco has fallen prey to the Gödelian dilemma, to the aporetic contagion that Deconstruction regularly diagnoses in the premises that compose the theory of positive disciplines, but whose discovery in itself is no reason to stop working on the theory.

> Even though we have reason to believe, as Derrida writes, that "the language of theory always leaves a residue that is neither formalizable nor idealizable in terms of that theory of language," there is no reason to stop work on the theory (Limited Inc., p. 41/209). In mathematics, for example, Gödel's demonstration of the incompleteness of metamathematics (the impossibility of constructing a theoretical system within which all true statements of number theory are theorems) does not lead mathematicians to abandon their work.[4]

Gödel's proof demonstrates "the impossibility of constructing a theoretical system within which all true statements of number theory are theorems"—that is, demonstrable propositions resulting from other propositions already in place such as definitions, axioms, postulates or principles. The impossibility of such a metamathematical, theoretical system means that there will always be a residue; there will always, of necessity, be some piece belonging within the system which cannot be formalized or idealized, says Derrida, in terms of the definitions, axioms, postulates, or principles which determine what the theory comprises. Whereas Gödel proves that assertion for number theory, Derrida is arguing here that the same impossibility affects all "language of theory" and, it goes without saying, all theory of language. Culler is correct to insist, as he does elsewhere, that Deconstruction no less than Gödel's proof, does not lead theoreticians to abandon their work: the discovery of some inherent principle of indeterminacy—as in mathematics or physics or critical theory—does not somehow invalidate the disciplined study of the theory of a science, let alone the scientific study itself. Indeed there are scientists who take some aesthetic or ethical pleasure from the fact that their systematic (their idealized, formal) constructs are inherently unsusceptible to totalizing, hence to totalitarian claims of control over the mass of phenomena they encompass and observe; just as there are deconstructors whose whole theoretical horizon is semiotics—the scientific study of linguistic signs and sign systems. The

4. Ibid., p. 133.

power of a theoretical system is not absolute over the elements it comprehends, but because not absolute it may no less be immensely powerful.

If there is no reason to stop work on the theory, yet by the same argument one ought not to abandon too quickly those residual indeterminacies—those moments of undecidability or "demonstrations of incompleteness." It is not as if, after much work having disclosed the existence of an aporia in the constitution or in the consequences of a theoretical system, one may simply ignore its implications and skeptically suppose that it is the self-identical, the same damn aporia that one has repeatedly and often discovered in the past. Such ignoring would be equivalent to what Hegel in the "Introduction" to the *Phenomenology* calls the one-sided perspective of radical skepticism, "a merely negative process," "which always sees in the result only pure nothingness, and abstracts from the fact this nothing is determinate, is the *nothing* of *that out of which* it comes as a result. Nothing, however, is only, in fact, the true result, when taken as the nothing of what it comes from; and it is thus itself a determinate nothing, and has a *content.*"[5] To ignore the content of the residue or all that is left of nothing, after the demonstration of incompleteness or following the aporia, falls back into something like the pre-Hegelian Pyrrhonism on which Hegel in the "Introduction" heaps scorn, calling it "this sort of conceit which understands how to belittle every truth . . . and gloats over this its own private understanding, which always knows how to dissipate every thought, and to find instead of all the content, merely the barren Ego."[6] Those who would be content merely to demonstrate the existence of a residue and to ignore its implications, *that out of which it comes as a result*, are condemned to casting all positive truth into "the same abysmal void," to discovering no ground upon which to found any systematic discipline but only tbe barren landscape of their own ego, says Hegel, of their own private understanding. Such an Ego conceitedlv knows only its own understanding of the nullity of everything, and gloating, ego-centrically invests (in) itself, aggrandizes itself by taking its particular private perspective for the ground of the negative universal truth.[7]

5. *The Phenomenology of Mind* (New York: Harper, 1967), p. 137.
6. Ibid., p. 139.
7. Deconstruction is not a nihilism, as Culler scrupulously demonstrates using the evidence of its two-handed gestures. *On Deconstruction*, pp. 17–182.

The implications of an aporia are often difficult to specify, but Culler is certainly right to suggest that those who accuse Deconstruction of wishing to abandon the work of theory once it discovers another piece of nothing, or residue, a locus of indeterminacy, accuse it of falling behind Hegel into a form of predialectical naiveté, the most vain and futile skepticism. On the contrary, the work must go on.

For example, it is not at all self-evident what would count as a paradox of misfire. Culler writes:

> *The bat is on my hat* would not be a signifying sequence if it were not possible to utter it falsely. Similarly, *I now pronounce you man and wife* is not a performative unless it is possible for it to misfire, to be used in inappropriate circumstances and without the effect of performing a marriage. [P. 114]

The difficulty of distinguishing absolutely between a constative statement and a performative may be observed in the first example, *"The bat is on my hat,"* which wants to be the most unambiguously falsifiable description of a state of affairs, as befitting constative statements, but strikes the reader as one of those artificially devised sentences that does not intend to refer to anything, so much as to instantiate a significant distinction and serve as a grammatical or phonological example. It refers only in so far as it enacts the small signifying difference between *hat and bat*, and means only in so far as it successfully performs the required speech act of exemplification. If the example which is intended to be able, par excellence, to lie, can be read as a successful performative, are there circumstances in which we might consider the statement, "I now pronounce you man and wife"—a "good" example, perhaps the best example, of a speech act—liable to be used in order to lie, capable of being judged to be true or false?

Is a misfire ever a lie, and vice versa? Not under normal circumstances, or not in the ordinary sense of those words. Culler writes:

> Consider what would happen if after apparently completing a marriage ceremony one of the parties said that he had been joking when he uttered his lines—only pretending, just rehearsing, or acting under duress. Assuming that the others believe his report of his intention, it will not in itself be decisive. What he had in mind at the moment of utterance does not determine what speech act his utter-

ance performed. On the contrary, the question of whether a marriage did indeed take place will depend upon further discussion of the circumstances. If the minister had said that there would be a full dress rehearsal immediately before the real ceremony, or if the groom can sustain the claim that throughout the ceremony the bride's father was threatening him with a pistol, then one might reach a different conclusion about the illocutionary force of their utterances. What counts is the plausibility of the description of the circumstances: whether the features of the context adduced create a frame that alters the illocutionary force of the utterances. [Pp. 122–23]

The point of this passage is rather exactly to deny the connection between misfire and lie. It does not matter whether one of the parties was actually joking when he uttered his lines, was "only pretending." To be sure, the pretense, the false appearance intending to deceive, and thus the joking may be morally reprehensible. But the question of what he had in mind at the moment of utterance is irrelevant, the passage argues, in determining "what speech act his utterance performed," whether the marriage actually occurred. Even so, matters of truth and falsehood, of verification and plausibility, are not entirely absent from the determination of the speech act's success. Invited to consider what would happen after the groom announced he had been only joking, we are led to envisage something like a judicial inquiry. What is "decisive" in determining what happened depends on "further discussion of the circumstances; the evidence may be used to "sustain a claim," or "reach other conclusions" for "what counts is the plausibility of the description of the circumstances." The determination of whether a speech act has been successfully performed depends on considering the context in an investigative light, as a state of affairs whose conditions may be the object of constative statements that are true or false, that are open to doubt or skepticism concerning their plausibility or truth. The language of inspection, of detection and inquiry is manifest enough in the example of the joking groom; what is not explicitly described is the anxiety which accompanies the epistemological uncertainty of the parties for whom resolving doubts and skepticism about whether this was a "real ceremony" is of more than theoretical interest. A misfire is not a lie; it is a determination made on the basis, not of truth and falsehood, but of success and failure. But misfire, as a principle of explanation or analysis, shares with the lie, the possibility of accompanying doubt and thus anxiety. Like anxiety, lie and misfire are conceived, in the temporality of Cartesian doubt, as being *vor etwas*, a theoretically necessary precondition of conceiving the possibility of avoiding danger, of telling the truth, of successfully performing a speech act.[8] The persistence of that Cartesian temporality makes detective fiction boring. One does not need to be required to specify *every* feature of a context, as would be the case for a theory of speech acts that dreamed, as Austin does, of mastering "the total speech act in the total speech situation," [Culler, 123] in order to acknowledge how difficult it might be, under many circumstances, to put aside our skepticism, allay our doubt and agree that a speech act, like a wedding, had been effectively performed. Specifying the context, judging whether appropriate circumstances have been maintained is both indispensable for determining the meaning or success of a speech act and in principle and in practice a potentially limitless task. "Meaning is contextbound, but context is boundless" is the powerful formula Culler reiterates throughout the final pages of the chapter, "Meaning and Iterability."

The paradoxical implications of that formula serve simultaneously to make possible and make impossible the determination of a speech act: possible because it says that the context is infinitely available for further description or specification and yet in the interest of meaning may be arbitrarily detached and defined, its margins unproblematically surveyed by investigation and represented by exact description; impossible because, in the first place, the same infinite disposability resists all efforts to ground meaning by exhaustively circumscribing the context of "a total speech act in the total speech situation," ("Meaning," writes Culler, "is determined by context and for that very reason is open to alteration when further possibilities are mobilized." [Ibid]) and, in the second place, because "any attempt to codify context can always be grafted on to the context is sought to describe, yielding a new context which escapes the previous formulation."

In this last connection, Culler cites the very interesting example of Wittgenstein's "bububu."

8. Cf. Sam Weber's brilliant discussion of *vor etwas*, the implications of the anticipatory structure of anxiety in Freud's account. *The Legend of Freud* (Minneapolis: University of Minnesota Press, 1982), pp. 114–27.

Attempts to describe limits always make possible a displacement of those limits, so that Wittgenstein's suggestion that one cannot say "bububu" and mean "if it does not rain I shall go out for a walk," has, paradoxically, made it possible to do just that. Its denial established a connection that can be exploited. [P. 124]

The attempt to cut off the context, to set limits on what the expression can be said to mean through the device of specifying the actual boundaries of the linguistic environment in which the expression normally and conventionally does not reside, has the paradoxical effect of creating a new context that denies the attempted denial, that accomplishes the meaning which its description was intended to deny. The logic of context is dialectical here, indistinguishable from the negation of negation we quoted earlier when Hegel dismissed the skeptical negation for failing to acknowledge that it is a determined negativity, one that acquires content, takes its signification from "that out of which it comes as a result."

In the case of Wittgenstein's suggestion that "the denial established a connection that can be exploited," the connection between "bububu" and "if it does not rain I shall go out for a walk" may be more complexly motivated than first appears, as a francophone would be likely to hear if in the interest of reinforcing the liquid intimations of that expression one slightly altered the sentence whose meaning is denied. If, denying the connection, one affirmed that "bububu" does not mean "If it does not rain I shall go out for a (drink)," it would actually be somewhat more difficult to claim that it was only the denial of that connection which established the link that now could be exploited for meaning. On the contrary, it now would seem that the argumentative motive of the denial takes its force from the quite plausible assumption that "bububu" is what is normally uttered by francophile Cambridge philosophers whenever they think of their pub. The absolute absence of motivation, the purely arbitrary relation, between the word and the conditional sentence it means, makes it more unambiguously possible to signal the one with the other, through the trope of denying their negative relation, *litotes*, than if between the word and the sentence there were evident contiguities or material ressemblances. A spoon is not a good sign for a fork, but it is a good substitute: the one might conveniently be put in the place of the other on a table, or substituted in a dream. If then Wittgenstein were to have said to his nurse that "bububu" did emphatically not mean "If it does not rain I shall go out for a (drink)," his companion might well have accepted this philosophical denial and retreated from an assumption that had previously been taken for granted. The trope of negating a denial would be disrupted in its easy functioning by a logic of negation.

The general principle, enunciated by Culler, that "any attempt to codify context can always be grafted on to the context it sought to describe" ought to give us the means for conceiving a "pragmatic" or performative paradox of semiotics on the model of the liar's constative paradox, which we found implicitly lodged in the sentence he quotes from Eco defining a sign as anything that can be used to lie. Culler, following Austin, provides the term equivalent to lie for a theory of performative speech acts—a similarly negative, or privative mechanism for delimiting the field of study:

> Similarly, *I now pronounce you man and wife* is not a performative unless it is possible for it to *misfire*, to be used in inappropriate circumstances and without the effect of performing a marriage. [P. 114]

In order to envisage a "pragmatic" paradox of misfiring, it might be well to begin by asking whether the sentence above could conceivably misfire, the way Eco's sentence was asked to lie, and what would be the logical consequences if it did. On the surface that appears to be an impossible request, since Culler's sentence, while it contains an exemplary performative statement embedded in it is itself a constative one, affirming a certain state of affairs. Yet we know, as Culler writes, that the distinction between performative and constative is not an absolute one:

> An utterance such as "I hereby affirm that the cat is on the mat" seems also to possess the crucial feature of accomplishing the act (of affirming) to which it refers. *I affirm X*, like *I promise X*, is neither true nor false but performs the act it denotes. It would thus seem to count as a performative. But another important feature of the performative, Austin has shown, is the possibility of deleting the explicit performative verb. Instead of saying "I promise to pay you tomorrow" one can in appropriate circumstances perform the act of promising by saying "I will pay you tomorrow"—a statement whose illocutionary force remains performative. Similarly, one can perform the act of affirming or stating while omitting "I hereby affirm that." "The cat is on the mat" may be seen as a shortened version of

> "I hereby state that the cat is on the mat" and thus a performative. But, of course, "The cat is on the mat" is the classic example of a constative utterance. [Pp. 112–13]

Far from being absolute, the distinction between performative and constative in Austin collapses to the point that the constative comes to be considered merely "a special case of the performative" (p. 113). But that being the case, the condition of the possibility of the special case may not be "similarly" symmetrical to that of the norm as one might expect. Suppose, for example, that we were to add to the original sentence the implicit performative verb and imagined it to be saying:

> I hereby affirm that . . . *I now pronounce you man and wife* is not a performative unless it is possible for it to misfire, to be used in inappropriate circumstances and without the effect of performing a marriage.

Logically, we might say that nothing here has been changed. Taken as a special case of the performative, as an act of affirming, the sentence does not appear to be logically altered when we specify the performative verb of affirming. But has its illocutionary force remained the same? If anyone actually said the above, with the affirmative verb so emphatically specified, would we not rather be inclined to imagine the sentence in a rhetorical context quite different from the one in which it appears in *On Deconstruction*. If we overheard the sentence with its rhetorical insistence on the verb of affirming, would we not suppose that, far from simply affirming anything, the sentence was probably being used with the illocutionary force of a menace, a negative promise to act, a threat of annulment, for example? Perhaps "The cat is on the mat," being a classic example of a constative utterance, is a misleading one, and that as a general rule, making explicit the implicit performative verb of affirming in the case of most constative statements changes the assumed context, altering its illocutionary force. It acquires the discursive force of contractual violence. *Affirm* goes from having the sense, "to express that something is" (*Toute proposition affirme ou nie.*) to meaning, under the influence of hereby: "to declare under oath, to swear or certify." It switches illocutionary functions and becomes its homonym or anaseme. Affirming *gives* something to be true, and the discursive force of that gift, which by degrees may go from the quiet letting go of expressivity to the conflictual blow of a declarative oath, is affected by the presence or absence of the explicit performative verb. Making the verb explicit gives it more force and changes its meaning; an increase in the quantity of discursive power changes the quality of the semantic reference. We would therefore have here a peculiarly paradoxical situation: the insertion of the explicit performative verb in a statement which, without it, accomplishes the act of affirming, causes the affirmative performance to misfire. The act of specifying, of explicitly publicizing the intention to act guarantees that the act will not be accomplished. Could we not then say that in this instance, the affirmative speech act did not fail to be accomplished because it misfired, but it misfired because it was accomplished. Precisely because one could publicly and correctly affirm that *I hereby affirm that* . . . , the felicity of that accomplishment results in its misfire.[9]

What sort of experience would correspond to such a "pragmatic" paradox? If an act were unable to misfire until it were accomplished, what would that do to anxiety, to the anxiety which normally arises in anticipation of the accomplishment of an act or the act of accomplishment, the anticipatory anxiety which proceeds on the assumption that a performance is not a performance unless it can misfire?

> Consider the following case. The military commander of a certain camp announces on a Saturday evening that during the following week there will be a "Class A blackout." The date and time of the exercise are not prescribed because a "Class A blackout" is defined in the announcement as an exercise which the participants cannot know is going to take place prior to 6.00 PM on the evening on which it occurs. It is easy to see that it follows from the announce-

9. This is the place to indicate how much this paper owes to a meditation on this passage in Shoshana Felman's powerful articulation of the performative scene in *Le Scandale du corps parlant* (Paris: Le Seuil, 1980), pp. 66–67: "La promesse, elle aussi, est une fuite en avant, dans la mesure où elle est du ressort de la fonction de la hâte: entre la limite et le but, point de fuite entre la fin en arrière et la fin au-devant, elle saute par-delà le manque du présent vers une anticipation de l'avenir, et par-delà le manque des moyens vers une anticipation de la fin. Constituée par l'acte d'anticiper l'acte de conclure, la promesse est symptomatique de la non-coïncidence du désir avec le présent. ["The promise too is a flight forward, in so far as it pertains to a function of haste: between the outer edge and the goal—the vanishing-point between the end-behind and the end-ahead—it leaps beyond the absence of a present towards an anticipation of the future, beyond the absence of means towards an anticipation of the end. The promise, constituted as it is by the act of anticipating the act of conclusion, is symptomatic of the noncoincidence of desire with the present."]

ment of this definition that the exercise cannot take place at all. It cannot take place on Saturday because if it has not occurred on one of the first six days of the week it must occur on the last. And the fact that the participants can know this violates the condition which defines it. Similarly, because it cannot take place on Saturday, it cannot take place on Friday either, because when Saturday is eliminated Friday is the last available day and is, therefore, invalidated for the same reason as Saturday. And by similar arguments, Thursday, Wednesday, etc., back to Sunday are eliminated in turn, so that the exercise cannot take place at all.[10]

A great deal would have to be said in order to clarify all of the issues[11] which are raised by this anecdote but it suffices to our purposes here merely to indicate that it presents the same temporal solution to anxiety that we had discovered in analyzing the action of the implicit performative verb of affirmation in relation to its becoming explicit. Similarly, the first attempts to solve the Class-A Blackout paradox insisted on the contradictory relation between the two requirements of the Commander's order, that a Class-A Blackout occur during a specified, delimited time period and that it be a surprise. The fact that the "participants" cannot know that the blackout is going to take place prior to 6.00 PM on the evening in which it occurs guarantees that if it happens it will happen by surprise: no logical deduction will allow them to deduce with absolute, or even with vital certainty, that the blackout will happen on a specific day of the week. The camp commander is there (in other versions of the paradox he is a hanging judge or a schoolmaster) to guarantee that we understand the force of the certainty with which we are expected to anticipate, as if it were absolute, the occurrence of an empirical event. For what allows the paradox to seem to work, to make a certain event impossible, is the strength of the certainty with which one can anticipate a certain future time, like a week: a precisely delimited, an arbitrarily devised, period of future time. About such a period of time deductions, alas, are possible, so that if I argue in relation to the week

10. D. S. O'Connor, "Pragmatic Paradoxes," *Mind*, vol. 57, July 1948, p. 358.
11. As Martin Gardner writes in *The Unexpected Hanging and other mathematical diversions* (New York: Simon and Shuster, 1969), p. 11: "That the paradox is indeed powerful has been amply confirmed by the fact that more than twenty articles about it had appeared in learned journals. The authors, many of whom are distinguished philosophers, disagree sharply in their attempts to resolve the paradox. Since no consensus has been reached the paradox is still very much a controversial topic."

like a mathematician would argue from the perspective of a solution—from the standpoint of its already having passed—I would not necessarily be committing some metaphysical mistake, as Paul Weiss thinks. He thinks, after Aristotle in *De Interpretatione*, 18b ff., that one cannot in principle know anything about the future with *distributive* certainty (whether this or that, specifically determined, will be the case) but only what can be *collectively* certain, grasped as a range of possibilities (including, comprehending this or that).[12] W. V. Quine makes the much more straightforward assumption that logical procedures may be applied precisely to delimited temporal periods: Past or future or future anterior.[13]

The solution to the paradox proposed by O'Connor and accepted by the logical community for several years until the appearance of Michel Scriven's radical rethinking of the problem,[14] locates a contradiction in the terms of the problem:

> Now though there is an obvious fault of definition in this case, the fault is not a fault of logic in the sense that the definition is formally self-contradictory. It is merely *pragmatically* self-refuting. The conditions of the action are defined in such a way that their publication entails that the action can never be carried out.[15]

This explanation locates the fallacy of the paradox in its definitions, thereby sparing the principle of formal noncontradiction from any menace to its coherence which would be feared if, following from noncontradictory definitions, logic led to contradictory conclusions. This example, O'Connor says is "rather frivolous" but for the next twenty-five years logicians did not stop discussing it. O'Connor's explanation, like those of the next two major contributors to the discussion L. Jonathan Cohen and Peter Alexander, assumes that the problem lies in the making explicit of an implicit decision to surprise at some future delimited time. The Camp Commander, without realizing it, had issued a contradictory order. The debate on that question is still not resolved, in the wake of Scriven's insight that the order as

12. Cf. Paul Weiss, "The Prediction Paradox," *Mind*, Vol. 61, April 1952, pp. 65–67.

13. W. V. Quine, "On a So-called Paradox," *Mind*, vol. 62, January 1953, pp. 65–67.

14. Michael Scriven, "Paradoxical Announcements," *Mind*, vol. 60, July 1951, pp. 403–07.

15. O'Connor, p. 358.

defined could perfectly well occur on Thursday evening and be seen after the fact to have occurred within the week as a complete surprise. After the fact one may observe that the Commander's order was perfectly noncontradictory, although before the fact it must appear as a contradiction. Hence the surprise.

But the real interest of the problem lies in its relation to the penultimate moment.

"La Pénultième est morte," repeats the demon of analogy in the ear of Mallarmé's narrator—compulsively reiterates with the insistence of a ritual obsession, with sublimely exasperated negative pleasure, the erroneous conclusions of anxious expectations.

> Je ne discontinuai pas de tenter un retour à des penséés de prédilection, alléguant, pour me calmer, que, certes, pénultième est le terme du lexique qui signifie l'avant-dernière syllabe des vocables, et son apparition, le reste mal abjuré d'un labeur de linguistique par lequel quotidiennement sanglote de s'interrompre ma noble faculté poétique: la sonorité même et l'air de mensonge assumé par la hâte de la facile affirmation étaient une cause de tourment.

> I did not discontinue trying to return to predilective ideas, alleging, in order to calm myself, that, to be sure, penultimate is the lexical term which signifies the next-to-the-last syllable of words, and its appearance the unrenounced remainder of a linguistical labor which my noble poetic faculty sobs to interrupt: the very sonorousness and air of lie assumed by the haste of facile affirmation was a torment.[16]

Facile affirmation like sentimental poetry, hastens too quickly ahead to the penultimate moment—the moment before the last moment at which something must happen. It leaps forward to the penultimate moment which is the last moment when one can still be anxiously anticipating, still in advance, the last moment when anxiety can do its work of bracing for the shock of the end, before it is not too late, to reduce and repair in anticipation the trauma of the anticipated certainty, blackout in the end. In facile affirmation, like this stubbornly repeated, bad little prose poem, "La Pénultième est morte," the sonorousness of its descending tone, the musicality of the *nul* in its center contribute to enhancing the odor of lie ("l'air de mensonge")

16. Stéphane Mallarmé, "Le Démon de l'analogie," *Oeuvres Complètes* (Paris: Gallimard [Pléiade], 1945), p. 273.

that the haste of a facile affirmation assumes or breathes as it rushes all too eagerly, easily to its fated conclusion.

> . . . une voix prononçant les mots sur un ton descendant: "La Pé-
> nultième est morte," de façon que
> > *La Pénultième*
> finit le vers et
> > *Est morte*
> > > se détacha de la suspension
> fatidique plus inutilement en le vide de signification.

> a voice pronouncing the word in a descending tone: "The Penulti-
> mate is Dead" so that *The Penultimate* ended the line of verse and *Is
> Dead* [like an enjambement] more uselessly detached itself from the
> fated suspension into the absence of meaning.[17]

The poet is returned by the demonic insistence to the moment before the moment it is too late, to the poetic idea of predilection, the Mallarmean luster of autumnal fading. But the rhetorical affirmation of the end from the penultimate position is all too easy, too full of the illusion of anticipated certainty as it contemplates the end. The narrator knows the lure and the error of that seductive confirmation of the last moment of anticipated certainty that anxiety deludes itself into obsessively repeating.

Anxious expectations love to leap forward, in advance, *vor etwas;* they poetically imagine over and over the illusory moment, when they can be sure that the end must occur next, because next is last. But to suppose that anxiety can anticipate the end with certainty is to fall victim to a wishful error, the wish to hide the deeper fear that even when the end is perfectly certain, we might yet have to live. Anticipating the end from the perspective of the penultimate moment, anxiety gives itself a posthumous, ghostly fiction which is the sentimental consolation of its facile affirmation, its eager facination with rhetorical images of the end. Anxiety that leaps forward to the next to the last moment protects itself from its doubt and uncertainty, from the paradoxical possibility that doubt may not be the measure of all certainty, that the value of some truths may not depend on their capacity to be doubted, to be examined skeptically, but on their anticipated certainty, the strength of the conviction that precedes them.

17. Ibid., p. 273.

Or as W. V. Quine says, "Thus K erred in his argument that $i \leq n-1$ (Mind, January 1953.) $n-1$ is the penultimate moment you imagine to be logically prior to the time, n, which is the last possible specified time at which something that must happen can happen. K concludes erroneously, says Quine, that i, the time during the week at which the blackout does occur, must be less than $n-1$, because he supposes that at $n-1$, the penultimate moment, he will know with anticipated certainty that $i = n$; for if the event has not happened by now, after six on Friday, $n-1$, it must happen tomorrow on Saturday, n, the last possible time it can happen if the Commander commands. But precisely because he knows this he knows nothing about whether the event will occur. For if K knew that it must happen tomorrow, as he does at $n-1$, the blackout would not then be a surprise and the Commander's command would not have succeeded in achieving its desired effect which included, in the case of the Class-A Blackout, the element of surprising the population.

But if the first half of the his command has proven in fact to be without the authority appropriate to the performance of commanding, there is no reason to believe that the second half of his command—that the event must occur within the specified time period—has any authority either. On the basis of having arrived at the penultimate moment, $n-1$, one is not entitled, according to Quine, to draw any anticipatory conclusions, any positively reassuring certainty about the future—at least in regards to the question of whether the predicted or promised event will actually occur. As he puts it with the sweet reasonableness of some earlier Harvard Transcendentalism:

> If K reasoned correctly, Sunday afternoon, he would have reasoned as follows. "We must distinguish four cases: first, that I shall be hanged tomorrow noon and I know it now (but I do not); second, that I shall be unhanged tomorrow noon and I know it now (but I do not); third, that I shall be unhanged tomorrow noon and do not know it now; fourth, that I shall be hanged tomorrow noon and do not know it now. The latter two alternatives are the open possibilities, and the last of all would fulfill the decree. Rather than charging the judge with self-contradiction [as did O'Connor, L. Jonathan Cohen, and Peter Alexander in Mind, July 1948; January, 1950; October, 1950.] let me suspend judgement and hope for the best."[18]

18. Quine, op. cit., p. 67.

The last two alternatives are the open possibilities, because at $n-1$, the penultimate moment, I can claim with equal pertinence, on the basis of what I know already about the possible occurrence of the event, that either I shall be unhanged tomorrow and do not know it now (since the Presiding Judge, having failed to fulfill the first part of his decree, has opened the possibility that the second half of the decree will not be accomplished) or that I shall be hanged tomorrow and do not know it now (which, if it occured, would, exactly fulfill the Commander Judge's sentenced promise that the hanging would take place sometime next week and K would not know when in advance). Thus Quine has proved that the decree can be fulfilled, i.e., that K can be surprised on the last day, precisely because he cannot be surprised. Precisely because he can have absolute anticipatory certainty, as much as one *can* have, in the authority of a Commander, he cannot be certain that he will be hanged, since if that authority appears to be contradicting itself before the event in ordering a surprise within a specified time period, after the event it may nevertheless perfectly well prove to have been entirely within its performative authority in ordering a surprise blackout or hanging.

The "pragmatic" paradox has the peculiar power of disrupting the normal pattern of logical procedure and the usual movement of experience. One normally goes from naiveté to experience, from mystery to truth, from being *in advance* to being *nachträglich* (deferred action) as Lukacher translates *après-coup* in Roustang's useful distinction in Freud: "Anyone who has resolved his transference ceases to trust *in advance*, that is, to trust anyone else with his future or regard him as the basis of his hopes."[19] The *im voraus* of in advance, the faith which one gives in advance of the truth is always criticized by the wisdom of "deferred action:" in both the German *träg* and the Latin *ferre* one hears the labor of the analytical work that drags the patient from naiveté to truth, from the belief in advance in the truth of the Other's judgement to a wiser understanding, a more skeptical relation to truth. We must learn the painful Cartesian lesson that all assertions should have their truth deferred, treated backwards as if that "so-called" truth had not already been heard and many times proven to be false. Wisdom treats the pronouncements of authorities as

19. Cf. François Roustang, *Dire Mastery*, trans. Ned Lukacher (Baltimore: The Johns Hopkins University Press, 1982), p. 20.

liable to be doubted before their truth is accepted; indeed its value as a truth depends upon its capacity to withstand the most rigorous examination of its claims. The naive is the one who trusts in advance; the wise defers judgement. The temporal priority of faith to skepticism reflects the dominant interpretation of experience that goes from dependance on the other to self-standing, critical autonomy, able to judge oneself. It is the movement too from love to desire, from instantaneous identification with the other to a restrained, that is mediated relation to the other whereby its possession may be infinitely postponed. As Stuart Schneiderman writes: "If, as Lacan put it, one ought to sustain desire and not seek an object that will gratify it and thereby erase it, the desire to die is best enacted when death is kept at a distance."[20] The Augustinian wisdom which consists in sustaining desire as distinct from seeking to gratify it and hence killing it obeys the same temporality of passing from a condition of being "in advance" which is mystified to being deferred which is wisdom.

The interest of the Class-A blackout paradox is that it appears to reverse that temporality: In order for one to be able to doubt that the Command will be fulfilled, it would appear from the paradox that it is first necessary to be absolutely certain, convinced absolutely in advance that the event must happen if this is a real command situation. This jussic paradox of command performance reverses the normal Cartesian relation to truth, which requires not certainty in advance as the test of the value of truth but doubt. Here in order to doubt whether the event will occur as commanded one first has to be anticipatorily absolutely certain that the command will be achieved. Only because the blackout must happen on Saturday, because we have arrived at Friday night after six only by hypothetically assuming that the command will be fulfilled can one acquire the certainty that, therefore, it can't happen. The degree of one's belief in the paradoxical solution, the possibility of something not happening depends on the necessity of its happening.

20. Cf. Stuart Schneiderman, *Jacques Lacan: The Death of an Intellectual Hero* (Cambridge: Harvard University Press, 1983), p. 23.

JAMES R. LAWLER

"An Ever Future Hollow in the Soul"

Amère, sombre et sonore citerne
Sonnant dans l'âme un creux toujours futur[1]

In a succinct formula Valéry defined what he held to be the difference between himself and Mallarmé: "For him, the work; for me, the self."[2] He seized upon a polarity, nurtured it from his Genoese night of revolt that determined a basic orientation. Where Mallarmé sought to turn the poem into an absolute that subsumed memories and dreams in the language of beauty, Valéry made self-awareness his matter and method whose unachievable consummation might yet be considered an ultimate goal, to be possessed "once and for all."[3] Forbears and descendants, past and future, had no place; what alone counted was the eventless time of inner constraint. "In a nutshell, I do not take up again, nor do I undertake."[4]

The notes he made during the drama of his twenty-first year show thus, first and foremost, the solitude he claimed with fierce obstinacy. Consciousness as island, the domain of the shipwrecked Robinson, would banish alien gods: "I am between self and self."[5] Pride refused allegiances, initiated rigor, rejected the thoughts of all and sundry. Yet this pursuit of self-sufficiency was marked by a critically anxious relationship to the past. Just as he explained Baudelaire with respect to Hugo and Poe, and Mallarmé with respect to Baudelaire, so he saw himself as the antithetical product of his predecessors. "Reading is a military operation," he wrote; again: "A man of value (in matters of the mind) is, in my opinion, one who has killed

1. "Bitter, dark and resonant cistern/ Sounding an ever future hollow in the soul" ("Le Cimetière marin"). All translations are my own.
2. *Cahiers* (Paris, Centre National de la Recherche Scientifique, 1957–1961), 24, 147.
3. The motto Valéry adopted in the nineties: "Une fois pour toutes."
4. *Cahiers*, 29, 627.
5. "Introduction biographique," *Oeuvres* (Paris, "Pléiade," Gallimard, 1957–1961), 1, 20.

110

beneath him a thousand books."[6] So it was that, when he addressed his debt to Mallarmé, he spoke in similarly strong metaphor of "the one head to be lopped off so as to decapitate all Rome."[7] Rimbaud was an element in his formation, the more so since the poet of "Le Bateau ivre" was a counterpoise to Mallarmé in the way that turbulence might respond to calm. But he maintained a fertile combat with Mallarmé for over fifty years. There could not be a clear break but an unresolved tension which, keeping him at a peak of alertness, underwent three subsequent crises—1898 (the year of Mallarmé's death, the "grief of the intellect," the "sadness . . . of not knowing something or of being unable to find,"[8] which was followed by his own silence as a poet), 1912 (the brusque confrontation with Mallarmé by way of Thibaudet's letters, and his own return to poetic creation), the early forties (the "Mallarmé question" took on grave resonance as shown in the notebooks and the last essay published in *Le Point* in early 1944)—that corresponded to pivotal moments in his life.[9] He did not speak of "influence" for the word was too vague, and the figure of a transferred liquid misleading. Instead, he named a "decisive spiritual conquest," an "instantaneous intimate scandal" by which he had been "converted into a fanatic."[10] The connection was analyzed in the notebooks and a series of essays, but the evidence of this revisionary bond is subtly inscribed in the whole range of his poetry itself. The structure—mind, poem—that resumes the world with a finality analogous to Mallarmé's "Work"; the mythical Narcissus who, like Hérodiade, discovers the terrors of an intrusive self-awareness; language, syntax, form; voice, tone, phrasing: all were explored with a jealous sidelong glance at the one poet he must, for his own reason's sake, resist.

The struggle, in a personality as egotistic as Valéry's, gave his thought unique denseness. We may apply to him the words he wrote of Verlaine: "His art, rather than heralding another, implies that a previous one is being fled."[11] Nevertheless the poetry of his fortieth

6. *Cahiers*, 11, 700.

7. *Lettres à Quelques-uns* (Paris, Gallimard, 1952), 95.

8. Manuscript note, October 1898.

9. I have attempted to trace this evolution in "Valéry et Mallarmé: Le Tigre et la Gazelle," *Colloque Paul Valéry* (Paris, Nizet, 1978), 85–116.

10. "Lettre sur Mallarmé," *Oeuvres*, 1, 637.

11. "Villon et Verlaine," *Oeuvres*, 1, 442.

year was not allowed to emerge of its own accord like some fruit of natural growth: external events intervened with the outbreak of the First World War that brought history to the forefront of his concerns. Public turmoil became a condition of the genesis of *La Jeune Parque* and, indeed, its constant accompaniment. From a study of the manuscripts we see that the substance and vital charge of his poem were found in 1914 and 1915, and that their development coincided with the early dark period of the war. "Who would believe that certain verse was written by a man waiting on news bulletins, his thoughts at Verdun and uninterruptedly so?"[12] "I well know I wrote it *sub signo Martis*. . . . I cannot conceive of its having been written otherwise than as a result of the war. . . . I had finally told myself I was carrying out a duty, paying homage to something about to disappear."[13] In this way the sphere of reversibility posited in 1892—not the act itself but "my inviolable *Pure Possibility*"[14] like the dice forever uncast—fractured under the pressure of the moment. Along the line by which the Young Fate would summon fresh resources and find the sensible dawn of her being, Valéry experienced poetry as temporal imperative.

It becomes important, then, to envisage *La Jeune Parque* and the group of poems composed in its margins as the expression of a disquietude that sought to encompass the authority of Mallarmé and much else. Valéry acknowledged a line of poets whom, in a sense, he wished to serve as guarantors: he named a cultural heritage, undertook to shore its imperilled state. Mallarmé was a preeminent part of this domain, but also Euripides, Virgil, Petrarch; and Racine, Chénier, Baudelaire; and Hugo, Rimbaud, Claudel.[15] From such a point of view there could be no question of looking to a future tradition and some throng of disciples. "I likened myself to those monks of the early Middle Ages who heard the civilized world crumbling about their cloisters and who no longer believed in anything but the end of the world; and yet they took great pains to write, in solid and obscure hexameters, grandiose poems with no readers in view. I confess that French seemed to me a dying language and that I made a point of considering it *sub specie aeternitatis*."[16] A series of fragments, mobile sheets, interchangeable digressions without beginning or end

12. *Lettres à Quelques-uns*, 123.
13. Ibid., 180.
14. *Cahiers*, 29, 8.
15. Ibid., VI, 508.
16. *Lettres à Quelques-uns*, 180.

were his multiple variations on the single motif of the mind entwining the body and playing out, to the extreme point of the attitudes implied, the quivering patterns of a severely constituted self-knowledge. *La Jeune Parque* could literally be developed at will and endlessly: "an infinitely extensible hydra that may also be cut up into pieces."[17] In the same manner, the poems of *Charmes* were at first arranged according to the alphabetical order of their titles, each no more than a moment of the ungraspable whole.

> Pris que je suis dans le corps de ce jour
> Comme le vers est pris dans le poème[18]

Yet if an elegance of diction and tone determines the crystal of thought, time's passage cannot be forgotten. The self of "Le Cimetière marin" begins its monologue with words of sensuous fullness, but it is led to savor the bitter waters of its inner sea. Such is the obverse of the instant, however pure: past and future are no solace to the mind for which consciousness is merely—the word is at the source of Valéry's notebooks—an abyss of "self-variance."

One poetic text of the very many that date from the war period illustrates the author's despair, in the face of which he pursued his creation. "Aux vieux livres," included in early lists of titles for publication in *Charmes*, did not finally appear until after Valéry's death. It is his elegy dedicated to literature which, in alternate alexandrines and hexasyllables, establishes the measure of a thwarted aspiration. A noble age is expiring: wisdom and imaginative depth are evoked in a sequence of legendary names—Delphi, Plato, the Swan; at the same time, we come to be aware that this language has lost its vitality. The movement delineates a fatal decadence as "murmuring marbles" and the "splendor of former suns" succumb to a barbarous age.

> Le parfum de Platon lentement s'évapore
> Du souvenir humain.[19]

The gravity of tone, the resonance of imagery are those of an achieved composition. Despite memorable lines, however, the text will not reach the promise of artistic unity it at times shows: it is as if the theme of civilization doomed had led lyricism to fail and to leave only its ruins.

17. *Oeuvres*, 1, 1615.
18. Manuscript draft of the eighth stanza of "Le Cimetière marin."
19. *Oeuvres*, 2, 1625.

Yet Valéry was not content to indulge in the disabused acceptance of fragmentation, and it is by this radical transition that his
work found a new maturity. *La Jeune Parque* was not abandoned to
its plurality of voices but brought to a final form: "J'y suivais un
serpent qui venait de me mordre." The wounded sensibility discovers
its past, past anterior, present, it calls forth the tear that reveals the
hidden islands of thought—"Mères vierges toujours . . ."—and an
expectancy of fulfilment. Such temporal articulations enabled Valéry
to transform his multiple moments of salvaged time—detached, reversible—into a continuum of the self that poignantly learns its fate
as commingling mortality and vibrant élan. The movement culmi-
nates in the discovery of sea, and sun, and reborn innocence:

> Alors, malgré moi-même, il le faut, ô Soleil,
> Que j'adore mon coeur où tu te viens connaître,
> Doux et puissant retour du délice de naître,
> Feu vers qui se soulève une vierge de sang
> Sous les espèces d'or d'un sein reconnaissant.[20]

A law is found in the tracings of body and mind, a linear progression
leads to light through an anxious maze: after being lost in her depths,
the Parque affirms her identity in the enactment of a solemn rite.

One may in this respect examine the dramatic evolution of a
single passage. The theme of spring comes towards the end of the first
half (ll. 218–42) and plays a crucial role in the Young Fate's process of
self-discovery. It can be traced back to a much earlier manuscript, the
paper and handwriting of which seem to indicate the late nineties or
shortly thereafter. Under the title "Avril," some of the characteristic
energy of the definitive text is already evident.

> Les arbres regonflés et recouverts d'écailles
> Aux plus jeunes des vents livrent d'âpres batailles
> Et brûlant de verdir jusques à l'horizon
> Meuvent sur le soleil leur entière toison,
> Montent dans l'air amer avec toutes les ailes
> De feuilles par milliers qu'ils se donnent (sentent) nouvelles,
> Et par tous les rameaux suprêmes de leurs fronts

---

20. *Oeuvres*, 1, 110: "Then, against my will, I must, oh Sun,/ Worsbip my heart
where you come to know yourself,/ Sweet strong return of birth's delight,/ Fire to
which a virgin of blood raises herself/ Beneath the golden species of a grateful breast."

Ils poussent à l'azur à travers mille troncs
Un fleuve tendre, immense et secret (vague) sous les herbes.[21]

The development has at first reading a splendid force; and, indeed, the first line will remain unchanged throughout several versions and in the final text; lines 4, 5, 6, and 9 will receive only slight modifications; while the general syntactical pattern will be retained. The group of alexandrines is caught up in a single forward scheme as nature is personified and as subterranean waters rise to unite with the sky. Grounded in an urgent dynamism, the enabling metaphor is that of martial struggle (". . . livrent d'âpres batailles," ". . . poussent à travers mille troncs") for which Valéry turned not to the Mallarméan tradition but to the Hugolian one of rhetorical and imaginative crescendo. And yet, when many years later the lines were considered for inclusion in *La Jeune Parque*, they were radically transformed. The working drafts that have come down to us show the poet taking his already reworked version and rehandling it as if it were a simple raw material. With ever more meticulous attention the trees come to be envisaged as bodies projecting their strength on high, delving into the humus of memory, dreaming the form that is the substance of their song to be.

Un chant spirituel
S'élève des châteaux de feuille et de vapeur[22]

This will lead to the theme of the later "Au Platane" of *Charmes* with its plane tree as the marvellous symbol of poetic creation; but it does not significantly further the assimilation of "Avril" into the corpus of the text. What Valéry needed was, first, the verbal play of "rameau" (branch) and "rame" (oar) which will underpin the sweeping curve of physical effort; secondly, the sexual element which will take priority over the martial and, consonant with a vast act of love, focus the tenderness discreetly suggested in the first draft ("Un fleuve tendre . . ."). He later wrote: "In order to soften the poem somewhat, I was forced to insert unplanned fragments which I wrote after the fact. All the sexual elements were added; for example the central passage on spring which now seems to be of essential impor-

21. This passage is photographically reproduced by F. de Lussy in her *La Genèse* de *"La Jeune Parque"* (Paris, Minard, 1975), 56.
22. Quoted by Octave Nadal in *La Jeune Parque* (Paris, Le Club du Meilleur Livre, 1957), 335. Nadal studies the spring theme in detail (329–67).

tance."[23] The sequence becomes richer in rhythmic and musical scope, and tributary—in the manner of no other passage in *La Jeune Parque*—to Rimbaud still more than to Hugo in the expression of a panic violence ("L'étonnant printemps rit, viole . . ." "Aux déchirants départs des archipels superbes . . ."). But a further aspect is of no less interest: the lines are now seen, not merely as renewal and reawakening, but also as a step consciously taken towards death: the Young Fate turns to the joys of the flesh and, at the same time, realizes the mortal sense of her yearnings and the bitter aftertaste of tenderness ("O Mort, respire enfin cette esclave de roi," "Un fleuve tendre, ô Mort . . ."). Hence her enthusiasm is inseparable from a pathos that reveals a wholly new dimension. The fragment can now have an organic place in the complex and equivocal evolution that forms the action of the poem.

In the case of *Charmes* the change from original to final versions was no less surprising. Valéry opted in 1922 for an arbitrary order ("L'Abeille," "Au Platane," "Aurore," "Le Cantique des colonnes," "La Ceinture" . . .), a scheme that held good for the first eighteen poems, the remaining four ("Le Sylphe," "Ebauche d'un Serpent," "Le Rameur," "Palme") spelling out a reversal of the pattern. But the two editions of 1926 offer a notable modification that was further adjusted in 1929 by the removal of "Air de Sémiramis" to the *Album de vers anciens*. The poet had rethought his entire collection; he had set the number of pieces in both the *Album* and *Charmes* at twenty-one so as to impose a balance; and, instead of the observance of the alphabet or—as for the *Album*—of the approximate dates of conception, he had written an implicit dynamics into the sequence. Pursuing the notion of the "livre composé" characteristic of the nineteenth century and elaborated by Baudelaire, he arrived at a scheme that may best be described in terms of his definition of the sonnet: "a rotation," he said, "of the same body around a point or axis."[24] For the poems are no longer treated separately but as constituent parts of a whole whose extremes are "Aurore" and "Palme"—the morning ode of the intellect and sensibility, the parable of the creative act as inner reward. Time enters the collection, which has both origin and goal: the poems are arranged in six groups around the focal drama of

23. *Lettres à Quelques-uns*, 124.
24. Ibid., 124. On the architecture of *Charmes*, see my *Lecture de Valéry: une étude de "Charmes"*, (Paris, P.U.F., 1963), 254–66.

"La Pythie," whose action engenders a new language in the manner of a dolorous parturition: "Honneur des Hommes, Saint LANGAGE . . ." We follow step by step the creative self as it explores the forest of the senses, its "forêt sensuelle" ("Aurore," "Au Platane," "Cantique des Colonnes"); plumbs the nature of desire ("L'Abeille," "Poésie," "Les Pas"); recognizes the tenuous interconnection between idea and image, death and life ("La Ceinture," "La Dormeuse," "Fragments du Narcisse"); seduces the sensibility with lucid art, and is seduced ("Le Sylphe," "L'Insinuant," "La Fausse Morte," "Ebauche d'un Serpent"); considers the interplay of poetry and abstract thought ("Les Grenades," "Le Vin perdu," "Intérieur," "Le Cimetière marin"); looks back at last on its achieved creation before turning to the artistic quest ever rebegun ("Ode secrète," "Le Rameur," "Palme"). Thus mind and senses, will and patience, revolt and submission, make the framework of a poem three times as long as *La Jeune Parque,* its structure more richly resolved than could be any chance accumulation. In "Aurore" a future is perceived that the reader will come to know; and the wisdom of "Palme," emerging from past endeavor, stands as the happy sign of self-integration.

We recognize that this ordered sequence goes beyond a particular anecdote or narrative curve or legendary progression in its depersonalization of the text. The self is seen—not in the partial fashion of the first *Charmes*—as universal; its acts are not those of one but of all. It is less than adequate to say that we here take to ourselves the poetic persona in the way of every great lyric expression, since Valéry builds into his writing a cycle of movements that discover mind and body in answer to the author's individually defined "knowledge of the living organism."[25] Attention, patience, will, erotic desire are those of the intellectual sensibility which, eschewing the all-too-human, shows language disengaged from the quotidian cursus of thought. In this sense, led as we are by the system of poems, we realize that the collection is not only exemplary but didactic. The word would no doubt have hardly satisfied Valéry but nothing corresponds more closely to his effort to transform the art of poetry into the reader's own complete spiritual act. The book of poems proposes the scheme of a full and free and ideal exchange of sensuousness, feeling, intellection, so that, as be wrote, "it is not sufficient to expli-

25. Cf. *Oeuvres,* 1, 1614.

cate the text, we must also explain the thesis."[26] In the revised *Parque* as in the definitive sequence of *Charmes*, this thesis is the implied one of sumptuous discovery of the resources of the self as it engages in the creative act. At the end of the collection, "Palme," with its Judeo-Christian symbolism and exultant register, gives voice to a moral borne by its sensible strain and thereby retroactively endows the twenty poems that precede it with an implicit orientation.

> Patience, patience,
> Patience dans l'azur!
> Chaque atome de silence
> Est la chance d'un fruit mûr![27]

again:

> Tu n'as pas perdu ces heures
> Si légère tu demeures
> Après ces beaux abandons . . .[28]

All has become as simple and necessary as the knowledge that loss is gain, that time is redeemed, that poetic meditation is the verdant season of a secret ripening.

Valéry's pronouncements on the theory and practice of poetry were frequent and various after the publication of *Charmes*. Strong with his own experience, he enunciated the principle of artistic creation as a law of annexation like Baudelaire faced by Hugo, himself faced by Mallarmé ("The lion is made of the sheep he digests")[29]; underlined the condition of poetry as verbal act; insisted on the inventive potential of strict forms ("I am free, *therefore* I fetter myself")[30]; defined the conditions of the alliance of fine sound and fine sense. His inaugural lecture at the Académie Française was a brilliant statement of classicism as conceived and justified by a writer who could not approach the rules in the fashion of a poet of Racine's time but for whom skepticism aroused the need for order. "Doubt leads to form."[31] The Surrealists found in him a figure of derision whose dicta they need merely reverse to express what they themselves believed;

26. *Cahiers*, 24, 117.
27. *Oeuvres*, 1, 155.
28. Ibid., 1, 156.
29. *Oeuvres*, 2, 478.
30. Ibid., 2, 536.
31. Ibid., 1, 740.

but he could condemn Surrealism for seeking "salvation by way of leftovers." Literary fashions, he knew, are of a day, and he might still address a future reader who would be his loyal adversary—"quelqu'un qui viendra après." "The poem must give the idea of a perfect thought"; "Thought must be hidden in the verse like nutritional virtue in a fruit . . ."; "A metaphor is *what happens* when we *look at things in a certain way*, just as we sneeze when we stare at the sun . . ."; "Poets . . . you may look down upon novelists, philosophers, and all who by credulousness are enslaved by words—those who *must* believe that their discourse is *real* by virtue of its contents and that it signifies some reality. But you know that the reality of a discourse is words alone, and forms. . . ."[32] His statements aim to cut the fat from a critical practice still obeisant to the nineteenth century, which was accustomed to explain the work by the man, or by the supposed feeling, or by the literary influence. Valéry spoke as an educator who could not but impart a lesson; he sought to *come clean* so as to ensure a future for art. At a time when poetry ran the risk of being engulfed, what was more urgent than to point to its myths?

From 1937 until a few months before his death in 1945, he was the Republic's official Professor of Poetics. In his courses at the Collège de France he developed ideas that had been sketched out in the notebooks but which lacked definitive shape. His teaching held poetry to be inseparable from awareness of the intellectual sensibility and the organically based laws of symmetry, complementarity and contrast; and herein lay the seed of a liberated rationale and practice. The paradox of this situation was only too apparent. The disabused skeptic had become a spokesman, the poet a draftsman of the poetics to be. His link with Mallarmé was in the final instance an earnest of the future: he could articulate a view alien to Surrealist and post-Surrealist tastes that could serve an art the exact character of which was as yet unclear. No doubt he felt painfully the end of his Europe and the imminent threat to values he had lived by; his anticipation was more and more enmeshed in anxiety. As he wrote in *Le Solitaire:* "I am weary of being a creature."[33] How could he turn his mind to what he took to be the most inconceivable of thoughts, that "there will be

---

32. *Cahiers*, 5, 871; *Oeuvres*, 1, 1452; ibid., 1, 1453; ibid., 1, 1456.
33. Ibid., 2, 402.

men after us"? And yet he continued to write and, on the last pages of his notebook, stated his belief in the work he had completed: "After all, I have done what I could"; again: "*I am sure of that worth. . . .*"[34] The presentiment of Europe's doom, his own "Maladetta primavera" of love, the futility of hope: this is the groundnote constantly recurring; yet the spirit of his writing runs ahead of despair. Equivocal in its intensity, the flame is his figure of an art that lights the future yet itself is consumed. Still more eloquent is the symbol of the bottomless ocean like the poem ever to be achieved, although inherently resonant with the cadence of death.

> Amère, sombre et sonore citerne
> Sonnant dans l'âme un creux toujours futur

His attempt to separate the pure from the impure was not viable for the generation that came after his own. Yet tradition cannot suppress one of its strongest links as found in a thought that cultivates the ceaseless potential of the intellect, and poetry—"creux toujours futur"—its poignant exemplum.

---

34. *Cahiers*, 29, 908.

JEANINE PARISIER PLOTTEL

Surrealist Archives of Anxiety

Once upon a time criticism discovered that new names for old forms
are like new clothes for insecure women or men. New names and
new clothes don't actually change the thought, the person, or the
thing they cover, but they make them seem different. Any French
schoolchild will tell you that an Anatole France, a Jules Romains, and
a Céline is bound to have a more distinguished literary career than an
Anatole-François Thibault, a Louis-Henri-Jean Farigoule, or a Louis-
Ferdinand Destouches. But would the other Thibaults, Farigoults and
Destouches be made uneasy by the fact that their names appear unsuited to the ambitions of those destined for success? How should
they react to seeing their patronym erased by outsiders?

An analogy can be made between French literary movements and
writers who change their names. If we consider surrealism for example, we can ask whether the name itself may be a new dress for the
fantastic, the incongruous, or the dreamlike. Is it just another ward-
robe for a familiar imagination that is characteristic of a more distant
past? Is it a modern costume worn by revolt, anarchy, dreams, horror,
nightmares, powerful feelings, self-expression and *Sturm and Drang*?

Let us suppose that the answer is: "Yes. Surrealism is a new term
for worn garments." The question is whether this claim would fill a
hypothetical surrealist with a sense of apprehension. Let Harold
Bloom be my guide here, and let me speak with his voice. I might
state that if the surrealist in question is a poet, and a strong poet, then
he will become anxious and transform his "blindness towards his
precursors into the revisionary insights of (his) own work."[1] If my

1. Harold Bloom, *The Anxiety of Influence* (New York: Oxford University Press,
1973), p. 10.

121

conjectural surrealist is not made "anxious" by what he has failed to create himself and if he idealizes what has come before, then he or she—Bloom doesn't actually say "she"—is a weak figure. The presumption then is that strong poets share the fantasy of being their own fathers. Bloom quotes Kierkegaard's aphorism at least twice in the *Anxiety of Influence:* "He who is willing to work gives birth to his own Father."[2] In other words, the strong poet cannot bear to have had a father, and will himself assume that role. The reasoning may go something like this: "I want to make myself what I am. I shall make anyone or anything that influences me in any way a part of myself. *Anyone* or *anything influencing me* is a metaphor of my father. Hence when I appropriate all influences for myself, I am appropriating my father and I make him become me." Such is the strong poet.

There is a failure to note that since the mother actually gives birth, the poet has also replaced his mother with the same sleight of pen that replaced the father, and so he has become his own mother. I would argue that for Bloom, Kierkegaard's aphorism about giving birth to one's own Father through work is a text that displaces a subtext that might be approximated as follows: "The Mother works to give birth. The Father, were he willing to work, might give birth too, but cannot, because he is a man. But if I, a man, were a woman then I could give birth. I will give birth anyway. But to be a man, I must become a Father. A man who is willing to work gives birth to his own Father." Bloom's insistence on this point suggests the hidden question: *Am I a man or a woman?* In fact, the anxiety of influence may not actually ask the question "what strong poet is in my text?" but whether the strong poet is a woman or man.

I am now going to give my hypothetical surrealist a name: André Breton. Breton deliberately sought out his sources. The first *Surrealist Manifesto* does not display a manifest anxiety in this respect, and names strong and weak writers, including one woman: Isidore Ducasse, Dante, Shakespeare, Young, Swift, Sade, Chateaubriand, Constant, Hugo, Desbordes-Valmore, Bertrand, Rabbe, Poe, Baudelaire, Rimbaud, Mallarmé, Jarry, Nouveau, Saint-Pol-Roux, Fargue, Vaché, Reverdy, Saint-John Perse, and Roussel. All his life, Breton continued to welcome precursors and fellow poets and artists to Surrealism. Viewed from Bloom's perspective, several possibilities

2. *The Anxiety of Influence*, p. 25.

arise. First, the fact that Breton admires and readily acknowledges the influence of older poets may indicate naiveté or a lack of talent. This may well be, but it is a suspicious assertion. If my own hypothesis is correct, once the anxiety of influence is deconstructed, the weak poet is simply the poet who doesn't appear to have any anxiety as to whether he is a woman or man. Be that as it may, I am reminded of the seventeenth- and eighteenth-century quarrels in France between the ancients and the moderns: one had to choose sides and there was clearly strength on both sides, strength of similar but different orders. In the ongoing dynamic of inescapable influence, intertextuality, like sexuality pervades all texts and all writers, the weak and the strong. The way in which one is stamped by tradition does not determine how strong one's own stamp will be upon the tradition that will follow.

Second, I can apply to Breton Bloom's own categories of poetic misprision, of which *clinamen* and *apophrades* are most pertinent. *Clinamen* is Bloom's term for the poet's swerve away from a precursor that takes the form of a misreading. *Apophrades* refers to the poet holding his own work up to the work of the precursor; the effect achieved is that the later poet has written the precursor's work. Breton, in misreading the poets and writers of the past, made them into surrealists. This, as Bloom suggests, is not an exceptional move; every reading of a text is necessarily a misreading. Even Pierre Mesnard's exact copy of *Don Quixote* in Borges' story is a misrepresentation of Cervantes' script. For the very definition of the copy hinges on its difference from the "original," in a repetition of a text that is always displaced.

The gesture of *apophrades* too is implicit in every act of reading and writing. "La bêtise n'est pas mon fort" may once have been Paul Valéry's sentence, but in my memory it belongs to me although I know that I appropriated it for my own use from *Monsieur Teste.* I cannot pretend that such a reading does not provoke anxiety. However, being a "weak" writer, a "weak" critic and of the "weaker" sex, my anxiety is not an anxiety of influence, or the anxiety of wondering whether I am a man or a woman. It is rather an anxiety of anticipation. *Monsieur Teste* anticipated my ideal. Although I have stolen his sentence, I am aware that this theft reflects a delusion, a delusion about the importance of intellect and intelligence. This anxiety of anticipation might be diffused if I could make myself the begetter of the anticipation in question.

But it is not my purpose to show how female writers and readers can achieve a state of "manhood" or androgyny. My main argument will be that just as Bloom perceives creative anxiety occurring between a poet and his strong predecessor, a writer can become himself and achieve his own voice, style, and manner by evicting major writers from the library's open shelves to make room for lesser known or even completely unknown minor figures.[3] It is not a question of "strong" or "weak" at all, but of taking a variable common to a series and regrouping the elements of that series according to the variable at hand. A poet or writer might have anticipated this variable, but since I defined it, my anxiety is neutralized. Furthermore, in defining this variable, I anticipate it in the future, and if I do feel anxious about my possible failure to control what will come, I may still entertain the illusion that I have determined the future through my shaping it around that same variable that I first identified.

Such was André Breton's procedure when he compiled his *Anthologie de l'Humour Noir*. While this book may appear to be a vaguely defined miscellany,[4] Breton is consistent in the criteria he uses for selecting the authors he presents. The clue to his surrealist logic is not so much in what he includes, as in what is deliberately left out. For one thing, he omits the major novelists who are usually required reading in the *General Text* of literature. One may look in vain to find novelists of the "first rank." We recall that following Paul Valéry, Breton scorned the genre that would use such sentences as "la marquise sortit à cinq heures." From this one might surmise that Breton simply did not like novelistic fiction. That, however, is not the case. There was at least one novel for which Breton had nothing but praise. He described it as wonderful, unforgettable, admirable, and a model of innocent grandeur.[5] He was not referring to *Don Quixote* nor to *La Chartreuse de Parme*, nor *Madame Bovary* nor

3. My use of the term "minor" reflects not my own value judgement, but the generally received opinions of "official" culture. Thus Breton's appreciation of *The Monk* runs counter to the critical tradition that mocked it, much like Mallarmé's appreciation of *Vathek*. For these authors, the books were minor masterpieces. I use the word minor the way Deleuze uses "mineur" in French to speak about "la littérature mineure" and Kafka.
4. Matthew Winston makes this point in "Black Humor: To Weep with Laughing," *Comedy: New Perspectives*, New York Literary Forum, vol. 1 (Spring 1978), p. 32.
5. André Breton, *Manifestes du Surréalisme* (1924) (Paris: Gallimard/Idées, 1972), p. 25.

War and Peace, nor to any other "major" novel, but to Lewis's *The Monk*, a Gothic novel publised in 1796. The first *Manifesto* analyzes it ostensibly in order to explain that the *marvelous* is an *aesthetic* category of the highest order. Breton especially admired *The Monk*'s miraculous, supernatural, bizarre and grotesque traits, those very traits that have usually elicited negative reactions from the critics. His extravagant praise no doubt functions strategically to protect his own anxiety of having been anticipated. But there is another explanation for Breton's singular support of this book.

The very features that Surrealism shares with *The Monk* were precisely those that the literary and artistic "cognoscenti" chose to deride the most. What better way to validate the specific targets of criticism than to inscribe them within the perspective of tradition? And for such a purpose, what better way to play the pedantic game than by citing a minor[6] work by a foreign author, published in a previous century? What might seem trivial when penned by a surrealist artist became exotic by virtue of its connection to Lewis. But Breton went further. It was not only *The Monk* that he singled out for praise. Like earlier French Romantics (especially the authors of *contes fantastiques*), he was wildly enthusiastic about Horace Walpole's *Castle of Otranto*, Maturin's *Melmoth the Wanderer*, and Clara Reeve's *The Old English Baron*.[7]

In French, the term for these Gothic Novels is *roman noir*, a term that is most probably implied in the *Humour noir* that Breton anthologized. The English translation of *Humour noir* as *Black Humor* is inadequate to express the specifically gothic quality that is the unifying principle behind all the authors Breton assembles in his anthology; indeed, *Gothic humor* seems the more apt term. If the quality of the gothic[8] is what gives this collection its coherence,

6. Cf. footnote 3.

7. Breton alludes to Horace Walpole's letter to the Rev. William Cole about the origin of *The Castle of Otranto* at least twice in print. See his preface to a reprint of *Melmoth* published in Paris by J.-J. Pauvert in 1954, reprinted in "Situation de Melmoth," *Perspective cavalière* (Paris: Pauvert, 1967), p. 24. Consult also "Limites non-frontières du Surréalisme," *La Clé des champs* (Paris: Pauvert, 1967), p. 24.

8. Cf. Webster's *Third International Dictionary:* "gothic: of or relating to a late eighteenth- and early nineteenth-century style of fiction characterized by the use of medieval settings, a murky atmosphere of horror and gloom, and macabre, mysterious and violent incidents. (2): of or relating to a literary style or an example of such style characterized by grotesque, macabre, or fantastic incidents or by an atmosphere of irrational violence, desolation and decay."

humor on the other hand is the principle of dispersion and fragmentation.

Humor may be located in the author, in the reader, or in both; as such it may be intentional or unintentional. Authors who aim to be funny, often do so in an ironic, "gothic" sort of way; similarly, in instances of unintended humor, we often come upon an effect that is unconscious gothic. Swift, for example, did not of course intend for anyone to cook and eat babies. If it is not too threatening to perceive the humor in this act of cannibalism, one can identify in it a decidedly gothic flavor. The same hold true of De Quincey's "Murder as One of the Fine Arts." The reader is meant to recognize the exaggerated humor of a gothic convention here—not to indulge in the surrealist act of dashing down the street to fire a pistol blindly into the crowd. Charles Fourier, on the other hand, was quite in earnest when he compared in his social system le *cocu*, la *cornette* and le *cornard* or when he contrasted the elephant with the dog. One may well ask how this fits into a gothic tradition generally replete with nightmares. What is typical of the gothic is precisely what makes Fourier seem so funny to us: the tenuous relation between reality and his quixotic perception of it. His comparisons have a stock and commonplace quality comparable to some of the narrative "claptrack" of the worst gothic fiction.

Another example: the following verses appear to be full of the commonplace conventions of a well-worn tradition:

> Que l'on est heureux quand on rêve! . . .
> Sans dormir, rêver c'est charmant.
> En moins d'une heure, ainsi j'achève
> Le plus agréable roman.
> Je me crée un monde à ma guise,
> Tous les meilleurs lots sont pour moi,
> Aussi jamais je ne m'avise
> De me choisir celui de roi.
>
> Tantôt dans une humble chaumière
> Heureux père et sensible époux
> J'ai près de moi ma bonne mère,
> Et mes enfants sur mes genoux;
> A l'ombre d'un épais feuillage,
> Je lis et j'écris tour à tour;

Mais, hélas! survient un orage,
Pourquoi ce rêve est-il si court?[9]

Breton includes this poem because its author is Pierre-François Lacenaire, the notorious nineteenth-century criminal. What makes these stanzas "gothic" is the contrast between the flat sentimentality of these trite verses that celebrate the pleasures of home and the evil criminality that the reader recognizes in the name of the exceptional poet-felon. The gothic element is produced by the theme of the double, and the suggestion of the split personality.

Gothic texts are not surrealist sources in the ordinary sense of the word. For Breton, they are artefacts upon which he projects and recognizes his own obsessions with dreams, the unconscious and madness. In seeing his own preoccupations anticipated, Breton is not weakly idealizing nor appropriating figures of a prior imagination. There is no hierarchy of ability here; rather an act of dissemination. When literature enters into the library of our culture, it spreads out into the past as well as the future. The gothic impulse today has become surrealist. I shall illustrate this point by taking up the question of inspiration and automatic writing.

André Breton had read Horace Walpole's account about the origin of *The Castle of Otranto* and quoted it in his writings. His repetition of Walpole prompts the modern reader to perceive in it an example of automatic writing and an expression of the unconscious:

I waked one morning in the beginning of last June from a dream, of which all I could recover was, that I had thought myself in an ancient castle (a very natural dream for a head filled like mine with Gothic story) and that on the uppermost bannister of a great staircase I saw a gigantic hand in armour. In the evening I sat down and began to write, without knowing in the least what I intended to say or relate. The work grew on my hands, and I grew fond of it—add that I was very glad to think of anything rather than politics—In short I

9. "How happy one is when dreaming! . . . /Without sleep, dreaming is charming./ In less than one hour, I can realize/ The most pleasant novel./ I freely create a world for myself/ All the best fortunes are reserved for me,/ But of the many lots I see/ I never choose the king's./ Perchance will I find myself in a humble shack/ Happy father and husband dear/ My aged mother at my side/ And children on my lap;/ Under the shade of fulsome trees,/ I read and write in turn;/ But alas! up stirs a sudden storm,/ Oh why must this dream end?"

was so engrossed with my tale, which I completed in less than two months, that one evening I wrote from the time I had drunk my tea, about six o'clock, till half an hour after one in the morning, when my hand and fingers were so weary, that I could not hold the pen to finish the sentence, but left Matilda and Isabella talking, in the middle of a paragraph.[10]

Reading surrealist texts has taught us to recognize in the chronology of Walpole's account the relation between the sleep that he had been roused from and the writing of the book in which he would attempt to rationalize his dream memories: "a very natural dream for a head filled like mine with Gothic story." On the contrary, the dream must have seemed *unnatural* or *supernatural.* Had it been natural, the dreamer would have scarcely needed to reassure his correspondent and himself about its naturalness. Nor would he have established a cause and effect relation between the morning dream and the evening writing. He assures his friend that he began to write without any premeditated plan. While on a conscious level he may have been unaware of the shape his story would take, on a different plane of consciousness the script was already written. The writer became a scribe whose task was to recover the absence of something lost in a dream. Surrealist reading suggests that the author was attempting to integrate the isolated fragments of his dream—a hand on the bannister of a great staircase—into a narrative structure that would rationalize and resolve the anxious impulse provoked by the initial dream. One would also want to focus on Walpole's avowed desire to be distracted from politics, which might suggest specific anxieties in the dream that would motivate the pleasant escape into fiction.

This is the direction a twentieth-century analysis would point to. It is not necessarily the best interpretation, nor the one eighteenth-century readers would have identified. A magical interpretation might accept the workings of a dark supernatural force that stirred the author to write one of the great literary successes of the century. Nevertheless, Breton was clearly not unsettled by Walpole's method of composition, so close to his own *Poisson soluble.* On the whole, he seems to have been relatively immune to the darker side of

10. "Introduction," *The Castle of Otranto.* Edited with an Introduction by W. S. Lewis. (London: Oxford University Press, 1969), p. ix.

gothic fiction. While he surely was alert to its possibilities for expressing "the problem of problems, the problem of evil"[11] he was most sensitive to the rich store of thematic material it provided. Supernatural drama, horror, violence, terror, miracles, uncanny events, artificial stock characters and monsters became the ornamental textures of dreamlike surrealist patterns. Unlike Stevenson and Wilde who were highly aware of the psychological stratagems implicit in gothic fiction,[12] and whose stories borrowed gothic motifs to incarnate various mental states, Breton perceived in these motifs naked expressions of automatic sense impressions.

It is tempting to speculate that for the surrealist writer the past was a source of reassuring authority rather than anxiety. At the same time we must note however that the gothic past not only displaced him in time, but in space as well. While Breton was pleased to cite an *English* authority in support of his own use of automatic writing, there is a hesitation to look closer to home. Surrealism is filled with allusions to German and English literature, but its own more immediate French sources remain strangely (or not so strangely) suppressed.

Breton may be dealing with the anxiety of influence by repressing his French father figures and replacing them with foreign dummies. To a degree this is certainly true. We have already noted his curious and surprising silence regarding the major novelists of his own native past. But Breton did not for the most part hide his literary debts, even to the French. Furthermore, whose anxiety exactly is at issue here? The anxiety of the author or the anxiety of the critic? In general, readers and students of Breton have preferred to deceive themselves by asserting the radical and anarchist aspects of the surrealist experience. In fact, it is their own anxiety of anticipation that is being repressed. For if the roots of an avant-garde movement lie within the confines of the traditional literary establishment, the confidence of being in the forefront of the new is threatened. Once the avant-garde movement has joined the ranks of tradition, however, the anxiety caused by its relation of indebtedness to specific forebears, ceases to be problematic. Critics may allow themselves to

11. *Perspective cavalière*, p. 91.
12. Elizabeth Mac Andrew, *The Gothic Tradition in Fiction* (New York: Columbia University Press), 1979.

retrieve what has been repressed from their own reading. Surrealism fed on the standard literary fare appropriate for its time. During his formative years, Breton particularly admired not only Mallarmé and Valéry, but also Marcel Schwob and lesser contemporaries. Two particularly interesting intertextual references have been suppressed by critics of surrealism: Hippolyte Taine and Jean Lorrain.

To my knowledge, no critic has followed up on the reference made by Breton to Taine's *De l'Intelligence* in the first *Manifesto*.[13] The context for this mention states that hallucinations and illusions are a source of considerable pleasure. Breton writes the following: "There are many evenings when I should be willing to tame the pretty hand that indulges in curious deeds at the end of Taine's *De l'Intelligence*. In Breton's own time Taine's idea that external perception is a true hallucination ("La perception extérieure est une hallucination vraie.")[14] had virtually entered into the language as an *idée reçue*. Taine explained that the sensation of someone hallucinating that he or she sees a shrunken head is exactly the same as the sensation they would have on actually seeing a shrunken head three steps away. When we walk in the street, houses, passersby, sidewalks and buses produce exactly the same sensations within our consciousness as would our hallucinations, were we sitting in a room and imagining ourselves watching a street scene. Taine claims that dreams, reality and delirium are all hallucinations. Such a claim is in clear sympathy with the tenets of surrealism that Breton expounds in the *Manifestoes*. What Taine calls the blend of dream and reality, *hallucinations*, Breton calls *surreality*, or absolute reality. When surreality and hallucination coincide, external perception and absolute reality become identical, and *surreality* becomes a variation on the "authoritative" theme of hallucination.

The imaginary and the unreal were also literary preoccupations of Jean Lorrain, a writer who has recently shown signs of emerging (or being retrieved) from oblivion.[15] There is no doubt that Breton read him and admired him a great deal. This is what he wrote to his friend Dr. Frankael about Lorrain's best known novel, *M. de Phocas*:

13. *Manifestes du Surréalisme*, p. 14.

14. Hippolyte Taine, *De l'Intelligence* (Paris: Hachette, 1906), vol. 2, p. 10.

15. Jean Lorrain—his real name was Paul Duval—lived from 1855 to 1906. Marguerite Bonnet has written the definitive book on Breton's early sources in her book, *André Breton, Naissance de l'aventure surréaliste* (Paris: José Corti, 1975).

Mais s'il est un roman pour lequel j'exalterai mon enthousiasme, ce sera *M. de Phocas*. Cette oeuvre admirable, à laquelle je ne vois rien d'équivalent dans notre littérature, suffit à fixer dans mon esprit, à côté de ces dieux de la poésie que nous avons, en somme, récemment découverts, une place exceptionnelle à Jean Lorrain, (si la phrase est déclamatoire, tant pis!) et pourtant c'est une oeuvre de folie: l'histoire d'un homme qui a "la hantise de prunelles émeraudées."—c'est d'une sensualité mystique et *follement troublante:* atmosphère malsaine, lourde en vapeur d'opium, d'éther; un esprit plus inquiétant encore quis'y meut, en proie à une demi-folie; obsédé d'un regard. Le tout est d'un charme extraordinaire. Si tu veux te donner une idée de l'atmosphère qui y règne, médite un instant le sonnet de Samain dans *Au Jardin de l'Infante.*

Le bouc noir passe au fond des ténèbres malsaines qui d'ailleurs y est cité. Il est presque impossible de se détacher de la lecture de ce livre; et le plaisir purement esthétique qu'on en ressent n'en demeure pas moins infiniment suspect.[16]

Monsieur de Phocas is the assumed name of the novel's protagonist, the duc de Fréneuse, a crazed, mysterious and depraved collector of precious gems. Before leaving for Asia he gives the narrator a journal that relates the story of his dissolute existence, and the novel reproduces that journal. The suggestiveness of this novel's unwholesome atmosphere and decadent self-indulgence appealed to prurient tastes of a certain reading public. Breton, emerging from a Symbolist context, looked for poetry in its ambiguous sensuality, in the dubious sense of reality and in the madness that masked corruption. Surrealism would go on deriving literary possibilities from the erotic, sadis-

---

16. The letter is unpublised, but is quoted in Marguerite Bonnet's *André Breton*, pp. 30–31. "If there is a novel for which I reserve my greatest enthusiasm it is *M. de Phocas*. This admirable work, which has, to my mind, no equivalent in our literature, alone merits for Jean Lorrain a seat of honor along with those gods of poetry whom we have only just discovered, (if this sentence sounds bombastic, too bad!). And yet it is a work of madness: the story of a man haunted by 'emerald green-pupils'—the book is sensually mystical and provocative in a madly erotic way: an atmosphere of rot, heavy with the scent of opium and ether; an even more disquieting soul who moves about, prey to demi-madness; obsessed with a gaze. The entire scene has extraordinary charm. If you want to get an idea of the pervading atmosphere, meditate for a moment on Samain's Sonnet in 'Au Jardin de l'Infante.' The black ram passes in the deepest darkness of unhealthy depths: this image in fact is quoted. One can hardly tear oneself away from the reading of this book; and the purely aesthetic pleasure which one feels is all the more suspect."

tic and frankly lascivious material that formerly served to arouse mainly responses of a less textual nature.

Lorrain himself suggested that the poetics of dreams, mystery and chance coincided with the literature of the future. He believed that naturalism was in agony, that romanticism was *dépassé* but that new possibilities were open: "peut-être l'étude du mystère de l'insaisissable et du pressenti qui nous entoure et toujours nous échappe. . . !"[17] The literature that he anticipated would give chills to the soul and would make tangible the rustlings of the invisible world. The following excerpt from *Masques d'Ombres* is characteristic of such a pre-Surrealist genre:

> Les poètes ne sont peut-être, après tout, que des âmes qui se souviennent, des âmes douées de mémoire, lesquelles à travers les réalités présentes évoquent et surtout savent évoquer et les vieux maux soufferts et les splendeurs vécues défuntes, dont les cadavres ont l'aspect très vivant.[18]

The idea that present reality expresses a living but defunct reality is not striking in its originality, but its expression here bears the uncanny mark of early Surrealist poetry. Another Lorrain story, "Lanterne magique," isolates more of the motifs that would take form in Surrealist art. A dialogue about the aesthetics of the future announces the return of the fantastic:

> Nous n'avons plus un brin d'illusion dans la tête, mon cher Monsieur. Un traité de mathématiques spéciales à la place du coeur, des besoins de goret à l'entour du ventre, des martingales et des tuyaux de courses dans l'imagination. . . . Vous avez tué le Fantastique, Monsieur.—Ah ça, faisait M. André Forbster en changeant subitement de ton, à demi tourné vers moi, est-ce sérieusement que vous parlez? Où avez-vous pris que nous avons tué le Fantastique, et que ce cher seigneur ait disparu de nos moeurs! . . . Mais, jamais, jamais à aucune époque, même au Moyen Age, où la mandragore chantait tous les minuits sous l'affreuse rosée dégouttant des gibets, jamais le Fantastique n'a fleur, sinistre et terrifiant, comme dans la vie moderne! Mais nous marchons en pleine sorcellerie, le Fantastique

17. Jean Lorrain. *Masques d'ombre* in *Masques et fantômes*. Edited with an introduction by Francis Lacassin (Paris: Union Générale d'Edition 10/18, 1974), p. 355.

18. Jean Lorrain. *Masques d'ombre*, p. 355. ["Poets are after all, perhaps nothing more than souls who remember, souls endowed with memory. Beyond the realities of the present they evoke and moreover, know how to evoke, ancient sufferings and the glory of past splendors, whose cadavers still seem surprisingly alive."]

nous entoure: pis, il nous envahit, nous étouffe et nous obsède, et il faut être aveugle ou bien de parti pris pour ne pas consentir à le voir.[19]

It is the fantastic, the fanciful and the uncanny that characterize the modern experience. Lorrain cites hypnotism, magnetism, suggestibility, Charcot's experiments at the Salpêtrière, sleepwalking and other such revelations. The poetics of Nadja's madness are not far away.

If I have chosen these examples almost at random, it is because insanity as a *ready-made* is everywhere in turn-of-the-century literature. Nerval's exalted tone of uncertainty, Baudelaire's fascination with evil had become the commonplaces of much standard literature. Once a topos is integrated into literary culture, it can be shown to have been anticipated throughout.

Surrealism and every other avant-garde movement, (and which movement does not see itself to some degree as avant-garde?) creates its own precursors from the most obvious, though too often unheeded, infratexts: the popular books, pictures, music, theater etc. that appealed to a general audience in their day, but that may no longer be held in particular esteem. Many of these texts may be doomed to oblivion in the dark stacks of the Library, except for the hidden traces they leave behind on the Cultural Text that survives. Our own present is generating staggering possibilities for the future, but we live in the anxiety of not knowing which are the texts that will define us for the future. Ultimately, the infratexts must be defined in an arbitrary way. We may say that our infratexts are the texts that we read and about which we talk in places of influence: New York, Paris, London, Hollywood or the university. As infratexts of our culture,

19. *Lanterne magique*, p. 329. [" 'My dear sir, we have absolutely no grain of illusion left in our head. A special treatise on mathematics in place of the heart, piggish needs in place of the stomach, racing whips and harness in the imagination. . . . Sir, you have killed the Fantastic.'

" 'Oh that,' M. André Forbster replied, suddenly changing his tone. And turning ever so slightly towards me: "You don't mean that seriously, do you? What makes you think that we have killed the Fantastic? That that dear old lord has passed from our midst! . . . To be sure, never, never in any age, even in the Middle Ages when the mandrake sang out at twelve each night beneath the horrid dew that dripped from the gallows, never did the Fantastic blossom forth in so sinister and terrifying a form as it does today in modern life! We walk through shadows of absolute sorcery, the Fantastic surrounds us everywhere. Worst of all, it overwhelms us, suffocates us, haunts us; one must be blind or very stubborn indeed, not to recognize it.' "]

they provide the setting for the supertexts, or rather, the algotexts that will eventually be written and will embody all the texts that sustain them. Anxiety, and it is the anxiety of the critic as much as the writer, is generated by the sense that everything has been anticipated and we are all too late.

Breton offers a kind of antidote to these anxieties in the last surrealist game he played, "l'un dans l'autre," [one into the other].[20] The main idea of the game is that any object can be contained in any other object, an act turned into another act, a person into someone else. The game was played more or less as follows: A person would leave the room and think of something he or she could be, a staircase, for example. Those remaining in the room would identify with another object, a bottle of champagne for instance. When the first person would re-enter the room, the group would tell him to what object he had become assigned. The object of the game was to sketch a portrait that was a synthesis and condensation of the identities of the two imagined objects.

We have played a similar game here. We have turned *The Monk*, Horace Walpole, Lacenaire, Hippolyte Taine and Jean Lorrain into André Breton, and Surrealists. Some transformations may of course generate more anxiety than others, but they are all part of a larger game. I myself would not mind being changed into Breton's champagne bottle, but Aragon's beer mug, for instance, would fill me with anguish. That feeling does not arise from the two objects in themselves, but from my own consciousness of them. So it is with the game critics play with influence and anticipation. The anxiety is located not at either pole of the relation between two subjects but in the relation that we define ourselves. The ultimate anxiety resides in the repression of the critic's perception of his or her own weakness and insignificance.

20. "L'un dans l'autre," Perspective cavalière, pp. 50–61.

Death-Defying Texts

STEVEN RENDALL

Montaigne under the Sign of *Fama*

Hört mich! denn ich bin der und der.
Verwechselt mich vor allem nicht!
—Nietzsche, *Ecce Homo*

Homme, est-ce de vous qu'on parle?
On vous prend pour un autre.
—Montaigne, *"Sur des vers de Virgile"*

INFLUENCE

Like most writers of his time, Montaigne looks back toward the Golden Age of classical literature far more than he looks forward to future developments. However, to indicate the limited relevance of Harold Bloom's theory to a reading of the *Essays* it is almost enough to point out that Montaigne, like Shakespeare, "belongs to the giant age before the flood, before the anxiety of influence became central to the poetic consciousness."[1] This does not mean that the problematics of influence is absent from Montaigne's text; on the contrary, it appears in nearly every chapter. But what Bloom says of Ben Jonson— that he still sees influence as health—seems equally applicable to Montaigne. When Jonson writes that to imitate is "to convert the substance or riches of another poet to one's own use" (quoted in Bloom, p. 27), it would be tempting to conclude that he is merely translating a famous page from "On the education of children" were it not that similar formulations could be found in any number of Renaissance writers. The notion of reading—and writing—as the incorporation of alien texts is a leitmotif in the *Essays;* refusing to accept the notion that ideas or language belong to those who first use them, Montaigne asserts his right to sign any text.[2] He frequently acknowledges the major influence other writers—especially Plutarch

1. Harold Bloom, *The Anxiety of Influence: A Theory of Poetry* (London and New York: Oxford University Press, 1973; rpt. 1975), p. 11. Subsequent references in text.
2. See my article, *"Mus in pice:* Montaigne and Interpretation," *MLN* 94 (1979), 1065.

and Seneca—have had on his work, and challenges his reader to find the places where he has reinscribed them into his text.

In all this there is an easy acceptance of the general superiority of the ancients and of the necessity of imitating them that seems a far cry from the oedipal struggles that mark Bloom's anxiety of influence. Yet passages like this one from "On some verses of Virgil" suggest that matters may not be as simple as they seem: "When I write, I prefer to do without the company and remembrance of books, for fear they may interfere with my style. Also because, in truth, the good authors humble me and dishearten me too much."[3] Montaigne's very insistence on the importance of appropriating these master texts and making them one's own can be seen as betraying his concern about the possibility of doing so. As Terence Cave has observed,

> However much the rewriting of the *topoi* may be ascribed to an author who, conveniently, claims to have thought of them independently, the exact convergence of what "Montaigne" is said to think and what "Plutarch" or "Seneca" is said to have thought threatens to erase the signs of Montaigne's identity. Hence the fear of repeating what others have said ("les argumens battus"); hence, above all, the insistent reversion to the mechanics of a deictic discourse which, as an empty *forme*, declares its mastery over the materials it encompasses. If this apparatus were removed, the *Essais* would revert to a florilege: an untitled one, since the word *essai* is one of the thematic motifs through which the personified author attempts to dominate his foreign materials.[4]

Thus there may after all be something like an anxiety of influence at work in the *Essays*. But there is also in them a related, equally pervasive anxiety that concerns not the text's relation to the past but its relation to the future. For Montaigne's problem is not just that his domination over the other voices in his text must constantly be reaffirmed and can never be assured. It is also that the possibility of appropriation, however limited, entails the possibility of expropria-

3. *The Complete Essays of Montaigne*, tr. Donald M. Frame (Stanford: Stanford University Press, 1965), p. 666; *Oeuvres complètes*, ed. A. Thibaudet and M. Rat (Paris: Gallimard, 1962), p. 852. Subsequent references to the *Essays* will be to these two editions, and will appear in the text in this form: (666; 852).

4. *The Cornucopian Text: Problems of Writing in the French Renaissance* (Oxford: Oxford University Press, 1979), p. 279.

tion. The iterability that makes it possible for Montaigne to rewrite the texts of others also makes it possible for others to rewrite—incorporate, quote, gloss, translate—the *Essays,* and thus dispossess him of what he considers most "his own."

FAMA

On the title page of Montaigne's personal copy of the 1588 edition of his book—the famous "Bordeaux copy" on which all modern texts of the *Essays* are based—the Latin words "viresque acquirit eundo" ["it gathers force as it proceeds"] have been added. Although experts agree that the handwriting is Montaigne's, the phrase does not appear in later editions. This is somewhat surprising, since there seems no reason to consider this "epigraph" less authentic than any of the hundreds of other marginalia—interpolations, additions, corrections—that have been incorporated into what we are now accustomed to think of as the definitive text of the *Essays.* No doubt its omission is the chief reason it has attracted so little attention from scholars and critics. But if its authenticity seems clear enough, there are good historical reasons for doubting that the phrase ought to be regarded as an epigraph in the modern sense or granted a privileged role in interpreting the *Essays.* As Antoine Compagnon has pointed out, in the sixteenth century the "perigraphy" (titles, tables of contents, prefaces, afterwords, indexes, etc.) that surrounds and encloses modern texts was still in the early stages of its development. Even the significance of titles—which were sometimes called "epigraphs"—long remained vague, so that one is seldom safe in assuming that the title of a sixteenth-century work can be taken as a guide to its general theme or focus.[5] The history of the epigraph is marked by a similar indeterminacy; not until 1762 did the French Academy recognize the word "épigraphe" as referring to "ces sentences ou devises que quelques Auteurs mettent au frontispice de leurs ouvrages, & en indiquent l'objet."[6] The word was first used (as early as 1694) to refer to a memorial inscription added to a monument or tomb—hence its in-

5. See Antoine Compagnon, *La Seconde main, ou le travail de la citation* (Paris: Seuil, 1979), pp. 328 ff.
6. The *Dictionnaire de Trévoux* listed a very similar definition of the word in 1752.

terchangeability with the older word "épitaphe." The epigraph thus marks the entrance to a textual monument or tomb.

Whatever the difficulties involved in determining the status and significance of Montaigne's "epigraph," it must still be read. When it is considered within the network of relations constituted by its placement on the title page, a reading seems to impose itself on us. The words "Cinquiesme edition augmentee d'un troisieme livre et de six cent additions aux deux premiers" have been crossed out, and "Sixieme edition" added underneath them. It thus seems that, as R. A. Sayce—one of the few critics to have commented on the subject—put it, "the epigraph *viresque acquirit eundo . . .* epitomizes Montaigne's growing confidence in the value of his book."[7] It would, in other words, refer to Montaigne's satisfaction in contemplating another, even more amply enlarged edition of his work, and to his conviction that it was growing not only in bulk but also in force or value. This reading meshes nicely with the usual modern interpretation of the *Essays,* which (since the work of Villey and Strowski early in this century) views the growth of Montaigne's book as an evolutionary process moving away from his early dependence on commentary and toward an increasingly complete and adequate realization of his fundamental goal of self-portraiture.

Since these words are a quotation (like all epigraphs), however, another context must be taken into account in reading them: that of the fourth book of Virgil's *Aeneid,* from which they are drawn. The passage in which they occur follows the "wedding" of Aeneas and Dido in the mountain cavern:

> That day was the first day of death, that first the cause of woe. For no more is Dido swayed by fair show or fair fame [*neque enim specie famave movetur*], no more does she dream of a secret love: she calls it marriage [*coniugium vocat*] and with that name veils her sin [*hoc praetexit nomine culpam*]! Forthwith Rumour [*Fama*] runs through Libya's great cities—Rumour [*Fama*] of all evils the most swift. Speed lends her strength, and she wins vigour as she goes [*virisque adquirit eundo*]; small at first through fear, soon she mounts up to heaven, and walks the ground with head hidden in the clouds."[8]

7. *The Essays of Montaigne: A Critical Exploration* (London: Weidenfeld and Nicolson, 1972), p. 13.

8. *Opera,* ed. and tr. H. R. Fairclough (Cambridge, Mass.: Harvard University Press, 1967), Vol. I, pp. 406–07 (lines 170–77).

The Virgilian context suggests a reading of Montaigne's epigraph almost the inverse of the one proposed by Sayce. For here what gathers strength and force as it proceeds is the rumor of Dido's liaison with Aeneas. Figured as the goddess Fama, it spreads with lightning speed across Africa and swells to monstrous proportions. It is an evil (*malum*) whose swift, malignant growth could hardly be considered cause for satisfaction.[9]

It cannot, of course, be assumed that the sense of these words in Virgil's text must necessarily be the same when they are transcribed onto Montaigne's title page. Montaigne frequently inserted quotations into his text in such a way as to give them meanings quite different from those they have in the texts from which he borrowed them.[10] It is even conceivable that he was enjoying a wry joke at his own expense by implicitly putting the *Essays* in the syntactical slot occupied by Fama in Virgil's poem (it is the elision of the subject of the clause—Fama—along with the enclitic conjunction -*que* that makes it possible to take the phrase as referring to the *Essays*). But if the Virgilian context cannot settle the question of how Montaigne's epigraph should be read, neither can it be ignored.[11] It would be premature to conclude that Fama has nothing to do with the essays that appear under her sign.

In Virgil's poem, Fama is first of all a figure of repetition, of the iterability or citationality of language. Dido speaks, names her liaison with Aeneas a marriage, and her words are repeated hundredfold as they pass from mouth to mouth. But this proliferation is also a dispossession, for the words cease to be "hers," escape her control— and the possibility, indeed the inevitability, of this dispossession shows that Dido's words were never under her control, never really hers. To the extent that rumor is a form of quotation (not only "Dido said . . ." but also "X told me that Dido said . . .") it can be consid-

9. Cave (op. cit., p. 298) notes the possibility of an "ironic" reading of Montaigne's epigraph, but does not develop it. I would like to thank Mr. William Clemente for drawing my attention to the source of the phrase.

10. See my article cited above, pp. 1064 ff.

11. Not only is there every reason to think Montaigne was aware of the Virgilian context of his epigraph—we know he owned a copy of the *Aeneid*, read the poem with pleasure (cf., e.g., his appraisal of Virgil's works in "Of Books," 298; 390), and (according to Pierre Villey) quoted it at least eighty-five times in the *Essays*—but the episode in which the phrase occurs was one of the most famous in the poem, and it is thus likely that even his readers might have recognized its source.

ered an example of a special kind of linguistic repetition that refers first of all to another enunciation and only secondarily to a non-linguistic state of affairs.

One of the peculiarities of quotation, as Compagnon has observed (op. cit., pp. 88–89) is that it displaces the question of truth. A false quotation is one that does not accurately reproduce the original; the truth of what it says is irrelevant to a determination of its authenticity. But since the words it repeats retain their referential value, the authenticity of the citation can always be confused with the truth of what it asserts—or rather, does not assert—and rumor is precisely this referential confusion. Hence in the *Aeneid* (IV, 184–90) Fama flies through the shadows of the night, midway between heaven and earth (*nocte volat caeli medio terraque per umbram*), promising truth but clinging to the fictive and the wrong (*ficti pravique tenax quam nuntia veri*), singing of fact and fiction and mixing them togeter (*pariter facta atque infecta canebat*). In an equally famous passage of Ovid's *Metamorphoses* (which Montaigne read and reread as a child), Fama dwells "t'wixt land and sea and sky" in a castle "built all of echoing brass. The whole place resounds with confused noises, repeats all words and doubles what it hears. . . . Crowds fill the hall, shifting throngs come and go, and everywhere wander thousands of rumors [*rumorum*] mingled with the truth, and confused reports flit about. Some of these fill their idle ears with talk, and others go and tell elsewhere what they have heard; while the story grows in size [*mensuraque ficti crescit*], and each new teller makes contribution to what he has heard."[12]

Fama, one might say, is language out of control, exercising a fictional potential paradoxically condemned by Virgil's fictional text. In moving away from its source, Fama gains in force and scope at the expense of its grounding in "fact"—that is, its referential truth. But what is the "fact"? In the *Aeneid*, what Fama repeats and replaces is not fact but another *fama*. Before the fatal day ("the first day of death") of her coupling with Aeneas in the mountain cave, Dido dreamed of a secret love (*furtivum Dido meditatur amorem*). But abandoning her concern for appearances and reputation (*specie famave*), Dido simultaneously voices and veils her desire under a new pretext by giving it the name of "marriage" (*hoc praetexit nomine*

12. *Metamorphoses*, ed. and tr. F. J. Miller (London and New York: Heinemann, 1916), Vol. II, Book XII, pp. 182–84.

culpam). Fame thus has its origin in an act of naming, or rather of predication: "I am married." But this naming is a renaming, since what it names is renown (*renom or renommée*); it replaces one appearance with another. The "truth" always disappears behind a name, and the only way to reveal it is to reveil it in another (potentially false) name.

Virgil's Fama thus links naming to repetition, and repetition to language's constitutive independence from its implied referential ground and from the context in which it is "originally" used. That is to say, Virgil's Fama, although disseminating itself by word of mouth, is a figure of writing in the sense Derrida has given that (non)term, a figure of the writing inherent in speech. To read the *Essays* under the sign of Fama is thus to read them under the shadow of repetition and dispossession.

PHYSIOGNOMY

According to the *Essays*, the dream of communication without the risk of dispossession could be realized only in the paradise of friendship. Montaigne claims his friendship with La Boétie was foreordained by some mysterious power, so that even before they met the two men embraced each other through their names. This nominal union was grounded in a substantial one, in a spiritual identity so complete, Montaigne says, that "neither of us reserved anything for himself [*rien qui nous fut propre*], nor was anything either his or mine" (139; 187). True friendship is incompatible with any consideration of gain or profit, any speculation on advantages that might be won or losses that might be incurred. Thus no debts can be contracted between friends: "Everything actually being in common between them—wills, thoughts, judgments, goods, wives, children, honor, and life—and their relationship being that of one soul in two bodies, according to Aristotle's very apt definition, they can neither lend nor give anything to each other" (141; 189). Friendship is not speculative but specular: in intercourse between friends, language becomes almost superfluous, since meanings are immediately reflected in the mirror of the friend's mind. Misinterpretation, the multiplication and loss of meaning, is impossible: "It is not in the power of all the arguments in the world to dislodge me from the certainty I have of the intentions and judgments of my friend. Not one of his actions could be presented to me, whatever appearance [*visage*] it might have, that I could not immediately find the motive for it . . . not only did I know his soul as well as mine, but I should certainly have trusted myself to him more readily than to myself" (140; 188). To speak to one's friend is like speaking to oneself. Words can be confined within the specular circuit, so that "the secret I have sworn to reveal to no other man, I can impart without perjury to the one who is not another man; he is myself" (142; 190). To repeat to a friend what one has been told by another is not to disseminate meaning but to conserve it.

The paradise of friendship is, however, a lost paradise. The depths of Montaigne's soul, which he says La Boétie plumbed with the certitude only a true friend can have, are inferred by others through the interpretation of an ambiguous surface. Not being grounded in the immediate communion of friendship, words lead in every direction, and whatever one says can be interpreted in a thousand different ways, repeated and not merely reflected.

What can prevent the dissemination of meaning over a verbal surface? Nothing, perhaps, unless it is the surface par excellence, the face—as Montaigne suggests in "Of Physiognomy." This essay seems to be one of those whose titles have only a tangential relation to their subjects, since Montaigne takes up his nominal theme explicitly only in the final pages. But from the outset, the discussion is organized by the figure of the "silenic" Socrates, the canonical emblem of the separation of surface and depth. According to the speech given in the *Symposium* by his friend Alcibiades (a speech on friendship), Socrates conceals beneath an ugly exterior a soul of rare worth and beauty, like the little figurine known as a *silenus*, and, Montaigne adds, like La Boétie, whose face, if not his body, was the ugly envelope of a beautiful soul (809–10; 1034–35). The friend—Alcibiades or Montaigne—can see through this deceptive exterior surface, because he knows by other, more intimate means what it conceals. But what of those who are not gifted with the insight of friendship, who are perhaps enemies? They may take the (sur)face for the depth, and lead others to do so, like those who had Socrates put to death for impiety. In such a case, it seems, one's face can determine one's fate.

Toward the end of the chapter, at the point where he turns to his titular subject, Montaigne contrasts his appearance with that of Socrates: "I have a favorable bearing [*un port favorable*], both in itself and in others' interpretation . . . one very unlike that of Socrates. It has often happened that on the mere credit of my presence and manner [*presence et air*], persons who had no knowledge of me have placed great trust in me, both for their own affairs and for mine; and in foreign countries I have derived singular and rare favors from this" (811–12; 1037). He then recounts two anecdotes concerning situations in which his face apparently saved his life. The first is about a neighbor who tried to take possession of Montaigne's chateau by claiming that he and his men were being pursued by a band of armed enemies and begging Montaigne to take them in. Once inside his walls, Montaigne notes, the man "saw himself master of his undertaking, and nothing remained but its execution." But the man suddenly remounted his horse and led his men out of the chateau because, as he later explained to Montaigne, the latter's face and frank speech (*mon visage et ma franchise*) "had disarmed him of his treachery" (813; 1039). In the second anecdote, Montaigne tells of being captured by enemy forces during a trip through a particularly dangerous part of the country. His money, horses, and equipment were taken from him, and the ransom for setting him free set so high, Montaigne says, "it was quite apparent that I was scarcely known to them" (813; 1039). While the men debated whether to kill him, Montaigne stood his ground, insisting that under the terms of the truce then in force, he was obliged to give them no more than what they had taken from him. At last they led him off alone into the forest, and the leader of the band then came to him "with gentler words," restored his belongings to him, and set him free, repeating several times, Montaigne says, "that I owed my deliverance to my face and the freedom and firmness of my speech, which made me undeserving of such a misadventure" (814; 1040).

These anecdotes stage a scenario in which the face guides the interpretation of character; that is, they describe physiognomy in action.[13] Physiognomy, we must remember here, is both the face and its interpretation; the word derives from Greek *phusis* (nature) and *gnomon* (interpreter). Aristotle discussed physiognomy as the art of interpreting character from physical features (e.g., in the *Prior Ana-*

---

13. It is surely significant that when Montaigne denies his interest in fame, glory, or what others think of him, he also denies the link between face and character: cf. "Of Glory," where he notes that "Any man can put on a good face outside, while full of fever and fright within. They do not see into my heart, they see only my countenance" (464; 608–09).

lytics, 70a–b), and his reflections were extended and elaborated on in the *Physiognomica*, a work by his followers long attributed to him. When Montaigne introduces his anecdotes by saying that he has a bearing favorable "both in itself and in others' interpretation" he links the two meanings of physiognomy: the face (or perhaps the whole surface of the body) as a sign of character and the interpretation of this sign. But it is worth noting that in these anecdotes the interpretive circuit is more complicated than the physiognomical model might suggest, for it includes another significant surface: speech. Thus, for example, the rebel leader tells Montaigne that he owes his freedom not only to his face but also to the freedom and firmness of his speech. Face and speech are intimately interdependent: "If my face did not answer for me [*Si mon visage ne respondoit pour moy*], if people did not read in my eyes and my voice the innocence of my intentions," Montaigne goes on in the same passage, "I would not have lasted so long without quarrel and without harm, considering my indiscreet freedom in saying, right or wrong, whatever comes into my head, and in judging things rashly" (814; 1041). The relation between them is not exactly symmetrical, however, since the face guides the interpretation of character, and the (correctly interpreted) character in turn guides the interpretation of speech. The circuit is not reversible: physiognomy guides the interpretation of words, but words do not guide the interpretation of the face. Physiognomy retains a privileged role in Montaigne's text: words alone could not have saved his life.

The essential attribute of both face and speech in this system is presence ("It has often happened that on the mere credit of my presence [*presence*] and manner . . . persons who had no knowledge of me have placed great trust in me . . ."). Thus Montaigne explains that his habit of speaking impulsively "may appear uncivil and ill adapted to our usage, but I have not known anyone who judged it to be injurious or malicious, or who took offense at my freedom if he had it from my own lips. Words when reported have a different sense, as they have a different sound [*Les paroles redictes ont, comme autre son, autre sens*]" (814; 1040). Here we rejoin Fama or the problematics of repetition and writing. For the negative converse of these remarks is the possibility of the repetition of words in the absence of the face and the personal voice, that is, in the absence of their author or speaker. This possibility exposes the author—and his words—to the threat of his death.

PORTRAIT

The project of self-portraiture in the *Essays* should be read in relation to this mortal threat. That it is more than a threat, more than a "mere" possibility, is suggested by the quotations from Terence and Maximianus Montaigne inserted into the middle of his assertion that unlike Socrates, he has a bearing "favorable in itself and in interpretation": "What did I say *have?* Chremes, I mean I had!" "You see, alas, only the bones of this worn body" (811; 1037). Like his friendship with La Boétie, this favorable bearing or (sur)face has fallen victim to time, it is irremediably *past.* It can no longer guarantee the correct interpretation of his character and speech—and therefore it never did, since the possibility of misinterpretation was always on the horizon. Moreover, since his words can be repeated in other contexts, they already declare him absent, dead. Unless, that is, they can be made "consubstantial" with his face, unless they live in it, and it in them.

Perhaps that is why the portrait metaphor is so frequently linked in the *Essays* with memory, and particularly with the memory of the dead—of *les absents*, as the French say. Thus, for example, in "Of Presumption" Montaigne mentions an experience in which one might be tempted to see the origin of his conception of the *Essays* as a self-portrait: "One day at Bar-le-Duc, I saw King Francis II presented, in remembrance [*pour la recommandation de la memoire*] of René, king of Sicily, with a portrait that this king had made of himself. Why is it not permissible for each man to portray himself with the pen [*se peindre de la plume*] as he portrayed himself with a pencil?" (496; 637). This portrait was presented as a means of keeping alive the memory of the good king René, who had died some eighty years before. The evident allusion to his own work suggests that Montaigne's written self-portrait is supposed to produce the same sort of result.

The epistle to Mme de Duras at the end of "Of the resemblance of children and fathers" seems to confirm this hypothesis. There we read:

> Madame, you found me at this point when you recently came to see me. Because it may be that these absurdities will someday come into your hands, I want them to bear witness that the author feels himself greatly honored by the favor that you will be doing them. You will recognize in them the same bearing and the same air that you have seen in his conversation [*vous y reconnoistrez ce mesme port*

et ce mesme air que vous avez veu en sa conversation]. Even if I had been able to adopt some other style than my own ordinary one and some other better and more honorable form, I would not have done it; for I want to derive nothing from these writings except that they represent me to your memory as I naturally am. These same traits and faculties that you have been familiar with and have favored, Madame, with much more honor and courtesy than they deserve, I want to lodge (but without alteration or change) in a solid body that may last a few years, or a few days, after me, in which you will find them when you are pleased to refresh your memory of them, without otherwise taking the trouble to remember them, as indeed they are not worth it. I wish you may continue the favor of your friendship to me for the same qualities that produced it. I do not at all seek to be better loved and esteemed dead than alive. [595; 763–64]

This passage—which served as a kind of coda in the 1580 edition of the *Essays*—weaves together all the motifs that have concerned us so far. It projects a reading of Montaigne's text in his absence (or rather, as the last lines suggest, after his death), and seeks to ground it in a recognition of the "bearing" and "air" his reader has seen in conversing with him. *"Port"* and *"air"* are, of course, the same words used in the later passage from "Of Physiognomy" that we have already examined, and they are again linked here with the physical presence of Montaigne and his voice. Just as Montaigne's references to the conversational character of his style (e.g., at the beginning of "Of the Useful and the honorable," where he echoes the classical *quicquid in buccam venit* topos: "I speak to my paper as I speak to the first man I meet") seek to ground writing in speech, the metaphor of the self-portrait seeks to ground speech in the representation of the face. Thus Montaigne, mixing his metaphors slightly, asks that Mme de Duras recognize in his writing the same bearing and the same air that she has seen (*veu*) in his conversation.

Montaigne insists on the identity of the textual surface with his face and what it represents—"the same bearing and the same air," "these same traits and faculties," "the same qualities"—and on his desire to "lodge" the latter *unaltered* in a durable body (*un corps solide*) that can outlast, however briefly, his mortal body. This insistence can be read as a clue to the role played by identification in the sequence of tropes constructed by the text. Montaigne's character (or nature, or self) is represented unaltered by his face—"my face immediately betrays me, and my eyes," he notes in "Of Experience" (842; 1040)—and his face in turn is represented unaltered in his written portrait. The identity or precise resemblance of the portrait and the face is the crucial link in this metaphorical chain because it connects the signifiers of presence (life, the face, the speaking self) with those of absence (death, the portrait, the written self) and posits the possibility of a transit or exchange between them. It gives a face and a voice to the absent self, and makes it possible for the latter to address the living from beyond the grave—as Montaigne does here, writing his own epitaph for the living to read.[14]

The vehicle of this mediation between presence and absence that restores the self is, of course, memory or recognition. The identity or resemblance of portrait and face is essential because it alone makes possible the recognition of the latter in the former and its restoration to life in the memory. Thus Montaigne asserts that even had he been able to write in a more elevated style, he would not have done so, "for I want to derive nothing from these writings except that they represent me to your memory as I naturally am." It is at this precise point that the textual system Montaigne develops in this passage reveals its limits, for the resemblance that makes re-cognition possible depends upon a previous knowledge. Thus it is no accident that, adopting the figure of prosopopeia, Montaigne addresses these remarks to a particular person, an acquaintance who already knows him, who has seen his face and heard his voice and can recognize them in his written portrait. For such a reader, the text would re-present Montaigne, revive or "refresh" a memory of his presence. The transparency of meaning Montaigne postulates in the face-to-face encounter is at once the cornerstone of his conception of a written self-portrait and the mark of its fragility.

For what of readers who have never seen or heard Montaigne "in person," who have not known the man but only his image on paper? For them his self-portrait cannot produce an experience of recognition, it remains dead and mute: "Whatever I may be, I want to be elsewhere than on paper. . . . Consequently I am so far from expecting to do myself some new honor by these stupidities that I shall do well if I do not lose any of what little I have acquired. For this dead and mute portrait, besides what it takes away from my natural being,

14. Cf. Paul de Man, "Autobiography as De-facement," *MLN* 94 (1979), 926ff. Subsequent references in text.

does not represent me in my best state, but fallen far from my early vigor and cheerfulness, and beginning to grow withered and rancid" (596; 764–65). As soon as Montaigne envisages a faceless reader, a reader who does not know his face, his text is described in terms of silence, alteration and loss.[15] For such readers, Montaigne's self-portrait is a death mask signifying his absence. As Paul de Man has pointed out, the deathly silence of the trope-as-picture always threatens to disrupt the specular language of cognition (op. cit., p. 930), and we may add that it is this threat that the resemblance and recognition of Montaigne's self-portrait is supposed to counter. But it must inevitably fail to do so when it is exhibited to those who cannot recognize its model.

This fact is probably related to the diffidence of the passages in which Montaigne considers whether he ought to have offered his book to the public at all, or denies that he ever meant it for anyone except himself or at most for his friends and family. This is perhaps clearest in the preface "To the reader," which seems to hesitate between offering and withdrawing the book it introduces. Montaigne denies that he has written his book for the (faceless) reader, adding that he has "dedicated it to the private convenience of my relatives and friends, so that when they have lost me (as soon they must), they may recover here some features of my habits and temperament, and by this means keep the knowledge they have had of me more complete and alive." Here we find the same themes we noted in the epistle to Mme Duras, and again they are linked with the resemblance of the text-as-portrait: "I want to be seen here in my simple, natural fashion, without straining or artifice, for it is myself that I portray." But having declared that he is himself the matter of his book, he half retracts his text in a self-deprecatory gesture that seems to conceal a certain anxiety behind its curious humor: "you would be

---

15. The *Essays* themselves are sometimes said to be faceless, as in the passage at the beginning of the essay on friendship, where Montaigne, comparing himself to a painter, says that his skill will not allow him to undertake "a rich and polished picture" but only the ornamental grotesques that surround it: "What are these things of mine, in truth, but grotesques and monstrous bodies, pieced together of divers members, without definite shape [*sans certaine figure*]. . . ." The allusion to a "monstrous body" further suggests the headless (and therefore faceless) Siamese twin described in "Of a monstrous child" (II, 10). As Jane Marie Todd has pointed out in an unpublished paper, this can be read as a figure of Montaigne's desire to retain an organic link to his headless twin text.

unreasonable to spend your leisure on so frivolous and vain a subject. So farewell."

Would it be better, perhaps, to remain silent, not to expose his words to readers whose interpretation of them will not be controlled and limited by their knowledge of his face and his voice? "But is it reasonable that I, so fond of privacy in actual life, should aspire to publicity in the knowledge of me?" (611; 783).

SE (FAIRE) CONNAÎTRE

In the seventy-sixth chapter of his *Verbum abbreviatum*, Petrus Cantor quotes lines 174–75 of the fourth book of the *Aeneid ("Fama, malum qua non aliud velocius ullum, mobilitate viget virisque adquirit eundo")* and then Ecclesiastes: " 'Fili, sine consilio' (hoc est lima discretionis) 'nil facias,' nil dicas, et post factum non poenitibus" [" 'Son, without deliberation' (this is the rule of discretion), 'do nothing,' say nothing, and afterward you will not have to repent."][16] Words are dangerous; silence—or at least brevity—is safer, less likely to lead to regrettable consequences. This is advice one might well give Dido, and one sees the point of Petrus's juxtaposition of the two texts. But one cannot escape being exposed by language, even if one neither speaks in public nor puts one's thoughts in writing, if only because one is born with a name (a name which, Montaigne notes in "Of Glory," is never sufficiently one's own, never sufficiently proper).[17] In "Of Some verses of Virgil," Montaigne writes: "I am hungry to make myself known [*je suis affamé de me faire connoistre*], and I care not to how many, provided it be truly. Or to put it better, I am hungry for nothing, but I have a mortal fear of being taken to be other than I am by those who come to know my name [je crains mortellement d'estre pris en eschange par ceux à qui il arrive de connoistre mon nom]" (643; 824).

This "mortal fear" links the Delphic injunction to know oneself (*se connaître*)—often taken to be the central preoccupation of the *Essays*—with the rhetorical project of making oneself known (*se faire connaître*). It thus concerns, we might say, the relation between the

16. J. P. Migne, *Patrologia latina* (Paris: Garnier, 1800–75), Vol. 20, p. 233. The English translation is my own.

17. On the problematics of the proper name in the *Essays*, see Antoine Compagnon, *Nous, Michel de Montaigne* (Paris: Seuil, 1980).

constative or cognitive functions of language and its performative—
or more precisely, its perlocutionary—functions. Whereas the successful formulation of a constative (e.g., "Dido is married") is governed by the rules of grammar, and the successful formulation of a
certain class of performatives (e.g., promising, warning, etc.) by the
relevant illocutionary rules, the success of another class of performatives—which Austin called "perlocutionary"—depends on the production of a certain effect on the addressee. Thus, for instance, one
can *persuade* someone only if he actually adopts beliefs or a course of
action in line with those which one has proposed. That is, whereas
the success of constatives and the first class of performatives depends
only on the fulfillment of conditions immanent to language (and thus
theoretically within the speaker's control), the success of a perlocutionary act depends upon the production of a specified effect that can
never be guaranteed, no matter how carefully or sincerely the speaker
satisfies the demands made upon him by the relevant illocutionary
rules. The passage from *se connaître* to *se faire connaître*, from
knowing oneself to making oneself known, leads across this slippery
terrain.

In the *Essays*, the danger of this passage is reflected in an anxiety
concerning the relationship between *name* and *fame*, and it can be
traced back as far as Montaigne's earliest writings. I am thinking here
less of his translation of Raymond Sebond, which he insisted on
publishing under his father's name,[18] than of a series of dedicatory
letters written between 1568 and 1570 in connection with his publication, as La Boétie's literary executor, of five volumes of his
friend's works. The constant theme of these letters is Montaigne's
desire to protect and preserve La Boétie's good name and to make his
qualities known to those who had not been acquainted with him.

The first of these letters is addressed to Henri de Mesmes, a well-
known general, statesman, and scholar who was also the friend and
protector of many of the most learned men of his generation.[19] In it,
Montaigne observes that while clever people (*fines gens*) often mock
the care we have for what happens on earth after our deaths, he finds
it all the same a great consolation for the weakness and brevity of our
life to think that it can be made more durable and prolonged by

18. *Oeuvres complètes*, p. 1360. References to Montaigne's letters will be accompanied only by the page numbers in the French edition. Translations are my own.
19. On Montaigne's correspondents, see Grace Norton, *Early Writings of Montaigne* (New York: Macmillan, 1904), pp. 31–53.

reputation and renown ("qu'elle se puisse affermir & allonger par la reputation & la renommee").[20] Moreover, Montaigne goes on, having loved La Boétie so much and considering him the greatest man of his century, he would be remiss if he knowingly allowed to evaporate and pass into oblivion a name so rich as that of his friend, and a memory so worthy of praise ("si à mon escient je laissois esvanouir & perdre un si riche nom que le sien, & une memoire si digne de recommendation"); if he did not, by publishing La Boétie's works, try to resuscitate and bring him back to life ("le resusciter & remettre en vie"). Indeed La Boétie has been preserved so whole and alive in Montaigne's memory that Montaigne can hardly believe him dead and buried. Hence, he continues, every new bit of knowledge he can give concerning his friend and his name multiplies this second life of his ("c'est autant de multiplication de ce sien second vivre"), and since La Boétie's name is ennobled and honored by the places in which it becomes known, it is up to Montaigne to ensure not only that it is a widely known as possible but also that it is given for safekeeping to people of honor and virtue.

In the other letters, as in this one, Montaigne insists on his peculiar qualifications for the task of presenting his friend's works to the public: La Boétie's spirit lives on in his, and he alone knows at first hand what others can only recall imperfectly or infer from La Boétie's writings. This gives him the right and even the obligation to make use of his friend's words to preserve his memory and his name (1365); he is the only person to whom La Boétie communicated himself fully (1368). The privileged, virtually immediate knowledge he claims to have of his friend corresponds to the privileged access to his own character and intentions which is the fundamental premise on which his claims to self-knowledge and the whole project of self-portraiture in the *Essays* rest.[21] But Montaigne observes, echoing a commonplace of the rhetorical tradition, the task of making known one's own true character or that of one's friend requires more than

20. This affirmation allows us to read against the grain the critique of fame in the *Essays.*

21. Among many examples, see the famous passage near the beginning of "Of Repentance," where Montaigne avers that "no man ever treated a subject he knew and understood better than I do the subject I have undertaken . . . in this I am the most learned man alive . . . no man ever penetrated more deeply into his material . . . or reached more accurately and fully the goal he had set for his work. To accomplish it, I need only bring to it fidelity; and that is in it, as sincere and pure as can be found" (611; 783).

knowing the truth about it, because truth, no matter how beautiful and acceptable it may be in itself, enters our belief only by means of the tools of persuasive rhetoric ("la verité pour belle & acceptable qu'elle soit d'elle mesme, si ne l'ambrassions nous qu'infuse & insinuee en nostre creance par les outils de la persuasion," 1368). Montaigne declares himself greatly lacking ("fort desgarny") not only in rhetorical skill, but also in the authority required to make himself believed and in the eloquence necessary to bring out the full splendor of his friend's character. Thus the danger is not that he may misrepresent La Boétie by adding something to his character, but that he may do so by taking something away from it. The very decision to publish works that his friend did not intend to leave to posterity is laden with risks and responsibilities. The executor's role is difficult, for he is charged not only with disseminating a dead author's works but also with ensuring that their true meaning and intention are communicated and preserved.

When he published La Boétie's *Oeuvres* in 1572, Montaigne omitted the only work generally known today, the *Discourse on Voluntary Servitude.* Apparently trusting neither the power of his protestations *in loco amicis* nor the protection of influential sponsors to control its interpretation, Montaigne was reluctant to "abandon" such a "delicate" and dainty" text to the "crude and dull" climate of the time (1366, n. 10). Instead, he planned to publish it as the centerpiece of his own *Essays*, with the chapter "Of Friendship" as an introduction. He did not do so, he explains, because in the interim it had been published (in 1576, without Montaigne's permission) in a collection of seditious pamphlets, and what is worse, those who published it "mixed his work up with some of their own concoctions" (144; 193). One is inclined to say that this is precisely what Montaigne intended to do by including La Boétie's text within his own. But Montaigne's claim is, of course, that whereas the Protestant dissidents who first published the *Discourse* did so "with evil intent" (144; 193) and distorted its meaning by appropriating it for their own ends, he intended to preserve its true meaning by inserting it into the *Essays*, which were to surround it like a protective frame, as Montaigne suggests at the beginning of the chapter on friendship (135; 181). This framing would be a proprietary gesture designed to protect his friend's work against the depredations of unauthorized interpreters.

A vivid image in "Of Vanity" indicates the nature of the menace: "Even the living, I perceive, are spoken of otherwise than they really are. And if I had not supported with all my strength a friend that I lost, they would have torn him into a thousand contrasting appearances [*visages*]" (752; 961). The scene of interpretive *sparagmos* conjured up by this passage would produce a fragmentation or disfiguration of the face (*visage*) by multiplying it a thousandfold, by repeating it in different contexts and interpreting it in an endless variety of ways until the "original" is lost in the welter of its reproductions. The essay "Of Friendship" can thus be seen as an abortive attempt to limit this fragmentation by providing an authoritative portrait of La Boétie's character and an authoritative context for his text. But only Montaigne's supposedly privileged and unparalleled knowledge of his friend could provide the ground for his claim that he alone is qualified to offer the true image of his friend's character and intentions. The latter could never be decisively determined from the texts alone.[22]

In the 1588 edition of the *Essays*, the passage concerning Montaigne's intervention to maintain the integrity of his friend's memory was followed by these lines: "I know well that I will leave behind no sponsor anywhere near as affectionate and understanding about me as I was about him. There is no one to whom I would be willing to entrust myself fully for a portrait: he alone enjoyed my true image and carried it away. That is why I decipher myself so painstakingly" (752, n. 14; 961, n. 3). After the word "portrait" Montaigne added and then crossed out "and if there should be any, I repudiate them, for I know them to be excessively prejudiced in my favor." Donald Frame, echoing the general opinion of Montaigne's modern editors, explains that "all this was deleted presumably out of consideration for Montaigne's 'covenant daughter,' and literary executrix, Marie de Gournay." But if this deletion leaves open the possibility of an authorized representative, it does not cancel the concern of the passage immediately preceding the reference to La Boétie. "After all this," Montaigne writes,

> I do not want people to go on debating, as I often see them troubling the memory of the dead: "He thought thus, he lived thus; if he had spoken as he was dying, he would have said, he would have

22. See my article referred to above, "Mus in pice" pp. 1056–62.

given. . . . I knew him better than anyone else." Now as far as decency permits me, I here make known my inclinations and feelings; but I do so more freely by word of mouth to anyone who wishes to be informed of them. At all events, in these memoirs, if you look around, you will find that I have said everything or suggested everything. . . . I leave nothing about me to be desired or guessed. If people are to talk about me, I want it to be truly and justly. I would willingly come back from the other world to give the lie to any man who portrayed me as other than I was, even if it were to honor me." [751; 961]

The anxiety that can be heard *en sourdine* finally surfaces (and is immediately displaced in the image of La Boétie's potential disfiguration) in the wish to be able to return from the dead in order to supervise what is said about him in his absence. Implicit in this wish is the recognition of the possibility that his self-portrait will fail to stabilize and control what is predicated of his name.

THE MORTGAGED TEXT

The risk inherent in the project of making onself known is indicated earlier in the same essay ("Of Vanity") in a passage where the specular metaphor of self-portraiture is inscribed within a larger speculative economy:

> Reader, let this essay of myself run on, and this third extension of the other parts of my painting. I add, but do not correct. First, because when a man has mortgaged [hypothequé] his work to the world, it seems to me he has no further right to it. Let him speak better elsewhere, if he can, and not adulterate the work he has sold [venduë]. From such people nothing should be bought until after their death. Let them think carefully before publishing. Who is hurrying them?
> My book is always one. Except that at each new edition, so that the buyer may not come off completely empty-handed, I allow myself to add, since it is only an ill-fitted patchwork, some extra ornaments. They are only overweights, which do not condemn the original form, but give some special value to each of the subsequent ones, by a bit of ambitious subtlety. [736; 941]

Two related figures organize this text: selling and mortgaging. Both compare the self-portrait to a commodity exchanged for compensation. Selling one's book is an alienation and a transfer of property through which the seller abandons his rights to what he has sold, as Montaigne points out.[23] But to describe this transaction as a mortgaging complicates it by suggesting that it involves both a risk and a lien on the future.

"Hypothéquer" (to hypothecate or mortgage) derives from medieval Latin legal terminology and was no doubt familiar to Montaigne from his experience as a jurist. To hypothecate one's property is to pledge it as security for a debt. In his translation of Sebond, Montaigne uses the term to refer to the debt man owes to God, a debt that can be repaid only in the currency most proper to man, namely his love;[24] it also appears at several points in the *Essays*, notably in "Of Husbanding our will,' where Montaigne declares his dislike of hypothecating his will to any person or institution (767; 980–81). It is not easy to see, however, just what sort of obligation or debt is incurred by publishing and selling one's book. I would suggest that the debt concerns the belief lent an author by his readers, for a creditor (*créancier*) is one who believes, who takes his debtor's word at face value, *pour de l'argent comptant*. This reading can be clarified by examining briefly another passage from the same essay which once again weaves together all the motifs that have concerned us here:

> I feel this unexpected profit [*proffit*] from the publication of my behavior, that to some extent it serves me as a rule. Sometimes there comes to me a feeling that I should not betray the story of my life. This public declaration obliges me [m'*oblige*] to keep on my path, and not to give the lie to the picture of my qualities [*ne desmentir l'image de mes conditions*], which are normally less disfigured and distorted [*desfigurées et contredites*] than might be expected from the malice and sickness of the judgments of today. The uniformity and simplicity of my behavior indeed produces an appearance easy to interpret [*un visage d'aisée interpretation*], but, because the manner of it is a bit new and unusual, it gives a fine chance to calumny [*mesdisance*]. [749; 958]

The obligation incurred is thus that of living up to the verbal image sold the public; to do otherwise would be to betray the story of his life

23. It should perhaps be recalled here that in Montaigne's time, when an author sold a printer the right to publish his book, he generally gave up any further rights to it.

24. *Le livre des creatures de Raymond Sebond*, in Montaigne, *Oeuvres complètes*, ed. A. Armaingaud (Paris: Conard, 1924), Vol. 9, p. 192.

and defraud the buyer or creditor. The profit expected from his speculation (presumably the revenue in money and the satisfaction of
making himself known) is accompanied by an unexpected gain in
self-consistency. But despite his book's presenting a face that is easy
to interpret, its novelty exposes him all too much to misinterpretation and ill fame.

The maintenance of this resemblance is moreover already a kind
of expropriation, since, as the passage just quoted suggests, the mimetic current is reversible. The written image controls and directs its
"original" instead of the other way round. The same reversal is implied in "Of Friendship," where Montaigne observes that "The true
mirror of our discourse is the course of our lives [*Le vray miroir de nos
discours est le cours de nos vies*]" (124; 168). In this formulation, life
becomes the image of discourse, and the inseparability of the two is
suggested by the *annominatio* "discours"—"cours." The written image of the author steadily shapes and displaces its extratextual original; that is to say, its repetition in writing constantly implies the
latter's existence while at the same time making its status as original, as extratextual, increasingly problematic. Moreover, this reversal cannot itself be reversed: there is no way the author can regain
control over his mortgaged text. Attempts to do so by adding explana-
tions, clarifications, further arguments or details succeed only in
raising further questions, offering more material for repetition in
commentary, interpretation, rewriting. And in accord with the rule
of Fama, this repetition can itself give rise to repetition, as the history
of midrash shows[25] and as Montaigne himself recognizes in his famous observation that "we do nothing but write glosses about each
other" (818; 1045).

An essential feature of hypothecation is, however, the debtor's
retention of the right to redeem his pledge by paying off the debt on or
before the date specified in the contract. For this reason the alienation of property is not unconditional, as in a sale; the debtor is entitled to reclaim it, he retains title to it subject to repayment of the
debt. But in the case of the mortgaged text, the debt can be paid off
only at the author's death; those who try to change, exchange, or
withdraw their pledge merely destroy their credit: "from such people
nothing should be bought until after their death." The author's name

25. See Frank Kermode, *The Genesis of Secrecy: On the Interpretation of Narrative* (Cambridge, Mass.: Harvard University Press, 1979).

on the title page is the mark of his claim to his text, but it is an empty claim, since it is precisely the fatal nature of words that they cannot be retracted—except by more words. Montaigne's assertion that he adds but does not correct acknowledges this fact, and confirms the law of Fama. Once the linguistic stake is on the table one cannot withdraw it but only raise the ante. And the stake is on the table from the beginning, as Montaigne points out, in the form of the name. Fama's game, it would seem, can be neither avoided nor won.

CARL PLETSCH

The Self-Sufficient Text in Nietzsche and Kierkegaard

Nietzsche and Kierkegaard have been coupled often enough, although they themselves were not great couplers in any sense of the word. They divorced themselves radically from every other thinker, and they gave birth, we assume, only to books. Yet they worried a great deal about who would finally grant them the status of fathers, by reading their books and becoming their disciples. And their worries were not unfounded, for their texts are fraught with the most multifarious seeds of thought and, one might say, profoundly heterozygous. In their texts they exposed themselves almost promiscuously to every interpreter and any interpretation that might be made of them. Yet each at the end of his career as an author insisted that he should not be misunderstood. This then is the spectacle at play: two quite recklessly daring, uninhibited and very prolific writers who seem to have drawn themselves up short at the ends of their careers, intent upon stifling mis- and multiple interpretations of their works.

The locus of this compulsive attempt to throttle other interpretations is in each case something like an autobiography. In a couple of the oddest autobiographical writings in occidental literature, Nietzsche and Kierkegaard both reviewed their authorship, to use Kierkegaard's term, apparently trying to specify how each text should be read. For Nietzsche this was *Ecce Homo: How one becomes what one is* (written in 1888 but not published until 1908); for Kierkegaard it was *The Point of View for my Work as an Author* (written in 1848 but not published until 1859) and several other shorter pieces written in the late 1840s and published with *The Point of View*.[1] These were among the last efforts of the two authors and

1. I shall refer to English translations of these two books: *Ecce Homo*, translated by Walter Kaufmann, in Friedrich Nietzsche, *On the Genealogy of Morals and Ecce Homo* (New York: Random House, 1967); and *The Point of View for my Work as an Author*, translated by Walter Lowrie (New York: Harper and Row, 1962). Page references to quotations from these two volumes are included in the body of the paper.

were published posthumously in each case. In spite of certain obvious signs of ambivalence about readers that mark these texts, it seems quite obvious that they were both intended for eventual publication and at least for some few readers. Thus we might equally well call these texts literary testaments as autobiographies; but rather than worrying over how to categorize them among the genres I should like merely to describe the thought process involved in them and try to locate that sort of thinking in the general world of self-consciousness exhibited by the typical genius of the nineteenth century.

The typical genius did not indulge in the sort of auto-interpretation exemplified by *The Point of View* and *Ecce Homo*. In fact, the typical genius affected the attitude that he did not need his readers at all, but that his readers needed him. Of course a genius would not be a genius if he were not recognized as such, and if his readers did not appropriate his vision of the world. But only in the sense that the genius is legitimated by the function he eventually fulfills for his readers does the genius evince any need for his readers. The typical genius of the nineteenth century thus assumed that his readers were fascinated by him and adopted a regal attitude toward being viewed by them: it was his duty to display himself to them. By contrast, Nietzsche and Kierkegaard, who teased their readers to think of them as geniuses in their earlier works, seem anxious in these last texts to fend off their readers' advances.

I

To speak of typical and atypical geniuses at all is to step back from the common discourse about originality and creativity and call the category of the genius itself into question, for the genius has always been defined by his uniqueness. But to understand the difference between the self-conscious auto-interpretive moves of Kierkegaard and Nietzsche on the one hand and the apparently naive or unself-conscious geniuses on the other, we must first acknowledge that the genius is not a natural category. The genius is a subcategory of the author, a function in a historically specific discourse.

The assumptions that have governed our thinking about intellectual and artistic creativity since the mid-eighteenth century may be called "the ideology of the genius." When we think within this ideology (and therefore within a discourse of individualism), we generally assume that individuals are the exclusive agents of cultural innovation, and that some individuals are born with the native capacity to create new things. This capacity differentiates geniuses in our minds from the merely talented, who seem to perform variations, however exquisite, upon inherited themes and within existing genres. This distinction between the genius and the talented cannot be found before the mid-eighteenth century, a fact of chronology that impels us to question the relationship of our conception of the genius to other components of modern ideology that emerged in the late eighteenth century. In fact, the notion of the genius is the cultural counterpart of the idea of the individual used in Enlightenment thinking about economy and society (e.g., by Turgot and Smith). In particular it legitimated the growing social and financial autonomy of individual artists and thinkers by providing an ontological basis and legal justification for their claims to private property in the books, paintings, music, etc. that they created. Copyright laws, for example, were unthinkable before the advent of the idea of the genius.

The characteristics ascribed to the genius since the late eighteenth century suggest that the concept was called into being not merely by the emergence of new social and material status for the artist and intellectual, however. It was fomented as well by the waning power of another set of beliefs about art and thought that had been used to explain cultural innovation in earlier centuries. According to the new ideology, the genius is supposed to be "born, not made." He[2] is purported not to have to learn his ability to create, but is believed to possess it inherently. The genius is also believed to be distinct and separable from his social context; indeed he is defined in part by his living in some sort of opposition to his contemporaries. Moreover, his works are thought to be "eternal" in an unspecified sense. It is also commonly assumed that geniuses are "original" and that they create, as it were, *ex nihilo*, independently of the influences of their predecessors and contemporaries. The "genius," in other words, emerged to replace God as the guarantor of artistic and intellectual novelty and of cultural innovation generally.

2. As to the gender of the genius: I use the masculine pronoun for the genius, not because I suppose that geniuses are in fact males, but in order to establish one more dimension of ironic distance from the category of the genius itself.

The category of the genius also has a narrative shape (for example see Joseph Campbell, *The Hero with a Thousand Faces*). We imagine the life of the genius to be a species of heroic journey and tend to plot the life of a particular genius upon the trajectory of the mythic journey. We assume that the hero-genius has so departed from his contemporaries that we can say the genius is "ahead of his time," and thus explain to ourselves why the genius is so frequently misunderstood. We assume that the life and works of the genius are coherent and all of a piece, which causes us to look for a point of emergence and a process of development in the works of a genius as well as in his life: we understand it as a story with a beginning, a middle, and an end. Thus the heroic journey of the genius is a story of the movement of the genius away from us or his contemporaries and into the virgin territory of his own mind—dangerous territory where discoveries are to be made only at great risk, often at the risk of madness. But it also involves a return, with the genius bringing his newly won vision back to the rest of mankind in his works.

This is a story that we nongeniuses tell ourselves about geniuses. It is a pervasive metatext of which we as readers are usually only subliminally aware. But this metatextual story (and the ideology of the genius generally) also governs the thinking of geniuses about themselves.

The genius too is aware of the metatextual life—acutely aware of it as the subtext of his own life. In the whole period during which the ideology of the genius has governed our thinking about cultural innovation, it has been possible to aspire to the status of genius. For the last two centuries, in other words, artists and intellectuals have known that they might be/become geniuses. It has proven an irresistible fantasy. Like all the other forms of mimetic desire, this has permitted and indeed constrained geniuses to live a particular type of life, a life suited for inclusion in the canon of geniuses. Thus from the moment he realizes his difference, the genius is condemned to an awareness that the eyes of his readers and even his biographers are upon him.

Living in anticipation of one's readers and biographers entails a degree and constancy of self-consciousness unknown before the eighteenth century. The modern genius knows that the eyes of his readers—even the yet unborn—are closely scrutinizing his whole life—even the portion he has still to live. This inevitably involves the genius in efforts to shape the way his life will appear to his readers, his biographers, and posterity generally. This striving to shape his own life is in fact an integral part of being/becoming a genius. The shapes of life that modern geniuses have striven for are various, for the preoccupation of the genius is his own uniqueness and capacity for innovation. But they all involve a troping or a turning of the conventions of autobiographic writing back upon the life itself. We customarily think of autobiography as a literary activity carried out towards the end of a life: writing a story of one's life near its end, a story modeled upon the life in some way. But in modern artists and intellectuals so constrained by the ideology of the genius, we are confronted with lives lived upon the general pattern of an autobiography imagined in advance, often when the subjects are quite young. Thus the literary figure of an autobiography—in this case the story of the culture hero's journey told by himself—becomes the model for lives yet to be lived. Consequently I call the life lived in anticipation of one's biographers an "autobiographical life."

An autobiographical life, needless to say, is not an autobiography, nor does living an autobiographical life necessarily entail writing an autobiography. The dialectic of the autobiographical life does not involve writing an autobiography at all: it lies rather in the relationship between desire and fantasy on the one hand and action on the other. Nonetheless, the dialectic of desire and action does frequently lead a genius to writing autobiographically. The resulting text constitutes a single moment of the dialectic, and cannot, of course, be considered a record of the autobiographical life in question. It is but one more fiction expressing the dialectical moment of the autobiographical life in its vector. Such texts originate within the parameters of the ideology of the genius and are plotted on the metastory of the life of the genius.

Having returned to the question of autobiographical texts, we can locate the auto-interpretations of Kierkegaard and Nietzsche in one of the dimensions of the autobiographical life of the genius: one characteristic that distinguished Nietzsche and Kierkegaard from typical geniuses is their peculiar and even obsessive concern with the reader.

Typical geniuses like Rousseau, Goethe, Wordsworth, Hugo, to take a few examples for the sake of argument, seem relatively unconcerned about their readers. They assume that their readers need and desire them, that their readers will inevitably interpret them, and that the resulting interpretations will reflect upon the readers rather than upon themselves. This attitude of the typical genius descends genealogically from the indulgent attitude of a god toward his worshipers. Typical geniuses seem, on the whole, quite comfortable being geniuses, and their complacency vis à vis their readers is relatively constant throughout their lives. Adapting Schiller's terms to my purpose, I therefore propose to call the typical geniuses "naive," for they give the impression of being unreflective about the problems of being interpreted by readers. (Of course Schiller had to create a fiction of Goethe to fill his category of the naive poet, as I am doing here too.)

Nietzsche and Kierkegaard on the other hand spent most of their careers seducing, provoking, and insulting their readers, but then finally declared themselves immune to interpretation. They are deviant geniuses in respect to their attitudes towards readers. They are "sentimental" in their painfully acute awareness of their readers, whether they are primarily concerned with seducing the disinterested, provoking the complacent, or finally just horrified at the prospect of what their readers might actually make of them. Their preoccupation with the reader is constant, intense, and volatile. This is perhaps most evident in their shifting styles. In Kierkegaard's case the pseudonyms together with the incredible difference in apparent intent among his writings actually deluded many of his contemporaries about his authorship. There are no pseudonyms on Nietzsche's title pages, but Derrida has shown us how various are Nietzsche's styles . . . as if there were not one Nietzsche but many. Thus we see that the virtual obsession with the reader seems to have at least partially broken down the category of the author in these two cases, and we can begin to understand that their late auto-interpretive moves may have been a response to anxiety about the disparate nature of their authorship: attempts to reconstitute themselves as authors.

A moment's reflection upon the relationship between the categories adapted from Schiller will point the way further. Nietzsche and Kierkegaard are "sentimental" in their obsessive concern with their readers. But as in Schiller's text, the sentimental variant deconstructs the naive one. For naive geniuses are also concerned about their readers. Their apparent equanimity is a pose dictated by the ideology of the genius. The dominant variety of genius, striving to exemplify the godlike independence of the unmoved mover, pretends to be uninterested in his readers. Living an autobiographical life, however, is by definition reflective, as a vital trope of autobiographic writing. The autobiographical life is a creature of intense concern with readers. Thus by flaunting their obsession with the reader, Nietzsche and Kierkegaard deconstruct the naiveté of the dominant variety of genius. Consequently, by examining the sentimental moves of Nietzsche and Kierkegaard in *Ecce Homo* and *The Point of View*, we may enhance our understanding of the category of the genius itself while illuminating the particular auto-interpretive strategies that they adopted.

In their apparent innocence and equanimity, sometimes elaborately pled for, the typical geniuses seem or try to seem oblivious to the reception accorded them by their readers. They exude confidence in their own difference, their originality, and their unique value to the rest of mankind. And if they make autobiographical gestures of self-justification at all, it is with apparent confidence that their readers will eventually do them justice too, or be damned as a consequence. Even Rousseau, whose confidence in the capacity of his fellows to understand and judge him fairly may seem the shakiest of all the great geniuses of the last two centuries, even Rousseau insists on the first page of his *Confessions* that he is unique among men. Embarked upon what he asserted was an unprecedented act of literary self-revelation, Rousseau presents himself as a moral mirror for his fellows to measure themselves against: were they as honest with themselves as he?

> Let the last trump sound when it will, I shall come forward with this work in my hand, to present myself before my Sovereign Judge, and proclaim aloud: "Here is what I have done. . . . So let the numberless legion of my fellow men gather around me and hear my confessions. Let them groan at my depravities and blush for my misdeeds. But let each one of them reveal his heart at the foot of Thy throne with equal sincerity, and may any man who dares, say "I was a better man than he."

In this passage and throughout *The Confessions*, Rousseau never lapses from his assumption that he is or would be transparent to a worthy judge. In fact his very transparence is what characterizes him as the genius of virtue. He does not explain himself, he seems to say, but merely shows himself to his readers—and for their benefit. This is also true, but with greater equanimity, of Goethe, Wordsworth, Hugo, etc.

The rhetorical strategies and emotional tone of Kierkegaard's and Nietzsche's fictions of themselves diverge radically from this general metalife lived to be displayed to the reader for the reader's edification. Nietzsche and Kierkegaard were "sentimental" in ways and degrees that would have astonished even Schiller. But what is of particular interest to me here is that in their late but apparently urgent desire to forestall and counter misinterpretations of their words, they are quite unlike the typical genius . . . unlike even Rousseau, who was so worried about how his former friends were deliberately misinterpreting him—and even more unlike Goethe, Wordsworth, Hugo, and the rest. Having done what they could in their writings to disorient their readers, Nietzsche and Kierkegaard finally insisted that they be recognized for who they truly were.

II

> In my career as an author, a point has now been reached where it is permissible to do what I feel a strong impulse to do and so regard as my duty—namely, to explain once for all, as directly and frankly as possible, what is what: what I as an author declare myself to be.
> —Kierkegaard, *The Point of View for my Work as an Author* [5]

> Seeing that before long I must confront humanity with the most difficult demand ever made of it, it seems indispensable to me to say *who I am*. Really, one should know it, for I have not left myself "without testimony." But the disproportion between the greatness of my task and the smallness of my contemporaries has found expression in the fact that one has neither heard nor even seen me. I live on my own credit; it is perhaps a mere prejudice that I live. . . .
> Under these circumstances I have a duty against which my habits, even more the pride of my instincts, revolt at bottom—namely to say: *Hear me! For I am such and such a person. Above all, do not mistake me for someone else.*
> —Nietzsche, *Ecce Homo* [217]

Thus the opening sentences of *Ecce Homo* and *The Point of View* evoke a crisis in the careers of their respective authors. Until the textual *now* of these passages a certain confusion has reigned, and the works of their authors have been grossly misunderstood or unappreciated. This is a matter of vital concern to the authors themselves, but until now they have been unwilling or unable to rectify the misunderstanding. Now the time has finally come for them to clear up their questionable identity and thus the meaning of their authorship as well. The occasion for this corrective presents itself in both cases at the completion of the *oeuvre*. At that point, self-clarification suddenly becomes the overriding duty.

In each case the movement of clarification consists of the author reading his own earlier works. In the course of these readings both Nietzsche and Kierkegaard indicate that misunderstanding and incomprehension of their works were induced by a species of silence that they themselves had inscribed in them. Their silences differ, of course. Kierkegaard's silence is dialectical, created only for the author to break it himself in *The Point of View*, whereas Nietzsche's silence only grows deeper in *Ecce Homo*. But in each case it is silence that gives rise to the auto-interpretive texts in question.

Kierkegaard asserts that until the moment of writing *The Point of View* he regarded a particular type of silence as his religious duty. This was not the silence of not publishing—he had published prolifically. Nor was it the silence of publishing exclusively under pseudonyms—he had indeed written a series of quite popular aesthetic books that appeared pseudonymously, but from the beginning he had also been heard as the author of religious or devotional works bearing his own name. The silence he had maintained was silence in regard to the meaning of his whole oeuvre or authorship: he had refrained from explaining the place of his individual works in his authorship. Now in *The Point of View*, he explains that "the reason I considered silence my duty was that the authorship was not yet at hand in so complete a form that the understanding of it could be anything but misunderstanding" (5). Kierkegaard envisioned a problem that most nineteenth-century authors never considered, least of all typical geniuses: that his works could not be understood until they had been explained by their author, and that they could not be explained even by their author until the authorship itself was complete. Thus in *The Point of View* Kierkegaard reads his individual works as parts of a whole that gives them their true meaning. Separately, however, they have other, diverse, and quite contradictory meanings; so if they are all parts of a single literary entity as Kierkegaard asserts, they were bound to be misunderstood when understood individually. In fact, according to Kierkegaard in *The Point of View*, they were *intended* to be misunderstood.

The silence that Kierkegaard reads in his authorship as he reviews it in *The Point of View* entails duplicity as well. This is nowhere more apparent than in Kierkegaard's reading of the pseudonymous books that he classifies as the *aesthetic* portion of his authorship, for example *Either/Or*. In this work of two volumes, the reader is confronted with the papers of two fictitious authors, A and B, edited by the pseudonymous Victor Eremita. The papers of A present arguments for an unrestrained sensuous life, concluding with the "Diary of a Seducer." The papers of B argue for a life of ethical restraint. Thus the book seems to pose the alternative: *Either* a sensuous life / *Or* an ethical one. But, according to Kierkegaard in *The Point of View*, this was a ruse. Taken in the context of the authorship as a whole, he argues, the function of *Either/Or* is to force the reader to take notice of his own condition, whether he prefers the ethical or the sensuous life. And this is only the first step in the larger project of preparing the reader to recognize a third alternative, the religious life. The duplicity of the aesthetic portion of Kierkegaard's authorship lies therefore in intentionally creating a false impression of the author's intentions. But Kierkegaard carried this duplicity beyond his writing, for he claims literally to have adopted disguises in order to facilitate such misunderstanding: for several years he went to the theater every night pretending to be a dandy, for example, giving plausibility to the suspicion that he shared the point of view of A in *Either/Or*, and causing readers to fall the more readily and surely into the intended misunderstandings of his main purpose, the purpose of the authorship as a whole.[3]

3. It is fitting that Kierkegaard chose to masquerade as a dandy, not merely because the dandy is an ironic figure paralleling the textual irony of Kierkegaard's aesthetic works on the social plane—cf. Sima Godfrey, "The Dandy as Ironic Figure," *Sub/stance* 36 (1982), pp. 21–33—but because the dandy is one of the limiting cases of the genius. The dandy has all the qualities and characteristics of the typical genius but one: his originality lies in doing nothing, creating nothing. The figure of the dandy may be said to deconstruct the typical genius ironically. But this irony of employing all the talents of the genius to do nothing is precisely the inverse of the irony deployed in Kierkegaard's authorship as a whole, for Kierkegaard's overarching irony was to do everything while seeming to be a mere dandy.

In *The Point of View*, Kierkegaard describes his previous relationship to the reader as *indirect communication*, and suggests that maintaining this stance for so long had been something heroic in itself: "seldom has any author employed so much cunning, intrigue, and shrewdness to win honour and reputation in the world with a view to deceiving it, as I displayed in order to deceive it inversely in the interest of truth" (49).[4] With his indirect communications, however, Kierkegaard created a textual situation in which he would ultimately find it necessary to resort to *direct communication* and explain *what is what*. That, of course, is the function of *The Point of View*.

Merely to indicate in *The Point of View* that his authorship was a simple whole was for Kierkegaard the principle act of auto-interpretation. This is true precisely because Kierkegaard regarded his authorship as having much the same kind of integrity as we were once accustomed to ascribe to an individual work. (We assumed that it would be impossible to interpret a poem or a novel without reading it to its end—a view that has broken down in the face of interpretive strategies that focus upon the fissures in writing rather than the units of writing or the boundaries between them. Thus while the claims Kierkegaard makes for the integrity of his authorship might strain our credence even more than the idea of the integrity of the individual work, they do reveal again—from the other side, as it were— the arbitrariness of that idea.) To state that his whole career as an author had been devoted to creating a single work of art/authorship, with his individual writings merely a series of fragments of this larger work, dispels the earlier misunderstandings. The authorship as a whole, Kierkegaard asserts, was present to his mind as a grand strategy during the writing of all of the individual works that constitute it. And although he kept the plan a secret, it was this projected authorship, rather than the individual works, that had defined him as an author from the first. In declaring *what is what* in *The Point of View*, he broke the silence in regard to his authorship and thus transformed the meaning of his earlier publications.

Much of *The Point of View* is dedicated to demonstrating how a

---

4. Not only his pseudonymous aesthetic works, but the religious works signed with his own name are understood as indirect communications. In the religious works the author is ironically self-righteous, and his disguise is that of an indignant defender of public morality—as in the affair of *The Corsair*.

single author could have written both such aesthetic works as *Either/Or* and the religious works, for example the *Two Edifying Discourses*. According to *The Point of View*, the question of whether this disparity in his authorship indicated that he was an aesthetic or a religious author, or that he had once been an aesthetic author and then became a religious one is superficial. Kierkegaard insists that he had always been a religious author:

> the contents of this little book [*The Point of View*] affirm . . . what I truly am as an author, that I am and was a religious author, that the whole of my work as an author is related to Christianity, to the problem "of becoming a Christian," with a direct polemic against the monstrous illusion we call Christendom . . . . [5–6] *Furthermore*, the duplicity, the ambiguity, is a conscious one, something the author knows more about than anyone else; it is the essential dialectical distinction of the whole authorship. [10]

The interesting questions, and the ones Kierkegaard does feel obliged to answer rather than merely negate, are the questions of why a religious author would have written the aesthetic works and what is their part in his religious authorship. How are they related to the problem of becoming a Christian?

The answer to his question is affiliated with what Nietzsche described as the disparity between the greatness of his task and the smallness of his contemporaries. For Kierkegaard, of course, the disparity was defined in religious terms: the disparity between Christianity and Christendom. He found his readers living in an aesthetic/ethical state, under the illusion that they were in a religious state—the condition Kierkegaard defines as Christendom. How can a religious author approach such readers? In Kierkegaard's view, a religious author who wants to lead his readers to Christianity "must find exactly the place where the other is and begin there" (29). From this basic principle Kierkegaard concluded that he must be both an aesthetic and a religious author. As an aesthetic author—as in *Either/Or*, where he demonstrated the parity of the aesthetic and the ethical points of view—he takes the reader where he is and forces him to acknowledge his true state. He forces him "to take notice." This, in a word, is what Kierkegaard claims he did in his aesthetic works, and claims he intended from the very first. His aesthetic works were seductive in that, while to an irreligious person they seemed to affirm that the aesthetic point of view was as legitimate as the ethical, they were really preparing such a reader for a third alternative, an alternative embodied in his religious works. This then was Kierkegaard's answer to the question of how a religious author could have made himself the scandalous author of such aesthetic works as he had written. It is also the explanation of his posing as a dandy. But the answer is less interesting, for my purposes, than Kierkegaard's mode of reply.

In order to answer the question, Kierkegaard thought it necessary to step into another role. He refused to defend himself directly from the charge of having been an aesthetic author and leading the virtuous astray—he cites Socrates as a precedent. For, as he writes in a remarkable passage of *The Point of View,*

> I have little confidence in [authorial] protestations with respect to literary productions and am inclined to take an objective view of my own works. If as a third person, in the role of a reader, I cannot substantiate the fact that what I affirm is so, and that it could not but be so, it would not occur to me to wish to win a cause which I regard as lost. If I were to begin *qua* author to protest, I might easily bring confusion to the whole work, which from the first to last is dialectical. [15]

As if his authorship were not sufficiently complicated by his deliberate aesthetic/religious duplicity, Kierkegaard insists in *The Point of View* upon stepping out of the role of author altogether and explaining his authorship from the point of view of the reader. Neither his assumption of the role of the reader nor his alleged objectivity can be understood simply, however. He continues to write in the first person (not "as a third person") and in his constant self-reference, the authorial persona of *The Point of View* is perhaps the most subjective of all Kierkegaard's personae. The adoption of the role of the reader and the asseverations of objectivity are rather to be understood dialectically, in the sense of reflection. Viewed dialectically, it is precisely the apparent subjectivity and self-reference that create the textual objectivity of *The Point of View,* for they are the reflections of yet another authorial persona upon the earlier works of the authorship.

The text in question might as well be entitled *Yet another Point of View in my Work as an Author.* And the root impulse of Kierkegaard's authorship begins to seem the multiplication of subjectivities. This is perfectly compatible with Kierkebaard's assertion that he always was a religious author having the one stated aim of leading his reader to becoming a Christian, i.e. sharing one point of view with him. For the multiplication of subjectivities can be understood—even in the case of the additional point of view of *The Point of View*—as serving the overarching purpose of leading author and reader to a single point of view: the point of view of the Christian. This presupposes a number of interesting ideas that would lead us astray here, such as the thought that the point of view of Christianity comprehends and transcends all other points of view and, more generally, that there is but one true point of view. But continuing my own line of reflection about Kierkegaard's auto-interpretive project, I confront a welcome paradox: the text that seems dedicated to revealing that Kierkegaard's authorship has only one point of view, can only operate by further fragmenting the authorship, by introducing still another authorial point of view. (For this additional point of view is that of a reader only in the sense that is the point of view of still another author reading the texts of the earlier authorial persona.) And although *The Point of View* bears the name of Søren Kierkegaard on the title page, it is a different "Kierkegaard" than the one who authored the religious works like the *Two Edifying Discourses*.

There are then three types of authorial persona in the authorship as a whole. First there are the various pseudonymous authors of the aesthetic works (among whom further distinctions can be made). Second, there is the Søren Kierkegaard, editor of *The Concluding Unscientific Postscript* and author of the religious works. And third, there is the Kierkegaard of *The Point of View*, the sole work in direct communication with the reader, and the book in which the author has become the reader of the works of the other/earlier authorial personae. This reduplication of authorial personae signals a disintegration of "the author" as a category and constitutes the necessary, equal, and opposite reaction to Kierkegaard's attempt to integrate his authorship as a whole as indicated above. There is, in other words, a further dialectical movement here (whether Kierkegaard was aware of it or not is immaterial): the authorship as a whole is integrated to an unprecedented degree precisely by an autobiographical life of duplicitous authorship and the disintegration of the author *qua* author. (And just as Kierkegaard's claims for the integrity of his "whole authorship" could be seen to contribute "from the other side" to the dissolution of the integrity of "the work," the fragmentation of his authorial personae in the interests of this authorship contributes to our decomposition of the category of the author *qua* author, again as if from the other side. For while we are engaged in decomposing the author into author-functions as we study a discourse—in this case the discourse on the genius and individual agency generally—we see Kierkegaard receding as an author in the other direction. Kierkegaard's duplicitous and self-replicating authorial personae are continuously extracting themselves ironically from every worldly discourse and striving to generate a discourse unto themselves. Nonetheless, decomposing the author *qua* author has the same ultimate effect, whether in Kierkegaard's shattering performance in *The Point of View* or in the programmatic study of discourse exemplified in the works of Michel Foucault.)

The illusory finality of this further fragmentation of Kierkegaard's authorship is revealed in Kierkegaard's inability to conclude *The Point of View.* For it has not one conclusion but two, and the second is not written by "Kierkegaard" in either of his two earlier guises. The first is called an Epilogue and oddly precedes what is entitled the Conclusion. It is written in a somewhat wistful voice that recognizes that the complexity of the whole project has now been deflated by the revelations of this last author who has explained that the disparate books of the (earlier) duplicitous authorship were all of a seductive piece. This voice recognizes that the authorship is no longer as interesting as it was before these revelations. But of course this interest was an aesthetic property that the author of *The Point of View* is willing to abandon, now that the religious purpose of that interest has been fulfilled. This author is attached neither to the pose of the *flâneur* nor to that of the ironically religious combatant. He finally adopts humility as his demeanor, the one attitude consistent with the authorship as a whole. So at the end of this Epilogue he can say that "With this present little book, which itself belongs to a bygone time, I conclude the whole authorship, and then as the author (not the author simply, but the author of this whole 'authorship') I advance to meet the future. . . . in humility and also in penitence" (98–99). Humility appears at this point in the text as the resolution of the textual dialectic, much as the turn to direct communication in *The Point of View* as a whole presents itself as a resolution of the dialectical movement between the aesthetic and religious moments of Kierkegaard's (former) authorship. This would seem to conclude Kierkegaard's work as an author and "the whole authorship," and in one sense it does. But this is still not the end of the little book.

There follows a Conclusion, which begins in the voice of the author of the rest of the book but immediately shifts to that of another: "I have nothing further to say, but in conclusion I will let another speak, my poet, who when he comes will assign me a place among those who have suffered for the sake of an idea, and he will say: 'The martyrdom this author suffered may be briefly described thus: he suffered from being a genius in a provincial town.' . ." (100). There follows a literary panegyric of several pages in the voice of "my poet." The book ends without a return to Kierkegaard's voice. Thus there emerges yet another fragmentation of Kierkegaard's authorship, still another authorial persona to comment upon and read the works of the earlier ones. This one, however, comes to read not only the earlier works, but the one in which his own voice is inscribed, *The Point of View*. The utterance of "my poet" is perhaps the most complex and fascinating to read of any in the whole authorship, for it is in one sense beyond and outside of "this whole authorship." I shall not attempt to read it here, however, but leave it as the loose end that Kierkegaard left it. Without entering upon a discussion of this voice of yet another, I may nonetheless point out that this final auto-interpretive act of Kierkegaard's demonstrates his awareness that he will be interpreted and read as a genius, no matter how clearly he may have announced "what is what: what I as an author declare myself to be." It is perhaps a humble recognition of the fact, but humble in a duplicitous sense once again, for as he has warned us, "seldom has any author employed so much cunning, intrigue, shrewdness . . . etc." His poet reveals him a genius triumphant in his humility.

In Kierkegaard's fragmented authorship we finally discern several autobiographical lives. In the authorship that he completed before writing *The Point of View*, there are a number of possibilities, the most prominent of which is that of an aesthetic author of salacious books who was converted and subsequently became a religious author of imposing self-righteousness. This autobiographical life is formally very much like the autobiographical life of the typical genius, inasmuch as it is implied in the authorship and susceptible to the perceptions of readers. It is not silent but audible. Until he wrote *The Point of View*, Kierkegaard pretended indifference to the reaction of his readers. In this too he was not unlike the typical genius, and in his

popular aesthetic works he was taken for precisely that. But his deception—a deception that contributes to constituting the typical genius as a genius—was itself a deception for Kierkegaard: he planned
all along to reveal that he cared passionately about the reaction of the
reader. The autobiographical life that was audible in his works was
itself a ruse. With *The Point of View* there emerges another autobiographical life that had formerly been silent. The silence itself sets
this story apart from the mythical life of the typical genius, but the
fact that it can and must be read by its author precisely at the completion of the authorship sets it even farther apart. Silence, fragmented
authorship, and auto-interpretation make Kierkegaard a genius
among geniuses and deconstructs—in one sense—the category of the
genius.

III

Nietzsche makes no extravagant claims about the integrity of his
authorship, nor does he ascribe the general incomprehension of his
works to his own duplicity. And although a parallel to Kierkegaard's
fragmented authorship can be found in the differences between
Nietzsche's own voice and that of Zarathustra, Nietzsche's authorship is not laid out as the work of a series of authorial personae, each
reading the writings of the one before. Furthermore, Nietzsche's
books are silent in a very different sense from Kierkegaard's. Thus
while one of my purposes is to demonstrate a certain parallel between
Nietzsche and Kierkegaard in their performance of disintegrated authorship, it must be understood that there are much deeper disparities between the two—disparities that give rise nonetheless to
the same effects: dissolution of the author, auto-interpretation, etc.

As Nietzsche depicts it in *Ecce Homo*, his authorship was not
dedicated to "deceiving [the reader] inversely in the interest of truth"
(Kierkegaard), but to disillusioning the reader in the truth itself. For
such a purpose neither secrecy nor deception was required: all
Nietzsche needed to do was to state his case against the truth repeatedly and he effectively initiated a discourse of silence. Nietzsche's
attacks upon the moral and metaphysical bases of the truth were just
so outrageous that they produced their own silence. For believing in
truth, Nietzsche's readers could only interpret his attacks as at-

tempts to establish different truths—truths at variance with the commonly accepted ones. Nietzsche therefore felt no compulsion to deceive his readers: they were already deceived by their own belief in truth, and he could rely upon their incomprehension. He found it equally unnecessary to disguise himself in any way, for, as he notes at the outset of *Ecce Homo,* "I only need to speak with one of the 'educated' who come to the Upper Engadine for the summer, and I am convinced that I do not exist" (217). He did not mean that no one had heard of his books, but that his contemporaries heard nothing even when they got his books into their hands and read them. Far from disappointing Nietzsche, this seems perfectly appropriate and even rewarding to him as he writes *Ecce Homo.* He does not go so far as to suggest that he intended to be misunderstood from the first, as Kierkegaard did, but the questions remains: how could he take pleasure in being incomprehensible?

In *Ecce Homo* Nietzsche does predict a great future for his works. Institutions would grow up to promulgate his teachings and academic chairs would be endowed for the interpretation of *Zarathustra.* And in his guise as the Antichrist the coming millenia would belong to him just as the foregoing ones belonged to Christ. However, he notes that "it would contradict my character entirely if I expected ears and hands for my truths today: that one doesn't hear me . . . is not only understandable, it even seems right to me" (259). Nietzsche explains this attitude with his own theory of silence.

> For what one lacks access to from experience one will have no ear. Now let us imagine an extreme case: that a book speaks of nothing but events that lie altogether beyond the possibility of . . . even rare experiences—that it is the first language for a new series of experiences. In that case, simply nothing will be heard, but there will be the acoustic illusion that where nothing is heard, nothing is there. This is, in the end . . . the originality of my experience. [261]

This Nietzschean silence is obviously very different from Kierkegaard's, for it disavows the author's influence over the reader altogether. It is nonetheless a judgment upon both his works and his readers. As far as his works are concerned, their incomprehensibility testified to the fact that he had had unheard of experiences and created a language for them as well.

As for his readers, he remarks with evident delight in *Ecce Homo* upon the "*innocence* of people who [have] said No to my writings. Only this past summer, at a time when I may have upset the balance of the whole rest of literature with my weighty, too weighty, literature, a professor from the University of Berlin suggested very amiably that I ought to try another form: nobody read such things." Reviewers fascinated him by demonstrating rather than elucidating his discourse: one "treated my Zarathustra, for example, as an advanced exercise in style, and expressed the wish that later on I might provide some content as well" (260). Nietzsche recounts such incidents ironically, but without bitterness. The complete failure of his contemporaries to grasp the significance of his attack upon truth itself reassured him. It confirmed his suspicions about his mission as well as about his contemporary readers, illustrating that "disproportion between the greatness of my task and the smallness of my contemporaries." His works had indeed fallen upon deaf ears, fallen, that is, into silence. And these public incidents of naive incomprehension showed him both how radical was his attack upon truth and how wedded were his contemporaries to their truth. What is more, the general incomprehension gave him a reason and an opportunity to explain himself (in silence) once again. This is the task of *Ecce Homo*.

What elicited *Ecce Homo* was not a dialectical tension between silence and misunderstanding in earlier works, as was the case with *The Point of View*, but the silence itself. Nietzsche's declaration of "*who I am*" has other motives, therefore, than to end (*aufheben*) a dialectically fragmented authorship. Nietzsche was not concerned to locate the fragments in a larger whole. It should come as no surprise then that his reading of his earlier works has none of the dialectical tautness of *The Point of View*. It is as loose as the rest of his authorship, a work of silence commenting in kind upon the silences of his earlier works. It is the most silent of Nietzsche's books, and therefore also the most forthright. It is a triumph that he earned the right to celebrate by having created a discourse of silence in his earlier works: the right to be even more silent henceforth.

Ecce Homo is more outrageous and incomprehensible than any of Nietzsche's earlier books. It remains difficult to hear even for those who have conceived a great enthusiasm for one or another of Nietzsche's ideas or other books. The arrogance of the chapter titles indicates the new source of silence: "Why I am so Wise," "Why I am so Clever," "Why I write such good Books," and "Why I am a destiny." The intensity of self-congratulation makes this book almost impossible to tolerate and creates a new species of silence akin to the obscene. In his earlier books Nietzsche at least had the good taste to attack truth from a variety of abstract and presumably objective points of view, or to ascribe his wisdom to the fictive voice of Zarathustra. But all along he substituted for truth the assertion that meaning is the subjective imposition of the (strong) individual. Now for the first time he illustrates this in *Ecce Homo*. The new vision substituted for truth is *Nietzsche's* interpretation. And anyone who breaks his silence and understands Nietzsche's project will have accepted Nietzsche's personal vision. In *Ecce Homo* Nietzsche flaunts his own role in the transvaluation of all values.

Nietzsche reviews his authorship in much greater detail in *Ecce Homo* than Kierkegaard does in *The Point of View*, but he makes no effort to show that his works are all of a piece. He does not speak of his "authorship." He makes no claim to have known what he was doing from the start. In reviewing his books title by title, Nietzsche leaves them in the same random order in which he wrote them. With two caesuras he merely arranges his books into three loose categories (that could of course be compared to Kierkegaard's categories). First come the books written before he realized what his mission was: *The Birth of Tragedy*, the *Untimely Meditations*, and, somewhat ambiguously, *Human all too Human*. The rest of his authorship—all in what might be understood as direct discourse—is divided into the "Yes-saying" and the "No-saying" books. The former include *Dawn*, *The Gay Science*, and *Thus Spake Zarathustra*; the latter include *Beyond Good and Evil*, *The Genealogy of Morals*, *The Twilight of the Idols*, and so on. Only the relationship between the Yes-saying and the No-saying works is assigned strategic importance and no explanation is given of why the No-saying books did not precede the Yes-saying, as might seem more logical. And the distinction itself is arbitrary. There is no tidying up in *Ecce Homo*, and what tidying up there is does little to clarify. What clarification there is is clarification by more audacious formulation.

Nietzsche apologizes for the minimal popularity of his early writings. He acknowledges that he himself had been deaf to the silence he had begun to create in them. So instead of taking credit for the notoriety he had achieved with *The Birth of Tragedy*, he notes that "its effect and fascination were due to what was wrong with it—

its practical application to Wagnerism. . . . In this respect, this essay was an event in the life of Wagner [rather than an event in Nietzsche's own autobiographical life]. . . . what people had ears for was only a new formula for the art, the intentions, the task of *Wagner*—and what was really valuable in the essay was ignored" (270). He takes credit for the incomprehension of his contemporaries, even here where he himself did not yet comprehend his larger mission. Nietzsche finds *The Birth of Tragedy* valuable when reading it in *Ecce Homo* nonetheless. It is the book that first gave him "the right to understand [himself] as the first *tragic philosopher*" (273), by which he means the first philosopher to negate being and affirm becoming. This much of his project was already embedded in *The Birth of Tragedy*, and it is the decisive component of the whole. But he was no more aware of the importance of his project or his own role in it than were his readers. Similarly, in his readings of his untimely essays on Schopenhauer and Wagner: he admits that the two essays do not depict their subjects; instead they unconsciously characterized himself—"Schopenhauer and Wagner, or in one word, Nietzsche." Unlike Kierkegaard, who was so concerned to read back a consciously calculated strategy into his early writings. He had not known what he was doing, but he had been doing it anyway. His works were as silent to him as they were to his readers, but consistent with his notion of *amor fati* he affirms them nonetheless.

The other caesura in Nietzsche's career as an author as he reads it in *Ecce Homo* comes after the completion of *Thus Spake Zarathustra:* "The task for the years that followed was now indicated as clearly as possible. After the Yes-saying part of my task had been solved, the turn had come for the No-saying, *No-doing* part: the revaluation of our values so far, the great war—conjuring up a day of decision" (310). On this reading, *Zarathustra* is the culmination of the Yes-saying or myth making portion of Nietzsche's authorship, and he reads it more extensively than any of his other books. He elaborates at length upon the theme of *amor fati* and notes that this is "the concept of Dionysus once again." But I prefer to call attention to a less well known dimension of Nietzsche's reading of Zarathustra:

> Zarathustra once defines, quite strictly, his task—it is mine too—
> and there is no mistaking his meaning: he says Yes to the point of
> justifying, of redeeming even all of the past. "I walk among men as
> among the fragments of the future—that future which I envisage.

And this is all my creating and striving, that I create and carry to-gether into One what is fragment and riddle and dreadful accident. And how could I bear to be a man if man were not also a creator and guesser of riddles and redeemer of accidents." [308]

With these words of Zarathustra, Nietzsche illuminates not only his concept of personal life as *amor fati*, but his authorship as well. His writings are fragments, riddles, and dreadful accidents redeemed by his Dionysian mission of raising the chaos of life from falsehood to the status of opportunity. The opportunity, of course, is to impose his own meaning upon the chaos—the chaos of his writings as well as the chaos of life.

The Dionysian vision is trained upon the author's own works. The fragments, riddles, etc., are Nietzsche's books, all fragmentary beginnings at a task that he has only gradually discovered and under-stood himself. *Zarathustra* exemplifies this. Nietzsche reads *Zarathustra* as involuntary writing, written at incredible speed and without forethought. Writing *Zarathustra* he was inspired, and, as he says, if one had the least residue of superstition one would call his experience "*revelation*." In this state, "one hears, one does not seek; one accepts, one does not ask who gives; like lightning, a thought flashes up, with necessity, without hesitation regarding its form—I never had any choice" (300-01). His authority is unconscious here too, but it is a different unconsciousness than what shrouded his early books in misunderstanding. There it was a dull unconscious-ness that overlay the deep but silent, i.e. incomprehensible, agenda with a superficial but distractingly readable Wagnerian agenda. In *Zarathustra* the unconsciousness is a state of writing that permits the new myths to emerge more fully than any conscious mind could manage or permit. Nietzsche does not of course ascribe this inspira-tion to any external source; it is the internal force of the self he is becoming that writes the book. This force is not the personal (Freudi-an) unconscious of course, but the unconscious as such.

After the completion of *Zarathustra*, according to Nietzsche in *Ecce Homo*, he lapsed into writing No-saying books. Unlike the im-perious Yes-saying books, these entailed a "slow search for those related to me, those who, prompted by strength, would offer me their hands for destroying. From this moment forward [from *The Geneal-ogy of Morals*, the first book after *Zarathustra*] all my writings are fish hooks: perhaps I know how to fish as well as anyone?—If nothing

was caught, I am not to blame. *There were no fish"* (310). Thus
Nietzsche turns to breaking up idols in order to prepare the path for
his own already formulated myths, *viz.* Zarathustra, *amor fati,* Eternal Recurrence, the Will to Power, etc. Naturally he writes polemi-
cally—in a style quite contrary to Zarathustra's mock biblical poetry—and polemic involves compromises with the reader. Nonetheless, there is silence here too, the silence of the fish hook. Nietzsche
attacks in full awareness of what he wants to destroy now, and there
is no longer the overlay of a more palatable agenda. He writes deliberately, even methodically in *The Genealogy of Morals* and *Beyond
Good and Evil.* So we now can speak easily of Nietzsche's "genealogical method." Partly for this reason, it seems, these books are the
most readable at present (excluding the early works like *The Birth of
Tragedy,* that are readable in a different sense). His polemics retain an
aspect of silence nonetheless. They do not search out the reader.
They lie waiting for the reader in deep water. And if no readers present themselves for the time being, Nietzsche's self-assurance as a
fisherman is undaunted. These are hooks upon which we can be
caught more than once.

This schematic division of Nietzsche's writings previous to *Ecce
Homo* makes his authorship seem more orderly than it actually appears in that final book. The earlier books appear there as fragments,
riddles, and so on. And what characterizes *Ecce Homo* is not these
two caesuras that I let stand for the plethora of breaks in his readings
of the earlier works. *Ecce Homo* has its own characteristic fissure:
two movements of interpretation—different styles of silence—that
cut across each other and produce the chiasma/paradox of his insisting that his discourse of silence be heard. Nietzsche affirms his earlier writings in all their silence while he cries out to be acknowledged
as the new Dionysos.

Ecce Homo is a performative declamation of the impossibility of
Dionysian truth. Not imposing a system of authorship upon his writings in *Ecce Homo,* Nietzsche treats them as Zarathustra treats the
past generally: he says yes to the point of justifying all his past writings. This is an effort of will that strives to supplant the truth with its
own meaning, creating an autobiographical life of riddles and accidents. It is Nietzsche's textual *amor fati,* saying yes to his writings,
just as he wrote them, without reordering or rewriting them. This is
the modest achievement of *Ecce Homo.* This style of silence makes

Ecce Homo a work of great restraint,[5] perhaps surprisingly, for it is more obvious that the book immodestly proclaims its author's power. Nietzsche's restraint is undercut by the other source of silence in *Ecce Homo:* the apparently megalomaniacal tendency of Nietzsche to equate himself with the god Dionysos and oppose himself to Christ. It is an extraordinary Wagnerian effort of will to impose *himself* upon the world. This (strident) agenda of *Ecce Homo* deafens the reader to the former silence of restraint. It is nonetheless another style of silence. Even faithful Nietzscheans find it an embarrassment. In his self-congratulation he seems to have gone too far. Thus the two styles/impulses of silence in *Ecce Homo* deconstruct each other, making it Nietzsche's most silent book.

In *Ecce Homo* Nietzsche prevents closure on a new truth. The silence or incomprehensibility of his books is based not merely upon their impossible contents—the assertion that truth is not—but upon their status as impulses and ultimately contradictory ones. Nietzsche's silence grows deeper in *Ecce Homo,* and yet he cries out "Hear me!" His silence is a provocation. He defies the reader to understand him, i.e., to find truth in his texts. And whenever one does, whenever the silence is broken, new avenues of discourse open up, new fictions become possible, and truth and reality recede yet again and farther.

As Nietzsche's silence deepens and he cries out "Hear me!" he seems to disappear as an author altogether behind the mutually deconstructing silences of *Ecce Homo.* This book is self-sufficient in the sense of auto-deconstructing, the ultimate reproach to the ideology of the genius.[6]

Nietzsche's silence, in his authorship as a whole as in *Ecce Homo,* is not silence in the strict sense. In one dimension it is simply the general incomprehension with which his works were received by his contemporaries. The parameters of such silence are just as Nietzsche described them: a new language for new experiences. But

5. In such a text, in such a situation of writing, it is an almost irresistible temptation for an author to indicate what his particular works mean, or what he wants them to have meant, and to ascribe a consciously intended meaning to the authorship as a whole, as we have seen Kierkegaard do. Nietzsche resisted.

6. Since completing this essay I have read Michael Ryan's excellent article on Nietzsche's *Ecce Homo:* "The Act," *Glyph* 2(1977), pp. 64–87. I am pleased to find myself in basic agreement with his more extended reading of this text.

Nietzsche's silence has been broken repeatedly, to the point where Nietzsche's books are now perhaps the most provocative master texts we have. Of course it is an increment of experience and a different blindness (not greater insight) that distinguishes our generation from Nietzsche's contemporaries. Thus the importance Nietzsche's texts have assumed for us is dialectically related to their silence after all. Indeed, I propose that dialectical silence of this type is precisely what distinguishes not only the works of Nietzsche, but a few other unusually fertile texts as well, from the works of even the greatest founders of scientific disciplines, systematic philosophers, initiators of literary genres, etc., including Kierkegaard's. The Nietzschean style of silence is what permits us to return to these few master texts in every generation and find ourselves provoked in totally unanticipated ways—when we manage to break it, of course. It is through their silence and the possibility of our breaking it that they renew themselves and open up whole new areas of discourse. Nietzsche never broke his silence, as Kierkegaard did, hoping ultimately to reveal the meaning of his texts himself. He kept his silence. So the dialectic is not within the authorship, as in Kierkegaard's case, but without it. We readers are left to break the silences of his authorship from our ever changing vantages. We can break them only momentarily and partially, however, never permanently or fully. Breaking these silences yields a peculiar form of knowledge or insight that cannot sustain itself, but has to be learned again and again. And the silence remains to be broken countless times again.

At the conclusion of his essay "What is an Author?" Michael Foucault writes of certain "initiators of discursive practices," and ascribes to their texts a peculiar potency that permits us to return to them and find wholly new discursive impulses.[7] (He takes Marx and Freud as his examples.) An enduring fertility distinguishes these texts from those of typical geniuses in the arts and sciences, inasmuch as we usually return to the works of founders of scientific disciplines and their like with essentially historic interests in the origins of a particular type of discourse: we want to see, for example, how Adam Smith launched modern economics. But we return to the works of the founders of discursive practices to find altogether new

7. Michel Foucault, "What is an Author?" in *Language, Counter-Memory, and Practice* (Ithaca: Cornell University Press, 1977), pp. 113–38, but especially pp. 131–36.

questions and to open whole new fields of inquiry. Foucault suggests that there is a qualitative difference between our rereadings, and the texts to which we return in the two types of cases. The distinction is of course overdrawn, both because we *do* return to the founders of scientific disciplines and literary conventions at times in the same way in which we return to Marx and Freud, and because the texts that seem to mark the inceptions of discursive practices are different at different times. Thus when we seek to determine what it is that distinguishes those texts that seem to mark the inception of discursive practices we must seek characteristics that a) are present in varying degree, rather than merely absent or present as seems to be implied in Foucault's essay, and b) seem to be more or less present depending upon the point in time, the generation, for example, from which they are being viewed or read. In conformity with these two criteria I suggest that what distinguishes Marx and Freud for us from even the greatest of their nineteenth-century rivals is something that Nietzsche distilled in even greater degree in his texts, namely their silence. The Nietzschean silence described in *Ecce Homo* explains to a remarkable degree why it is possible for us to return to the texts of these three authors so frequently and still discover wholly uncharted discursive territory.

One trait that unites the first chapter of *Capital*, for example, with Nietzsche's texts is its tenacity as a *beginning* of a discursive practice that would be impossible either to complete or to make systematic. (There is a certain aspiration to the status of system in the works of Marx and Freud, of course, but their texts occasionally belie this aspiration and entail a refusal of the system.) This is approximately what Foucault means by his concept of the "constructive omission," when he tries to categorize how Marx and Freud "cleared a space for the introduction of elements other than their own." But the unrealized discursive potential of the texts of Marx and Freud are much sparser than those of Nietzsche's. It is therefore curious that in "What is an Author?" Foucault should have excluded Nietzsche from his usual series—Marx, Nietzsche, Freud. The reason that he does exclude Nietzsche, I speculate, is that Nietzsche's texts not only refuse systematization, but are broken down into the greatest possible number of the smallest possible points of departure so that they are virtually immune to institutionalization. For as we know, there are no analogues of orthodox institutes of psychoanalysis or authoritarian governments grounded upon the texts of Nietzsche. We cannot even speak of Nietzsche-ism. Nietzsche's silence seems to guarantee that no such institutions can grow up upon his texts. From one perspective this might seem a debility of Nietzsche's discourse. But Marxist governments and institutes of psychoanalysis are not testimonies to the fertility of the ideas of Marx and Freud; they are testimonies to the degree to which Marxist and Freudian discourse can be frozen and turned to repressive purposes. Such institutionalization is precisely what inhibits the particular sort of return to these master texts that Foucault values so highly. Of course we have seen that Nietzsche was not immune to the fantasy that institutions would indeed grow up around his texts. But this is an easily deconstructed fissure in *Ecce Homo*. Just as the tenacity with which the discourses initiated by Marx and Freud insist upon repeatedly beginning again frustrates their authors's aspirations to system, Nietzsche's texts are preserved from institutionalization by their overwhelming silence. This silence, as we have seen, grew out of Nietzsche's repeated assaults upon truth itself and upon the postulate of reality. Each attack is a new beginning and a steadfast refusal of completion. Nietzsche did initiate a discourse, therefore, but it is the closest thing we have to a discourse of silence. And this silence, present in certain texts of Marx, Freud, and others (perhaps to *some* degree in *all* texts), is what permits us to return to them in the way Foucault quite accurately describes our doing.

This reading of Nietzsche's silence extends Foucault's critique of the category of the author into the crucial subcategory of the genius. For when Foucault writes that "the subject must be stripped of its creative role and analyzed as a complex and variable function of discourse," he outlines a program that can only be carried out on the territory of the genius. Yet in his essay he is obliged to call precisely upon the authority of two particular creative geniuses—Marx and Freud—to underwrite his general critique of the creative subject/author/genius. In my terms, he has to cite the authority of two (sentimental) geniuses distinguished by their moments of silence in order to call into question the authority of typical or naive geniuses. This is of course no reproach to Foucault, but an explanation of why it must be so. We can see this more clearly in the case of Nietzsche: those who break his silences are forced to reconstitute him as an author/genius at precisely those moments when they recognize how he has effectively deconstructed the genius by establishing the disintegrating authority of silence. My own essay is a performance of this.

The auto-interpretive strategy of both Nietzsche and Kierkegaard was an obvious one: to write one additional text in which the author usurps the role of the reader. This gesture was nothing more than a further radicalization of the role of the genius. For unlike the typical genius, who remained tied to the reader only through his function of illuminating the world, Nietzsche and Kierkegaard liberated themselves from the last vestige of dependence upon the reader with this act. They said—differently of course—that they did not need to enlighten the world in order to have been geniuses. They were textually as well as sexually self-sufficient. As obvious as this step may seem now, it was a radical innovation; it was an act of originality. Radical and original, it challenged the ideology of radical originality.

In their self-sufficient texts—*The Point of View* and *Ecce Homo*—each author gives a reading of his earlier writings, one by one. In so doing, however, he naturally raises more questions in the minds of other/subsequent readers than he answers or allays. These new questions give rise to further interpretations. Thus these texts are literally counterproductive of that single interpretation of their author's works to which they are apparently dedicated. They provide not merely one additional reading or interpretation of their authors's works, but call into question and fructify every other interpretation, provoking whole new generations of hybrid interpretations that would never have arisen without the additional seeds of these auto-interpretive texts. They demonstrate in the most literal and performative way the futility of that strife for a single right interpretation of a text in the terms of the author's supposed intentions. For here the author's intentions are redoubled and immediately riven. Yet when we realize that these texts are not the solutions to anyone's doubts about how to interpret the authors's earlier writings, we are left with the question: why *did* they write these books?

In usurping the role of the reader in their autobiographical texts, Kierkegaard and Nietzsche were acting out a fantasy that Nietzsche had recorded in an adolescent sketch of an autobiography: "to write a book and read it myself." Nietzsche expresses this remarkably innocent narcissistic fantasy again in an epigram that he placed at the front of *Ecce Homo* thirty years later. Reviewing the literary production of his forty-fourth year he asks himself, "how could I fail to be thankful to my whole life? — and so I tell my life to myself." Telling their lives to themselves and reading their books to themselves was an enduring fantasy that promised some deep satisfaction to Nietzsche and, I conjecture, to Kierkegaard as well. Once we have undermined the impression of apparently compulsive attempts to forestall the importunate advances of readers and their vulgar interpretations, this particular textual pleasure looms. An analysis of the naive genius's relationship to the reader would equally well deconstruct the textual self-sufficiency of *Ecce Homo* and *The Point of View.*[8] But the beauty of these texts is that they can do it themselves. This is the onanistic pleasure of the self-sufficient text.

8. Rousseau is obviously not the naive genius that I constructed above. Cf. Jacques Derrida, *De la Grammatologie* (Paris: Minuit, 1967), pp. 145ff; and Paul de Man, "The Rhetoric of Blindness," in *Blindness and Insight* (New York: Oxford University Press, 1971), pp. 102–41, and all of the essays on Rousseau in *Allegories of Reading* (New Haven: Yale University Press, 1979) but especially the one entitled "Excuses," pp. 278–301.

LAWRENCE D. KRITZMAN

Barthesian Free Play

J'aurais souhaité que la sémiologie ne prît ici la place d'aucune
autre recherche, mais au contraire les aidât toutes, qu'elle eût pour
siège une sorte de chaire mobile, joker du savoir d'aujourd'hui,
comme le signe lui-même l'est de tout discours.

La Leçon

The goal of the Barthesian quest is to challenge the privilege of a
transcendent or systematic model of conceptual thought.[1] Barthes'
writing therefore liberates itself from an entropic rhetoric that would
engender the critic's sense of omniscience and authority. The anxiety
that comes to dominate Barthes' later work emanates from the fear of
institutionalization, a phenomenon that would preempt the possibility of futurity and thus threaten the writer's ongoing libidinal
energy. Adjectivization, the totalizing self-definition, prefigures
death and as such threatens an opening-out toward the otherness of
the original work of art.

> Il supporte mal toute *image* de lui-même, souffre d'être nommé. Il
> considère que la perfection d'un rapport humain tient à cette va-
> cance de l'image . . . un rapport qui s'adjective est du côté de l'ima-
> ge, du côté de la domination, de la mort. [*RB*, p. 47][2]

1. "It is my hope that semiology will replace no other inquiry here, but will, on
the contrary help all the rest, that its chair will be a kind of wheelchair, the wild card of
contemporary knowledge, as the sign itself is the wild card of all discourse." "Inaugural Lecture, College de France," *A Barthes Reader*, ed. Susan Sontag (New York: Hill
and Wang, 1982), p. 474.

I quote from the following texts: *Mythologies* (Paris: Seuil, 1970; Collection
Points, 1970) (*M*); *Sur Racine* (Paris: Seuil, 1963) (*SR*); *Essais critiques* (Paris: Seuil,
1964) (*EC*); *Critique et vérité* (Paris: Seuil, 1966) (*CV*); *L'Empire des signes* (Genève:
Skira, 1970) (*Ep.S.*); *S/Z* (Paris: Seuil, 1970) (*S/Z*); *Le Plaisir du texte* (Paris: Seuil, 1973)
(*PT*); *Roland Barthes par Roland Barthes* (Paris: Seuil, 1975) (*RB*); *Fragments d'un
discours amoureux* (Paris: Seuil, 1977) (*FDA*); *La Leçon* (Paris: Seuil, 1978) (*L*); *La
Chambre claire* (Paris: Cahiers du cinéma Gallimard-Seuil, 1980) (*CC*); *Le Grain de la
voix* (Paris: Seuil, 1981) (*GV*).

2. "He is troubled by any *image* of himself, suffers when he is named. He finds
the perfection of a human relationship in this vacancy of the image . . . a relationship
which adjectivizes is on the side of the image, on the side of domination, of death."
Roland Barthes by Roland Barthes, trans. Richard Howard (New York: Hill and Wang,
1977), p. 43.

189

What Barthes actually creates is an anxiety that precedes all real threats, the fear of being trapped within a description or a classification. In self-defense, he conceptualizes an idealized theory of writing as an activity which refuses all settled doctrines and is consequently open-ended.

> *Fiché*: je suis fiché, assigné à un lieu (intellectuel), à une résidence de caste (sinon de classe). Contre quoi une seule doctrine intérieure: celle de l'*atopie* (de l'habitacle en dérive). L'atopie est supérieure à l'utopie (l'utopie est réactive, tactique, littéraire; elle procède du sens et le fait marcher). [*RB*, p. 53][3]

The essential problem may be defined as the tension established between authority, stability and origin and an avant-garde in a perpetual state of reconstruction through the desedimentation of the discursive constraints that menace it. In terms of the Barthesian idiolect, *atopia* is conceived of as an ideality, a dynamic textual enterprise whose kinetic energy prevents it from being transformed into a relic or monument of thought. Instead of establishing the authority of instruction, the Barthesian critical essay becomes a new form of experimental literature that destabilizes accepted meanings and subverts the power inherent in traditional categories:

> Le Texte . . . est apparu comme l'index même du *dépouvoir*. Le Texte contient en lui la force de fuir infiniment la parole grégaire . . . il repousse ailleurs, vers un lieu inclassé, atopique . . . loin des *topoi* de la culture. [*L*, p. 34][4]

In *Roland Barthes par Roland Barthes* the *topos* of the absent father makes explicit the inadequacy which ultimately generates his creative energy: ". . . pas de père à tuer, pas de famille à haïr, pas de milieu à réprouver: grande frustration oedipéenne!" (*RB*, p. 49).[5] But to obviate this lack, Barthes inscribes the critic in a history in which the bastard son invents an Oedipal struggle, a conflictual tangle, with the canon and the cultural *doxa* that are transcribed metaphorically

---

3. "Pigeonholed: I am pigeonholed, assigned to an (intellectual) site, to residence in a caste (if not in a class). Against which there is only one internal doctrine: that of *atopia* (of a drifting habitation). Atopia is superior to utopia (utopia is reactive, tactical, literary, it proceeds from meaning and governs it). *RB*, Howard, p. 49.

4. The Text . . . appeared as the very index of *nonpower*. The Text contains in itself the strength to elude gregarious speech . . . it procrastinates elsewhere, towards an unclassified, atopic site . . . far from the topoi of politicized culture." "Inaugural Lecture," Sontag, p. 472.

5. ". . . no father to kill, no family to hate, no milieu to reject: great Oedipal frustration!" *RB*, Howard, p. 45.

as figures of the father. The effort of an Imaginary order to reshape a personal relationship reveals itself through the writer's refusal to accept the various fictions of authority that the dominant ideology maintains. Barthes cultivates a critical rhetoric which glorifies originality, negatively by its apparent break with the past, and positively by its willingness to leave the future of the modern undefined.

The Barthesian refusal of oedipalization seeks to free critical discourse from its dependence on an authoritarian voice whereby the critic would become the guarantor of the values of society: ". . . il lâche le mot, la proposition, l'idée, dès qu'ils *prennent* et passent à l'état de solide, de *stéreotype* (*stéréos* veut dire *solide*) (*RB*, p. 63).[6] Thus, the only valid critical authority is one which denies its origins and the institutionalization of inheritance as Law. Barthes' forfeit of continuity with the past disengages his critical praxis from the symbolic adaptation of the discourse of the Other. As a writer he will never have a true sense of identity since the absence of the father will prevent the son from being able to guarantee the authenticity of his origin and therefore bequeath the law; the absent father affords Barthes the space in which he explores a self in opposition to the powerful Other. The abandonment of paternal law fetters Barthes' proper symbolic identification with the *potestas patris* and the subsequent integration into the social and symbolic order. The idealized portrait of the Socratic mentor that Barthes projects in *La Leçon* associates the binding energy of creativity and the swerve away from "death" with the desire to know; the prefiguration of death must be equated with the benumbing force of authority and institutionalization which is indeed the place of the father. "Il [le professeur] dévie de la place où l'on attend, qui est la place du Père, toujours mort, comme on le sait; car seul le fils a des fantasmes, seul le fils est vivant" (*L*, p. 44).[7] The incorrigible son opts for the transcription of the Imaginary into critical fictions, a rhetoric enabling a desacralization of a unifiable and didactic transmission of culture.[8]

6. ". . . we abandon the word, the proposition, the idea, once they *set* and assume the solid state, *stereotyped* (in Greek, *stereos* means *solid*). Ibid, p. 58.

7. "He [the professor] thereby turns from the place where he is expected, the place of the Father, who is always dead, as we know. For only the son has fantasies; only the son is alive." "Inaugural Lecture," Sontag, p. 477.

8. "The Imaginary, therapeutic discourse of the teacher as analysand is directed explicitly against the "name-of-the-Father" (the law) that is inherent in the Symbolic order of language." Gregory L. Ulmer, "The Discourse of the Imaginary," *Diacritics* (Spring 1980), 65.

At the heart of Barthes' epistemological critique may be found a pedagogical imperative which emphasizes the movement away from a scholarly mode of discourse responsible for the interpretation and elucidation of texts. The rejection of scholarly lucidity, in favor of the apparently more a-topical seminar space of free play, motivates Barthes to formulate a theory obtrusively critical of what he terms *le discours du maître*. He decenters the tyrannical spatial hierarchy in which we traditionally see the brutal side of guardianship and the debilitating effects of dependency; there is no privileged standpoint as guarantee of certainty.

> Il faudrait, substituer à l'espace magistral d'autrefois, qui était en somme un espace religieux . . . un espace moins droit, moins euclidien, où personne, ni le professeur ni les étudiants, ne serait jamais à *sa dernière place.* . . . Dans l'espace enseignant, chacun ne devrait être à sa place nulle part.[9]

Barthes does not conceive of pedagogy as a foundationalist enterprise which establishes what is objectively certain. The idealized pedagogical topography that he seeks to create is predicated not only on the avoidance of domination, but also on the adherence to a paradoxical epistemological imperative designed to destabilize sedimented knowledge.

> En somme, dans les limites mêmes de l'espace enseignant, tel qu'il est donné, il s'agirait de travailler à tracer patiemment une forme pure, celle du *flottement* . . . il se contenterait de désorienter la loi: les nécessités de la promotion, les obligations du métier . . . les impératifs du savoir, le prestige de la méthode, la critique idéologique, tout est là, *mais qui flotte.*[10]

The progressive subversion of authority inaugurates a critical activity where no "real" father can be identified and which functions through the process of unlearning. The seminar space can be defined

9. Roland Barthes, "Ecrivains, intellectuels, professeurs," *Tel Quel,* 47 (1971), 12. "We need to substitute for the magisterial space of the past—which was fundamentally a religious space . . . a less upright, less Euclidean space where no one, neither teacher nor students, would ever be *in his final place.* . . . In the teaching space nobody should anywhere be in his place." "Writers, Intellectuals, Teachers," Sontag, pp. 393–94.

10. Ibid., 18. "In short, within the very limits of the teaching space as given, the need is to work at patiently tracing out a pure form, that of a *floating* . . . which would be content simply to disorientate the Law. The necessities of promotion, professional obligations . . . imperatives of knowledge, prestige of method, ideological criticism—everything is there, but *floating.*" Ibid., pp. 402–03.

as a *locus* where freedom of invention forbids the debilitating assignment of a signified to a signifier. The learning process, for Barthes, produces new perceptual abstractions, equivocal and always inviting the participant to prevent language from "sticking." Clearly, the unanchored motion that Barthes terms *flottement* implies the recognition by the writer of the importance of the process of creation itself: the Imaginary is no longer repressed or dissimulated at the expense of authority, but allowed to develop freely and like the act of writing to become a critical fiction. "L'espace du séminaire est phalanstérien, c'est-à-dire, en un sens romanesque" (*RB*, p. 173).[11]

Against the oppressiveness of language whose ultimate task is to define knowledge, Barthes advances the notion of *Le Neutre* which defies the establishment of taxonomies and ascribes to the notion that productivity of meaning is dependent on its manipulator more as a playful intellectual than as a scientist.

> *Le Neutre*, catégorie éthique qui vous est nécessaire pour lever la marque intolérable du sens affiché, du sens oppressif. Et le sens lui-même, lorsque vous le regardez fonctionner, c'est avec l'amusement presque puéril d'un acheteur qui ne se fatigue pas de faire jouer le déclic d'un gadget. [*RB*, p. 128][12]

It is the decision to revoke the legality of language—the reductionist representation of reality limiting the plurality of meaning—that affords the playful subject the *jouissance* derived from the emptying-out of preexistent conceptual molds. To represent the integrity of meaning in language is to respect the laws of the binary system and unquestionably deny the lack which constitutes desire. Playfulness therefore exploits the independence of language from its bonds of reference to engender polymorphous forms. "Ne jamais assez dire la force de *suspension* de plaisir: c'est une véritable *épaché, un arrêt qui fige au loin toutes les valeurs admises. . . . Le plaisir est un neutre (PT*, p. 102).[13] The suspension of meaning activates the euphoria

11. "The space of the seminar is phalansteric, i.e., in a sense fictive, novelistic." *RB*, Howard, p. 171.

12. "*The Neutral*, an ethical category which is necessary to you in order to erase the intolerable scar of the paraded meaning, of the oppressive meaning. And meaning itself—when you watch it functioning, you do so with the almost puerile amusement of a buyer who never tires of pulling the switch of some gadget." Ibid., p. 124.

13. Roland Barthes, *The Pleasure of the Text*, trans. Richard Miller (New York: Hill and Wang, 1975). "Pleasure's form of *suspension* can never be overstated: it is a veritable *épaché*, a stoppage which congeals all recognized values. . . . Pleasure is a *neuter . . .*" p. 65.

derived from an eroticized language whose multiple transfers and leaps fetters the plenitude associated with orgasmic pleasure. "Chez lui, le désir du mot l'emporte, mais de ce plaisir fait partie une sorte de vibration doctrinale" (*RB*, p. 78).[14] Barthes evokes the transport of being caught up in a signifying system whose deferred action liberates language from the numbing lubricity of parasitism. Clearly, the drive towards quiescence—the plague of meaning which invests objects—provokes anxiety and as such threatens the kinetic energy of Eros.

> Dès lors que l'alternative est refusée (dès lors que le paradigme est brouillé), l'utopie commence: le sens et le sexe deviennent l'objet d'un jeu libre, au sein duquel les formes (polysémiques) et les pratiques (sensuelles), libérées de la prison binaire, vont se mettre en état d'expansion infinie. Ainsi peuvent naître un texte gongorien et une sexualité heureuse. [*RB*, p. 137][15]

The castrating gesture that shifts meaning from the negative mode of the distinction of difference to the positive mode of the assertion of identity limits rebellion against conventional discourse and the process of the spending of desire.

Under Barthes' pen the creation of an eroticized discourse, radically severed from the laws of contingency, renders the text free of contextual determinants and the conditions of narrative transitivity; "textual writing" is a self-sufficient activity incapable of transcending itself. "La littérature est au fond une activité tautologique, comme celle de ces machines cybernétiques construites *pour elles-mêmes* (l'homéostat d'Ashby)" (*EC*, p. 148).[16] Just as writing must affirm meaning without specifically articulating it, Barthes adapts the sexual metaphor of prostitution in order to delineate a relationship in which the domination/submission paradigm is abandonned for a gratuitously "playful" sexuality suspended somewhere between the satiety of pleasure and the complete absence thereof. The ideal to

14. "In him the desire for the word prevails, but this pleasure is partly constituted by a kind of doctrinal vibration." *RB*, Howard, p. 74.

15. "Nevertheless, once the alternative is rejected (once the paradigm is blurred) utopia begins: meaning and sex become the object of a free play, at the heart of which the (polysemant) forms and the (sensual) practices, liberated from the binary prison, will achieve a state of infinite expansion. Thus may be born a Gongorian text and a happy sexuality." Ibid., p. 133.

16. "Literature is at bottom a tautological activity, like that of those cybernetic machines constructed *for themselves* (Ashby's homeostat)." "Authors and Writers," Sontag, p. 187.

which Barthes subscribes is to escape from the contingency of a priori roles so that the demythologized love relationship would portray a fiction without names, a game in which no one player would have a hold over another.

> Le modèle du bon contrat, c'est le contrat de Prostitution. Car ce contrat . . . libère en fait ce qu'on pourrait appeler les *embarras imaginaires* de l'échange . . . le contrat supprime ce vestige; il est en somme la seule position que le sujet puisse tenir sans tomber dans deux images inverses mais également abhorrées: celle de l'"égoïste" (qui demande sans s'inquiéter d'avoir rien à donner) et celle du "saint" (qui donne en s'interdisant de jamais rien demander): Le discours du contrat élude deux plénitudes; il permet, d'observer la règle d'or de toute *habitation,* déchiffrée dans le corridor de Shikdai: *"Aucun vouloir-saisir et cependant aucune oblation."* [RB, p. 64][17]

Prostitution, like writing, provokes a special form of gratification through gratuitous play. It is a contract that keeps desire alive, an intransitive relationship which may be regarded as symptomatic of a signifying process publicizing its categorical disembodiment from the limits of interpretation and the problems of classification. The desiring subject takes on a position with a vacant slot, a grammatical category no longer in compliance with the pitfalls of meaning; play therefore prevents the coagulation of significance and thus lures us towards the free circulation of disengagement.

CRITICAL PLAY

As early as the 1950s Barthes aimed at elucidating the process by which cultural mythologies are produced and the means by which the bourgeoisie seeks to persuade and exercise a monopoly over our modes of thought. Barthes' critique had as its objective the massive

17. "The model of the good contract is the contract of Prostitution. For this contract . . . liberates in fact from what might be called the *imaginary embarrassments* of the exchange. . . . The contract eliminates this confusion: it is in fact the only position which the subject can assume without falling into two inverse but equally abhorred images: that of the 'egoist' who demands without caring that he has nothing to give) and that of the 'saint' (who gives but forbids himself ever to demand): thus the discourse of the contract eludes two plenitudes; it permits observing the golden rule of any *habitation,* discerned in the Shikidai passageway: *no will-to-seize and yet no oblation."* RB., p. 59.

effort to define cultural stereotypes and to demystify the petrified dogma of bourgeois fables. In short, mythology is the force identified with the totalization of knowledge and the massive effort to control culture through the legislation of rhetoric. Barthes decodes the mythical material so that he may uncover the science of false discourse and introduce a diacritical process which would set formalized bourgeois ideology off-center.

From the beginning Barthes sets out to discover how signs reify the world and institutionalize power by imposing an eternal form on the ephemeral. In *Mythologies* he depicts a self-enclosed world in which the "artefacts" of bourgeois culture come under attack for projecting a nature that equates accident with essence. Barthes forces the dominant ideology into a role corresponding to that of a parental authority prescribing acceptable modes of behavior and establishing "une interdiction à l'homme s'inventer" (*M*, p. 244).[18]

Barthes' brand of sociosemiology involves ideological choices even when it proclaims itself to be "value-free." Working under the influence of the Marxist concepts of alienation and class, he adapts a radically critical stance in order to reveal the paucity of innocence in our daily routines. In an essay on toys in *Mythologies*, Barthes is severely critical of most French toys which he claims are cultural commodities for initiation into the world of bourgeois consumption; he shows the role they play in the consecration of the social order, enabling children to conform and become deprived of their creative instincts.

> Que les jouets français préfigurent *littéralement* l'univers des fonctions adultes ne peut évidemment que préparer l'enfant à les accepter toutes, en lui constituant avant même qu'il réfléchisse l'alibi d'une nature qui a crée de tout temps des soldats, des postiers, des vespas. . . . Seulement, devant cet univers d'objets fidèles et compliqués, l'enfant ne peut se constituer qu'en propriétaire, en usager, jamais en créateur; il n'invente pas le monde, il l'utilise: on lui prépare des gestes sans aventure, sans étonnement et sans joie . . . on ne lui donne jamais rien à parcourir. [*M*, p. 59][19]

18. "a prohibition for man against inventing himself." *Mythologies*, trans. Annette Lavers (New York: Hill and Wang, 1972), p. 155.
19. "The fact that French toys *literally* prefigure the world of adult functions obviously cannot but prepare the child to accept them all, by constituting for him, even before he can think about it, the alibi of a Nature which has at all times created soldiers, postmen and Vespas. . . . However, faced with this world of faithful and

Barthes puts into question the authority of the existing social order on the grounds that it is an artificial, human creation subservient to the bourgeois ideals of homogeneity and socialization. The notion of the character type conserves the essentialist myth of man and as such hermetically seals social reality.

Even though Barthes' social critique avoids the terrorism and political orthodoxy often associated with Marxist analysis, he expresses, nevertheless, a deep dissatisfaction with the solidification of culture. His article on toys proposes a countermodel, one which recognizes the importance of play and the centrality of the process of creation itself.

> Le moindre jeu de construction, pourvu qu'il ne soit pas trop raffiné, implique un apprentissage du monde bien différent: l'enfant n'y crée nullement des objets significatifs, il lui importe peu qu'ils aient un nom adulte: ce qu'il exerce, ce n'est pas un usage c'est une démiurgie: il crée une vie, non une propriété; les objets s'y conduisent eux-mêmes; ils n'y sont plus une matière inerte et compliquée dans les creux de la maison. [M, pp. 59–60].[20]

The child's ludic effort must be practiced without its father's guarantee; it must constantly be projected against a wide range of contexts, no single one of which should be regarded as the sole or appropriate one. Barthes proposes the use of a toy that would furnish the child the possibility of actively fabricating new meanings and referentially free forms. To be sure, play is a structuralist enterprise, a combinatory practice that refuses the re-production of socially sanctioned behavior and prefabricated meanings.

Consciousness of the creative act and of originality itself develops out of Barthes' awareness of structuralism, a sense of the signifying machine's multiple combinations that question the theological conception of man: ". . . l'écrivain s'emploie à multiplier les signi-

---

complicated objects, the child can only identify himself as owner, as user, never as creator; he does not invent the world, he uses it: there are, prepared for him, actions without adventure, without wonder, without joy . . . he is never allowed to discover anything from start to finish." *Mythologies*, pp. 53–54.

20. "The merest set of blocks, provided it is not too refined, implies a very different learning of the world: then the child does not in any way create meaningful objects, it matters little to him whether they have an adult name; the actions he performs are not those of a user but those of a demiurge . . . he creates life, not property: objects now act by themselves, they are no longer an inert and complicated material in the palm of his hand." *Ibid.*, p. 54.

fications sans les remplir ni les fermer et qu'il se sert du langage pour constituer un monde emphatiquement signifiant, mais finalement jamais signifié" (*EC*, p. 265).[21] Literature, as Barthes conceives it, is not a product to be apprehended by an inert consumer. Instead, he offers a new role and status to the reader which in many ways is analogous to the child's creative play. The reader participates in playing with and in re-creating the fabrication of a work which derives its meaning from the interplay of multiple codes: "l'oeuvre propose, l'homme dispose" (*CV*, p. 52). Like Lévi-Strauss' *bricoleur*, Barthes' critic elucidates the science of forms and the logic of relations which make works exists; he reforms the always already formulaic so that he may reveal how the game of literature is played out. What is at stake in his structural analysis is a method which allows the reader to comprehend through the processes of substitution and denomination; his methodological investigation allows him to localize meaning so that he may become the creating and knowing operator of a signifying system. In *Sur Racine*, for example, Barthes describes each of the individual tragedies as part of what he terms a Racinian anthropology. The system which he delineates reveals through his analytical procedures psychological structures hereto repressed by bourgeois academic criticism. Ironically enough, the generative force of Racine's tragedies may be found in the myth of the primal horde and the authoritarian relationship that is established between fathers and sons.

> Qui est cet autre dont le héros ne peut se séparer? . . . c'est le Père. Il n'y a pas de tragédie où il ne soit réellement ou virtuellement présent. . . . Dire que le Père est immortel veut dire que l'Antérieur est immobile: lorsque le Père manque . . . tout se défait; lorsqu'il revient, tout s'aliène: l'absence du Père constitue le désordre; le retour du Père institue la faute. [*SR*, p. 48][22]

Barthes engages himself in an attempt to re-write and appropriate the

---

21. "It means that the writer is concerned to multiply significations without filling or closing them, and that he uses language to constitute a world which is emphatically signifying but never freely signified. *Critical Essays*, trans. Richard Howard (Evanston: Northwestern University Press, 1972, p. 268).

22. "Who is this Other from whom the hero cannot detach himself? . . . it is the Father. There is no tragedy in which he is not actually or virtually present. . . . To say that the Father is immortal means that the Anterior is motionless: when the Father is . . . absent, everything falls apart; when he returns, everything is alienated. The Father's absence constitutes disorder; his return initiates the transgression." *On Racine*, trans. Richard Howard (New York: Octagon Books, 1977), pp. 38–39.

Racinian *gestalt* as his very own: the dilemma of the son's refusal of oedipalization. The critical performance enables Barthes to reshape the raw material of the Racinian anthropology and to fabricate a new world in which formal imitation renders the aesthetic object intelligible through the critic's own intellection.

Barthes' critical praxis, however, forbids science to become law. In principle, the *bricoleur* does more than construct a mere simulacrum of the original. In *S/Z*, more than in any other work, Barthes expresses his repugnance for a logically organized corpus and the teleological character of most structuralist methodologies. He opts, instead, for critical play in which the critic's active participation attests to the infinite transcriptibility of an aesthetic object. This is perhaps best illustrated by Barthes' exhaustive analysis of Balzac's *Sarrasine* where the critic skillfully decomposes the story in 561 fragments (*lexias*) placed within one of five codes or systems of meaning. What this process of fragmentation puts into question is the unsettling authority of a text's integrity. The violent force exercised against the "naturalness" of a text is designed to make it a work that has a rhapsodically plural character; the act of narrative subversion precludes totalization and as such fragments the space constituting the textual fabric.

> Le commentaire, fondé sur l'affirmation du pluriel, ne peut donc travailler dans le "respect" du texte: le texte tuteur sera sans cesse brisé, interrompu sans aucun égard pour ses divisions naturelles . . . le travail du commentaire . . . consiste . . . à *malmener* le texte, à lui *couper la parole*. [*S/Z* pp. 21–22].[23]

By placing particular emphasis on the reader's subversive manipulation of a text, commentary no longer reflects anything but a textual practice designed to frustrate the quest for intelligibility and the utopian moralistic dream of totalization. "Le texte . . . le système est en lui débordé, défait . . . ce qui est débordé, cassé, c'est l'*unité morale* que la société exige de tout produit humain (*PT*, pp. 49, 52).[24]

---

23. "The Commentary based on the affirmation of the plural, cannot therefore work with 'respect' to the text; the tutor text will ceaselessly be broken, interrupted without any regard for its natural divisions . . . the work of the commentary . . . consists . . . in *manhandling* the text, interrupting it." *S/Z*, trans. Richard Miller (New York: Hill and Wang, 1974), p. 15.

24. "The Text . . . the system is overcome, undone. . . . What is overcome, split, is the moral unity that society demands of every human product." *PT*, Miller, pp. 29, 31.

Barthes renders the very nature of interpretation problematic and establishes a tension between the intelligible and the equivocal. He distinguishes between two textual modes: the readerly (*le lisible*), in which meaning is conceived of as the transparently natural representation of reality as it will forever be, and the writerly (*le scriptible*) which functions independently of a priori models of intelligibility and acknowledges the plurality of which a text is composed. In short, the readerly text establishes the unequivocal authority of a particular signifying mode whereas the writerly text discredits the so-called "innocence" of an aesthetic object and demands that the reader become a writer capable of liberating energies otherwise repressed. If the readerly may be considered a product to be passively consumed, then the writerly transforms the reader into a cultural aggressor whose corrosively turbulent reading "n'est plus consommation, mais jeu (ce jeu qui est le retour du différent)" (*S/Z*, p. 23).[25]

To read Barthes on Balzac is to encounter a critical activity far too complex to be subsumed by the symmetrical patterning of readerly vs. writerly; alongside a rigorous reading, a free-floating reading takes place demonstrating how a text is at once structured and dismantled at the moment when the critic enters into its system of language. Barthes chooses to analyze a classic example of the so-called readerly text not only to illustrate how a "work" escapes from itself and becomes a "text," but also to reveal—perhaps unconsciously—the critic's latent desire "to reduce difference to identity."[26] The fear of succumbing to a reductive or unifying process that would immobilize the critic's desire provokes an endless rhetorical play undermining the potential foreclosure of meaning.

Barthes' persistent concern here is to challenge the authority of any model that would openly repress critical play and therefore replace it with the typological ordering of a mechanistic cataloguer. For Barthes, the shift from structuralism to reader response may be accounted for by a move from the idealism of formal cognition to the deconstructive activity of grammatological play; the desire for knowledge puts the critic in touch with a world differentially trans-

25. "is no longer consumption, but play (that play which is the return of the different)." *S/Z*, Miller, p. 16.

26. Barbara Johnson demystifies the blindness inherent in Barthes' own critical approach. "The Critical Difference: BartheS/BalZac," in *The Critical Difference. Essays in the Contemporary Rhetoric of Reading*. Baltimore: Johns Hopkins University Press, 1980, pp. 3–12.

formed by the reading act itself. To be sure, the drive of desire is dependent on a rhetorical negativity which brings textuality into play and represents it as an expression of Eros. "Il n'y a d'autre si-gnifié premier à l'oeuvre littéraire qu'un certain désir; écrire est un mode de l'Eros (*EC*, p. 14).[27]

Barthes seeks to allegorize his notion of critical play by adapting the myth of Jason and the Argonauts who sail in quest of the Golden Fleece. The playful critic, no longer obeying fixed or supposed rules of signification, takes on a role analogous to that of the Argonauts who re-placed each piece of their vessel so that they ultimately ended up with an entirely new ship. Barthes' ludic praxis consists in moving the fixed point of representation; he thus liberates the signifying process from any constraining context or point of reference by ena-bling multiple combinations within a sole form.

> Ce vaisseau Argo . . . fournit l'allégorie d'un objet éminemment structural, créé, non par le génie, l'inspiration, la détermination, l'évolution, mais par deux actes modestes . . . la *substitution* (une pièce chasse l'autre, comme dans un paradigme), et la *nomination* (le nom n'est nullement lié à la stabilité des pièces): à force de com-biner à l'intérieur d'un même nom, il ne reste plus rien de l'*origine*: Argo est un objet sans autre cause que son nom, sans autre identité que sa forme. [*RB*, p. 50][28]

The process of infinite differentiation—the aleatory order of frag-ments—is never ending by its very definition.[29] The critical function of play is to prevent the reassuring enclosure of a signified within a veil of reified meaning; play is not to be understood, but practiced. In this sense, Barthes posits the impossibility of pure knowledge; no first text, not even a pre-text which acts as a model of that which is supposed to be represented. The practice of critical play constructs in

27. "There is no other primary *significatum* in literary work than a certain desire: to write is a mode of Eros." *Critical Essays*, Howard, p. xvi.

28. "This ship *Argo* . . . affords the allegory of an eminently structural object, created not by genius, inspiration, determination, evolution, but by two modest ac-tions . . . *substitution* (one part replaces another, as in a paradigm) and nomination (the name is in no way linked to the stability of the parts): by dint of combinations made within one and the same name, nothing is left of the origin: *Argo* is an object with no other cause than its name, with no other identity than its form." *RB*, Howard, p. 46.

29. On the hypothesis of vertiginous displacements in Barthes see Stephen Heath, *Vertige du déplacement* (Paris: Fayard, 1974) and Steven Ungar's "RB: The Third Degree," *Diacritics* (Spring 1977), 75–77.

its very inscription a principle of repetition, where repetition does not imply identity but alterity and the rejection of the privileged position of the Father. "Le texte est (devrait être) cette personne désinvolte qui montre son derrière au Père Politique" (*PT*, p. 84).[30]

THE SELF AS PLAY

The form of the Barthesian self-portrait represents the theoretical principles it describes: the writer projects the image of a protean self whose elusiveness is heightened through fragmentation. The integrity of a totalized self-portraiture is obliterated by the fusion of multiple selves that precludes the possibility of classification. "Dès qu'une victoire se dessine quelque part, il a envie de se porter *ailleurs*. . . . Vous n'êtes plus classable, non par excès de personnalité, mais au contraire parce que vous parcourez toutes les franges du spectre" (*RB*, pp. 51, 147).[31] Each fragment of the Barthesian *speculum* reflects a self that is isolated from the others. "Vous êtes une marqueterie de réactions. Y a-t-il en vous quelque chose de *premier*" (*RB*, p. 146).[32] Barthes' enterprise enfolds within itself the perpetual movement of thought towards its own negation: the subject is a mediator through which multiple ideologies converge and disengage from one another within structures of differentiation. Working successively under the aegis of the multiple cultural codes of critical dandyism—marxism, structuralism, telquelism—the self refuses definition and is unable to take on a discrete form. "Formations réactives: une *doxa* (une opinion courante) est posée, insupportable, pour m'en dégager, je postule un paradoxe; puis ce paradoxe s'empoisse, devient lui-même concrétion nouvelle, nouvelle *doxa*, et il me faut aller plus loin vers un nouveau paradoxe" (*RB*, p. 75).[33] Barthes' dialectical mode of thinking subverts, in its incessant movement, the reification of knowledge and the totalization of the self-image; he speaks of an urgent need for detour and oscillation.

30. "The Text (should be) that uninhibited person who shows his behind to the Political Father." *PT*, Miller, p. 53.

31. "Whenever a victory appears somewhere, he wants to go somewhere *else*. . . . You are no longer classifiable, not out of an excess of personality, but on the contrary because you pass through all the fringes of the phantom." *RB*, Howard, pp. 46, 143–44.

32. "You are a patchwork of reactions: is there anything *primary* in you?" Ibid., p. 143.

33. "Reactive formations: a *Doxa* (a popular opinion) is posited, intolerable; to free myself of it, I postulate a paradox; then this paradox turns bad, becomes a new concretion, itself becomes a new *Doxa*, and I must seek further for a new paradox." Ibid., p. 71.

In order to create a portrait that would be the antithesis of non-desiring immobility, Barthes seeks to effect multiple displacements which generate self-dispersion and a movement toward ontological emptiness.[34] The anxiety emanating from the fear of a totalized self-image forces him to substitute for the "whole" person shifting perspectives that underscore his fragmented posture. Barthes uses fragments of discourse—discrete, self-contained entities—to forstall closure: he conceives of an open-ended discursive *praxis*, a series of new beginnings manifesting a preference for discontinuity.

> Aimant à trouver, à écrire des *débuts*, il tend à multiplier ce plaisir: Voilà pourquoi il écrit des fragments: autant de fragments, autant de débuts, autant de plaisirs (mais il n'aime pas les fins: le risque de clausale rhétorique est trop grand: crainte de ne savoir résister au *dernier mot*, à la dernière réplique). [*RB*, p. 97][35]

The anxiety of the possible suppression of mobile energy, the fear that the portrait might no longer reflect the movement of self-extension, causes Barthes to express endlessly the insatiable need to cast meaning adrift: "je procède par addition, non par esquisse; j'ai le goût préalable (premier) du détail, du fragment, du *rush*, et l'inhabilité à la conduire vers une 'composition' " (*RB*, p. 87).[36]

The unmitigated attempt to undermine the authority inherent in discourse shapes the rhetoric of Barthes' self-fashioning. "La visée de son discours n'est pas la vérité" (*RB*, p. 53).[37] The writer transforms himself into an object incapable of articulating a singular mode of thought; self-depiction at all levels is characterized by a rupture

34. "La dérive barthésienne est exactement l'équivalent du *Cogito* cartésien, son revers ou son absence: *là ou j'écris, je ne suis pas*. La place exacte où le sujet barthésien de l'écriture se trouve est donc celle où il se perd." ["The Barthesian drift is the exact equivalent of the Cartesian *Cogito*, its reverse or its absence: in *the site where I write, I am not*. The exact site where the Barthesian subject of writing happens to be is therefore the one in which he gets lost."] Serge Doubrovsky, "Une écriture tragique," *Poétique*, 47 (1981), 333.

35. "Liking to find, to write *beginnings*, he tends to multiply this pleasure: that is why he writes fragments: so many fragments, so many beginnings, so many pleasures (but he does not like the ends: the risk of the rhetorical clausule is too great: the fear of not being able to resist the last word). *RB*, Howard, p. 94.

36. "I proceed by addition, not by sketch; I have the antecedent (initial) taste for the detail, the fragment, the *rush*, and the incapacity to lead it toward a 'composition.' " Ibid., p. 94.

37. "The aim of his discourse is not truth . . ." Ibid., p. 48. "Barthes' books are not expositions of ideas but verbal gestures, *action writing*; they count intransitively by the very act of their production." Tzvetan Todorov, "The Last Barthes," trans. Richard Howard. *Critical Inquiry*, 7 (1981), 451.

which comes from the impossibility of representing a portrait consubstantial to the man. Barthes therefore becomes entirely absorbed with the preoccupation of presenting himself as Other, a *mise en jeu* of identity and a refuge from being pigeonholed. "Tout ceci doit être considéré comme dit par un personnage de roman—ou plutôt par plusieurs . . . l'imaginaire est pris en charge par plusieurs masques (*personae*), échelonnés selon la profondeur de la scène" (*RB*, p. 123).[38] Barthes' discourse does not arise from the immediate presence of the speaker. The voice that narrates the self-portrait is a hybrid, discontinuous collage of stolen language ("on vole au langage, sans cependant vouloir l'appliquer jusqu'au bout" [p. 96]) undermining the supposed unity of authorial voice and pointing to the impossibility of establishing a singular identity.[39] Barthes unquestionably remains "un effet de langage" within the script of contemporary intellectual thought.

The order of Barthes' writing in the so-called self-portraits is encyclopedic; it dislodges the sacred character of linear writing and returns the text to a prediscursive level following the unmotivated but unarbitrary order of an alphabet which suppresses all origins. The alphabetic sequentiality of rhetorical commonplaces presents a broken image of the self, a corpus which is a *corps morcelé* of disseminated fragments. The ego thus constituted through the encyclopedic form is not founded in any one dominant voice, but in the deferred action of an echo effect.

> Par rapport aux systèmes qui l'entourent, qu'est-il? Plutôt une chambre d'échos; il reproduit mal les pensées, il suit les mots; il rend visite, c'est-à-dire hommage, aux vocabulaires, il *invoque* les notions, il les répète sous un nom, il se sert de ce nom comme d'un emblème . . . et cet emblème le dispense d'approfondir le système dont il est signifiant. [*RB*, p. 78][40]

38. "All this must be considered as if spoken by a character in a novel—or rather by several characters . . . the image repertoire is taken over by several masks (personae), distributed according to the depth of the stage." Ibid., pp. 119–20.

39. "Barthes a cherché l'élasticité maximum, par contrainte de rester piégé dans son 'imaginaire'." "Barthes has sought maximum elasticity, constrained as he is to remain trapped in his image repertoire.'" Philippe Lejeune, *Je est un autre*. (Paris: Seuil, 1980), p. 49.

40. "In relation to the systems which surround him, what is he? Say an echo chamber: he reproduces the thoughts badly, he follows the words; he pays his visits, i.e., his respects, to vocabularies, he *invokes* notions, he rehearses them under a name; he makes use of this name as of an emblem . . . and this emblem dispenses him from following to its conclusion the system of which it is the signifier." *RB*, Howard, p. 74.

Thus in eliminating an immediately identifiable self-image, Barthes comes to think of himself as actually ceasing to exist: "la vacance de la 'personne' sinon annulée, du moins rendu irrepérable—l'absence d'*imago*—la suspension de jugement, de procès—le déplacement—le refus de se donner une contenance" (*RB*, p. 136).[41] The writer has been evicted from his locus as origin of his work, and instead, becomes a public scribe whose re-writing of the *topoi* of critical fashionability problematizes the very production of the self-image. The grafting of fragments from alien discourses and their encyclopedic redistribution makes Barthes become "ni un texte de vanité, ni un texte de lucidité, mais un texte aux guillemets incertains, aux parenthèses flottantes" (*RB*, p. 110).[42]

The very essence of self-portrayal for Barthes is a rhetorical free play which recognizes the fictional foundation for Being.[43] His text functions through multiple voices that reverberate in an isolated speaker who produces the illusion of a theatrical presence. The endless rhetorical choreographics between third and first person narration permit Barthes to stage the Imaginary and transform the self into a text representing the modulations of a polytonal narrative voice; the passage from "I" to "He" inscribes Barthes in a kind of anonymity that distances the producer of writing from the subject of the work. Barthes' will to play devises the self as a fiction which celebrates its distance from ontological plenitude.

> *Je suis celui qui ne parle pas de lui* . . . je parle de moi . . . à la façon de l'acteur brechtien qui doit distancer son personnage: le "montrer," non l'incarner, et donner à son débit comme une chiquenaude dont l'effet est de décoller le pronom de son nom, l'image de son support . . . je suis ailleurs que là où j'écris. [*RB*, pp. 171–72][44]

41. "the vacancy of the 'person', if not annulled at least rendered irretrievable—absence of *imago*—the suspension of judgment, of due process—displacement—the refusal 'to keep oneself in countenance.'" Ibid., p. 132.

42. "neither a text of vanity, nor a text of lucidity, but a text with uncertain quotation marks, with floating parentheses." Ibid., p. 106.

43. "Le propre de l'autoportrait est d'intégrer son propre commentaire en une tentative toujours déjouée et différée de "donner un sens" à l'entreprise sans fin." [It is the property of the self-portrait to integrate its own discourse in the always undermined and deferred attempt to 'give meaning' to an endless enterprise.] Michel Beaujour, *Miroirs d'encre* (Paris: Seuil, 1980), pp. 19–20.

44. "*I am He who does not speak about himself*. . . . *I am speaking* about myself . . . in the manner of the Brechtian actor who must distance his character: 'show' rather than incarnate him, and give his manner of speaking a kind of fillip whose effect is to pry the pronoun from its name, the image from its support. . . . *I am elsewhere than where I am when I write*." *RB*, Howard, p. 169.

To make the self appear even more complex, the Barthesian "character" is not perceived in a rapid and finished manner: the figuration of
the self is in a process subject to a perpetual revision of the autograph.
The portrayed subject liberates itself from the structural constraints
that a transcendental ego would impose and refuses to privilege any
one of the many fictional characters that shuttle back and forth
across the scriptural space:

> Le livre ne choisit pas, il fonctionne par alternance, il marche par
> bouffées d'imaginaire simple et d'accès critiques. . . . La substance
> de ce livre, finalement, est donc totalement romanesque . . . que
> l'essai s'avoue *presque* un roman, un roman sans noms propres."
> [*RB*, pp. 123–24].[45]

These constant shifts in narrative focus loosen the apocryphal bond
between voice and *persona* and as such blur the identity of the tex-
tualized self. To speak of oneself as Other permits the unmarked
narrative voice to seek self-knowledge through the infinite rearrange-
ment of its constitutive parts. Like the vessel Argo, the self maintains
its identity through the endless process of reconstitution.

The will to play prevents Barthes from being locked in the reified
structures of personality; it is an assertion of freedom against the
agony of solidification. Barthes therefore transforms the self into a
text of *jouissance*, a creature of paper who shatters the illusory foundation of Being through the gaps in the text's discursive fabric. The
pleasures of absence and incompletion are compulsively evoked
since they catalyze the dialectics of desire and function as a delaying
tactic giving way to imaginary visions rather than self-immobiliza-
tion. The self-portrait is in a constant state of tension between wholeness and the bliss of disintegration. "Il jouit de la consistance de son
moi (c'est le plaisir) et recherche sa perte (c'est sa jouissance). C'est
un sujet deux fois clivé, deux fois pervers" (*PT*, p. 26).[46] Fragmentary
discourse dislocates the ground Being is anchored in and represents it
as a pure manifestation of erotic drives. "L'écriture, c'est la main,

---

45. "The book does not choose, it functions by alternation, it proceeds by impulses of the image-system pure and simple and by critical approaches. . . . The substance of this book, ultimately, is therefore totally fictive . . . let the essay avow itself
almost a novel: a novel without proper names." Ibid., p. 120.

46. "He enjoys the consistency of his selfhood (that is his pleasure) and seeks its
loss (that is his bliss). He is a subject split twice over, doubly perverse." *PT*, Miller, p.
14.

c'est donc le corps: ses pulsions, ses contrôles, ses rythmes, ses pesées, ses glissements, ses complications, ses fuites . . ." (GV, p. 184).[47] The breakdown or interruption in self-representation promotes orgasmic delight emanating from the impossibility of recuperating the self's integrity. Entry into the world of play through the activity of self-dissipation is thus dependent on the erasure of a *telos* that would provide the stability which Barthes desperately seeks to escape.

Barthes' endless activity of play functions as a mimesis of his struggle to keep himself alive and consequently defer the death of desire. Writing therefore provides a feeling of safety whereby the text functions as a transitional object giving reassurance that while the sense of a concretized self might be made to vanish on a temporary basis, it could not be annihilated permanently.[48] The transitional space in which Barthes reshapes his self-image is caught in a desiring machine which decelerates the telic movement of time:

> L'écriture est une création; et dans cette mesure-là, c'est aussi une pratique de procréation. C'est une manière, tout simplement, de lutter, de dominer le sentiment de la mort et de l'abolissement intégral. Ce n'est pas du tout la croyance qu'on sera éternel comme écrivain après la mort, ce n'est pas ce problème-là. Mais, malgré tout, quand on écrit, on dispense des germes, on peut estimer qu'on dispense une sorte de semence et que, par conséquent, on est remis dans la circulation générale des semences. (GV, p 339)[49]

The psychodynamics of desire and self-transcendence are indissociable here. To forsake desire would imply succumbing to entropy and the silence and petrification that is death. Writing enables Barthes to attain a certain freedom which allows him to escape the fiction of immortality and yet at the same time characterize his scriptural quest as a polymorphous enterprise always in the process of re-creation. His textual project characterizes itself as a form of re-production that undermines the inanimate brutality associated with death.

---

47. "Writing's the hand, hence the body: its drives, its restraints, its rhythms, its pauses, its slippery mouvements, its complexities, its flights . . ."

48. The psychological sources of Barthes' attraction to game were perhaps bound up with his difficulties in maintaining a feeling of his own personal selfhood. Barthes declares that he is in search of a "sexualité heureuse".

49. This remark was taken from Barthes' last interview, "La crise du désir," Le Nouvel Observateur, 20 avril 1980, propos recueillis par Philip Brooks.

As long as Barthes writes himself as text, his textual existence goes beyond itself and swerves away from the annihilating potential of narrative quiescence.

THE DEATH OF DESIRE

Barthes' last work, *La Chambre claire,* an apparent meditation on photography, serves, however, as a pretext for the writer to reflect on his growing apprehension of death. In the wake of his bereavement over his mother's death, he reveals his present impoverishment, his life almost fatally frozen. No longer having a reason to exist, he experiences a collapsing within himself which may be regarded as the dissolution of the playful subject. "Elle morte, je n'avais plus aucune raison de m'accorder à la marche du Vivant supérieur (l'espèce). . . . Je ne pouvais plus qu'attendre ma mort totale, indialectique" (*CC,* p. 113).[50] The mourning for the mother—the figure of plenitude and Being—fetters Barthes' creative impulses and transforms the abandonned son into a simulacrum of a lover suffering from separation anxiety. "L'amoureux qui n'oublie pas *quelquefois,* meurt par excès, fatigue et tension de mémoire. . . . Enfant, je n'oubliais pas: journées interminables, journées abandonnées, où la Mère travaillait loin" (*FDA,* pp. 20–21).[51] The loss of the loved one annihilates the desire to know and the security of symbiotic dependency. Barthes' inability to separate from the mother as object of nurturing dramatically reveals his inability to accept freely the anxiety of passively awaiting his own death; he suddenly feels as if a wall has been constructed in front of him beyond which he cannot go.[52] "La seule "pensée" que je puisse avoir, c'est qu'au bout de cette première mort, ma propre mort est

50. "Once she was dead I no longer had any reason to attune myself to the progress of the superior Life Force (the race, the species). . . . From now on I could do no more than await my total, undialectical death." *Camera Lucida,* trans. Richard Howard (New York: Hill and Wang, 1981), p. 72.

51. "The lover who doesn't forget sometimes dies of excess, exhaustion, and tension of memory. . . . (As a child, I didn't forget: interminable days, when the Mother was working far away" *A Lover's Discourse,* trans. Richard Howard (New York: Hill and Wang, 1978), p. 14.

52. "L'admirable testament qu'est *la Chambre claire* met soudain l'écriture au-delà du principe de plaisir jusque-là régnant; elle s'inscrit désormais dans la mouvance du *Todestrieb.*" ["That admirable Testament that *Camera Lucida* is, suddenly transports writing beyond the heretofore dominant pleasure principle; from that moment on writing is inscribed into the flow of the *Todestrieb.*" Doubrovsky, 352.

inscrite; entre les deux, plus rien, qu'attendre; je n'ai d'autre ressource que cette *ironie*: parler du "rien à dire" " (*CC*, p. 145).[53]

The interpretation of photography as a microexperience of death points to Barthes' fear of and preoccupation with paralysis, his inability to function as a free and autonomous Being in the absence of the maternal. An implicit analogy is delineated between the photographic self-portrait which contains within it the signs of the self's crystallization at the moment of death and the image of an indolent self which Barthes uses to describe the effect on him of his mother's death. The photograph does indeed emblematize death: it says "this has been" and can no longer be:

> La Photographie est indialectique: elle est un théâtre dénaturé où la mort ne peut se "contempler", se réfléchir et s'intérioriser . . . [elle est] le théâtre mort de la Mort. . . . La Photographie transformait le sujet en objet, et même . . . en objet de musée . . . lorsque je me découvre sur le produit de cette opération, ce que je vois, c'est ce que je suis devenu Tout-image, c'est-à-dire la mort en personne. [*CC*, pp. 141, 29, 31].[54]

The essay on photography, through its semitheoretical detours, inscribes within the text a mirror which clearly portrays the writer's immobilized self-image: Barthes becomes, in effect, a photograph, an image unable to escape from the past, and condemned to death. Barthes' existence, like the very nature of photography itself, is now characterized as being totally undialectical; he can no longer anticipate his own possibilities directed toward the future.

By the time of his own death Barthes was indeed no longer able to glorify the freedom of invention. The unresolved mourning for the idealized maternal object resulted in a deceleration of the energy producing tension between the female (the Imaginary) and the male (the Symbolic). The anaclitic relationship with the mother which was privileged at the expense of the authority implicit in the "name-

53. "The only 'thought' I can have is that at the end of this first death, my own death is inscribed; between the two, nothing more than waiting; I have no other resource than this *irony*: to speak of the 'nothing to say'." *Camera Lucida*, Howard, p. 93.

54. "The Photograph is undialectical: it is a denatured theater where death cannot be 'contemplated,' reflected and interiorized. . . . [it is] the dead theater of Death. . . . Photography transformed subject into object, and even . . . onto a museum object . . . when I discover myself in the product of this operation, what I see is that I have become Total-Image, which is to say, Death in person." Ibid., pp. 90, 14, 15.

of-the-Father" allowed free play to develop and find new representational modes. But now the futurity of the protean self had finally become annihilated, the anxiety realized. Perhaps the final desire to write a novel in memory of things past was nothing more than an antiproject and a sign of defeat, an insignificant gesture to an inert and immobilized world.

Contributors

MARY ANN CAWS is Distinguished Professor of French and Comparative Literature at Hunter College and the Graduate Center, City University of New York. She is the author, editor and translator of numerous books on modern French poetry; among the most recent, *The Eye in the Text: Essays on Perception, Mannerist to Modern, A Metapoetics of Passage: Architectures in Surrealism and After, The Prose Poem in France* (coeditor), and, forthcoming from Princeton University Press, *Radical Frames.*

PATRICK COLEMAN is Associate Professor of French at the University of California at Los Angeles. He has published articles on eighteenth-century French literature and contemporary literary theory. His book *Rousseau's Political Imagination* (Geneva: Droz) will be appearing later this year.

SIMA GODFREY is Assistant Professor of French at the University of North Carolina at Chapel Hill. She has published articles on Flaubert, Baudelaire and Gautier and is presently completing a book on Baudelaire's poetry and art criticism.

RICHARD KLEIN is Associate Professor of French at Cornell University. He is currently editor of *Diacritics.* He has published articles on contemporary critical theory in *Enclitic* and *Modern Language Notes.*

LAWRENCE KRITZMAN is Associate Professor of French at Rutgers University. He is the author of *Destruction/ Découverte: le fonctionnement de la rhétorique dans les "Essais" de Montaigne* and the editor of *Fragments: Incompletion and Discontinuity.* He has published articles on Renaissance literature, contemporary French intellectual history, and literary theory.

JAMES LAWLER is Professor of French at the University of Chicago. He

211

has published widely on Paul Valéry, René Char and twentieth-century French poetry and poetics. His books include *The Poet as Analyst: Essays on Paul Valéry,* and *René Char: The Myth and the Poem.*

LOUIS MACKENZIE, JR., is Assistant Professor of French at Princeton University. He has published articles on seventeenth-century French literature and is writing a book on Pascal and authority.

CARL PLETSCH teaches intellectual history at the University of North Carolina at Chapel Hill. He is completing a book on Nietzsche and the Ideology of Genius.

JEANINE PARISIER PLOTTEL is Professor of French at the City University of New York. She has written extensively on twentieth-century French literature and is currently editor of the *New York Literary Forum.*

STEPHEN RENDALL is Professor of Romance Languages at the University of Oregon. He is Associate Editor of *Comparative Literature* and has published numerous studies on French and Spanish literature of the sixteenth and seventeenth centuries. He has recently edited a volume of essays on Montaigne and current issues in criticism. He is the translator of Michel de Certeau's *Arts de faire.*

RICHARD SHIFF is Associate Professor of Art History at the University of North Carolina at Chapel Hill. His book, *Cézanne and the End of Impressionism* will be published this year (Univ. of Chicago Press).

The following issues are available through Yale University Press, Customer Service Department, 92 A Yale Station, New Haven, Conn. 06520.

63	The Pedagogical Imperative: Teaching as a Literary Genre	$10.95
64	Montaigne: Essays in Reading	$10.95
65	The Language of Difference: Writing in QUEBEC(ois)	$10.95

The following issues are still available through the Yale French Studies Office, 315 William L. Harkness Hall, Yale University, New Haven, Conn. 06520.

19/20 Contemporary Art	$2.50	49 Science, Language, & the Perspective Mind	$2.50
23 Humor	$2.50	50 Intoxication and Literature	$2.50
32 Paris in Literature	$2.50	53 African Literature	$2.50
33 Shakespeare	$2.50	54 Mallarmé	$3.00
35 Sade	$2.50	57 Locus: Space, Landscape, Decor	$5.00
38 The Classical Line	$2.50	58 In Memory of Jacques Ehrmann	$5.00
39 Literature and Revolution	$3.50	59 Rethinking History	$5.00
40 Literature and Society: 18th Century	$2.50	60 Cinema/Sound	$5.00
41 Game, Play, Literature	$2.50	61 Toward a Theory of Description	$5.00
42 Zola	$2.50	62 Feminist Readings: French Texts/ American Contexts	$5.00
43 The Child's Part	$2.50		
44 Paul Valéry	$2.50		
45 Language as Action	$2.50		
46 From State to Street	$2.50		
47 Image & Symbol in the Renaissance	$2.50		

Add for postage & handling

United States		Foreign countries	
	$ .75	(including Canada)	$1.00
Each additional issue	$ .50	Each additional issue	$ .75

YALE FRENCH STUDIES

315 William L. Harkness Hall
Yale University
New Haven, Connecticut 06520

Please send me the following issue(s) of Yale French Studies:

Issue no.   Title   Price

_____   _____   _____

_____   _____   _____

_____   _____   _____

                                            Postage & handling   _____

                                                        Total   _____

A check made payable to YFS is enclosed.

_____

NAME

_____

NUMBER/STREET

_____

CITY   STATE   ZIP

The following issues are now available through Kraus Reprint Company, Route 100, Millwood, N.Y. 10546.

36/37 Structuralism has been reprinted by Doubleday as an Anchor Book.

55/56 Literature and Psychoanalysis has been reprinted by Johns Hopkins University Press, and can be ordered through Customer Service, Johns Hopkins University Press, Baltimore, MD. 21218

Yale French Studies is also available through: Xerox University Microfilms, 300 North Zeeb Road, Ann Arbor, MI 48106.

american journal of
SEMIOTICS

A Quarterly Journal of the Semiotic Society of America

Editors: Irene Portis Winner and Thomas G. Winner

Editorial Board: Jean Alter, Eugen Baer, Jerome Bruner, Jonathan Culler, Paul Ekman, Irene R. Fairley, Max Fisch, Kenneth Ketner, Shelagh Lindsay, Ladislav Matejka, Leonard Meyer, Daniel Rancour-Laferrière, Donald Preziosi, Irmengard Rauch, Meyer Schapiro, Robert Scholes, Charles Segal, Milton Singer, Edward Stankiewicz, Henri Zerner.

The *American Journal of Semiotics* is a broadly interdisciplinary journal concerned with the nature and role of sign processes — with special attention to human sign systems and the messages they generate.

From the contents of Volume I, (1982)

Eugen Baer
The Medical Symptom

Jerome Bruner
The Formats of Language Acquisition

Jonathan Culler
Semiotics of Tourism

Daniel Patte
Greimas's Model for the Generative Trajectory of Meaning in Discourse

David Lidov
The Allegretto of Beethoven's Seventh

Jerzy Pelc
Theoretical Foundations of Semiotics

Thomas A. Sebeok
Dialogue about Signs with a Nobel Laureate

Milton Singer
On the Semiotic of Indian Identity

George Steiner
Narcissus and Echo

Volume II, Nos. 1-2 (Spring 1983) is a special issue on Peirce's semiotic, edited by Kenneth Ketner (Texas Tech), which addresses a broad range of topics and includes articles by Hanna Buczynska-Garewicz, Carolyn Eisele, Max Fisch, Kenneth Ketner, Roberta Kevelson, and others. This issue will be of special interest to philosophers, logicians, mathematicians, linguists, and aestheticians.

Volume II, No. 3 (Summer 1983) will be devoted to Roman Jakobson's contribution to semiotics.

Subscription is included in membership in the Semiotic Society of America. Annual dues are $30; Students and emeriti $15, Institutions $40. Foreign membership/subscription: add $5. Joint membership: add $10 to the dues category of the highest paying member to receive Journal. Please enter my membership/subscription to the AJS:

☐ Individuals $30   ☐ Students/emeriti $15   ☐ Institutions $40   ☐ Joint $_____

Name _____

Address _____

City _____ State _____ Zip _____

Please send check made payable to Semiotic Society of America to:
Subscription Manager, Semiotic Society of America, P.O. Box 10, Bloomington, Indiana 47402

REVUE FRANÇAISE D'ETUDES AMERICAINES

10, RUE CHARLES V — 75004 PARIS

A Journal published since 1976 by the French
Association for American Studies (AFEA)
A tri-annual from February 1982

Nº	1	April 1976	The Contemporary American Novel
Nº	2	October 1976	American Radicalism
Nº	3	April 1977	Civilization, Literature & Psychoanalysis, Literature & Ideology
Nº	4	October 1977	American Humor
Nº	5	April 1978	Transcendentalism & the American Renaissance
Nº	6	October 1978	Ideology & the Mass Media in the US
Nº	7	April 1979	Arts & Society in the US
Nº	8	October 1979	Aspects of Modernity in the US
Nº	9	April 1980	Otherness in American Culture
Nº	10	October 1980	The Theaters of America
Nº	11	April 1981	The City in American Culture
Nº	12	October 1981	Religion in the US
Nº	13	February 1982	French Historians of the US
Nº	14	June 1982	Autobiography in America
Nº	15	November 1982	Contemporary American Poetry
Nº	16	February 1983	Intellectuals in the US
Nº	17	May 1983	North-American English

. . . .

Fill out and send to : RFEA, 10, rue Charles V - 75004 PARIS

Please   ● send .... copies of Nos 2, 3, 4, 5, 6, 7, 8, 9, 10, 11, 12, 13, 14, 15
         ● enter my subscription for 19...

NAME : ....

ADDRESS : ....
....
....

o Price per issue : 35 FF (air mail)

o One-year subscription for the 1982 issues :
   — individuals : 90 FF (105 FF air mail)
   — institutions : 105 FF (120 FF air mail)

HUMANITIES IN SOCIETY

HUMANITIES IN SOCIETY is an interdisciplinary journal concerned with the role of ideas in modern society. It aims to situate intellectual endeavors in a social context and to explore the power relations that govern society. How do certain currents of thought gain legitimacy both within the academic community and outside it and how and why do these currents either reinforce the power of particular groups at the expense of others or challenge the domination of hegemonic groups by proposing alternative perspectives on the past, the present, and the future? Recent and forthcoming issues deal with Psychoanalysis and Interpretation, the Politics of Literacy, Militarism and War (double issue), Michel Foucault (double issue). Future issues being compiled include the following, for which submissions are requested. These should be sent by the date indicated to the guest editor, in care of the Center for the Humanities address below.

RELIGION AND POLITICS: What types of roles does religion play in political cultures, in various times and places? How do religious ideology and political practice interact? (Robert Booth Fowler, June 1, 1983)

RACE, CLASS, AND CULTURE: What is the significance of the current racial and class crisis? What perspectives and insights can the humanities offer which might aid in developing a non-racist and democratic society? Do the norms, myths, symbols, and popular culture that humanists study and promote help to eradicate the crisis or deepen it? (Manning Marable, August 1, 1983)

MARXISTS AND THE UNIVERSITY: What are Marxists doing in American universities? Have Marxist critics of society lost their real voices of opposition? Is the university, a workplace that produces cultural commodities, being significantly changed by Marxists— or are they being changed by it? (Robert M. Maniquis, September 1, 1983)

SEXUALITY, VIOLENCE, AND PORNOGRAPHY: What are the relationships between pornography and sexual oppression, freedom of speech, crimes of violence? What is the relationship between sexuality and political awareness and commitment? What forms might a new truly liberated sexuality take? (Marie-Florine Bruneau and Gloria Orenstein, October 1, 1983)

LITERARY EAST-WEST EMIGRATION: What are the effects of emigration to the West by writers of the Soviet Union, Eastern Europe, and East Germany—upon the writers themselves, their home countries, and their adopted countries? (Olga Matich and Arnold Heidsieck, October 1, 1983)

-- --

HUMANITIES IN SOCIETY

☐ $20.00 individual rate for one year   ☐ $32.00 individual rate for two years
☐ $26.00 institution rate for one year   ☐ $ 8.00 single issue (specify)
   (add $4.00 postage outside the U.S.)   ☐ $10.00 double issue (specify)

Name _____ _____

Address _____

City_____ State_____ Zip_____

Make checks payable to: Humanities in Society

Mail to: Department Q, Center for the Humanities, Taper Hall of Humanities 326, University of Southern California, Los Angeles, CA 90089-0350

PRAXIS

Praxis #6: Art and Ideology (Part 2)

Michel Pecheux, **Language, Ideology and Discourse Analysis: An Overview**

Douglas Kellner, **Television, Mythology and Ritual**

Nicos Hadjinicolaou, **On the Ideology of Avant-Gardism**

Kenneth Coutts-Smith, **Postbourgeois Ideology and Visual Culture**

Marc Zimmerman, **Francois Perus and Latin American Modernism: The Interventions of Althusser**

Fred Lonidier, **"The Health and Safety Game"** *(Visual Feature)*

Forthcoming issues:

Praxis #7: Antonio Gramsci   Praxis #8: Weimar and After

Single copy: $4.95   Subscription (2 issues): $8.00
Make checks payable to "the Regents of the University of California"
Praxis, Dickson Art Center, UCLA, Los Angeles, CA 90024 USA

Exile and Change in Renaissance Literature

A. Bartlett Giamatti

These seven essays by a scholar noted for his wit and eloquence
consider two recurrent themes in Renaissance literature—the sense
of exile as a precondition to identity and the preoccupation with
change or mutability. They provide insights into the transit of a
cultural and literary vision from Italy to England that readers will find
especially rewarding. $14.95

The Yale Review

Autumn 1983/Winter 1984:
"The Telling of Lives"

The Autumn 1983 and Winter 1984 issues of *The Yale Review* are
devoted to the uses of biography and autobiography in fiction,
poetry, history, literary criticism, and ethnography.

The list of contributors to "The Telling of Lives" includes
Daniel Aaron, Robert Coles, Terrence Des Pres, Erik H. Erikson,
Seamus Heaney, John Hersey, R.W.B. Lewis, James Olney,
Arnold Rampersad, Jonathan Spence, and C. Vann Woodward.
$4.50/issue $12.00/year individuals; $18.00/year institutions.

New Haven   *Yale University Press*   London